Christopher

with best wishes

Virginia Surtees, London,
1984

THE LUDOVISI GODDESS

Also by Virginia Surtees

DANTE GABRIEL ROSSETTI, A CATALOGUE RAISONNÉ

SUBLIME AND INSTRUCTIVE

CHARLOTTE CANNING

A BECKFORD INHERITANCE

REFLECTIONS OF A FRIENDSHIP

THE DIARIES OF GEORGE PRICE BOYCE

THE DIARY OF FORD MADOX BROWN

THE LUDOVISI GODDESS

THE LIFE OF
Louisa Lady Ashburton

VIRGINIA SURTEES

MICHAEL RUSSELL

© Virginia Surtees 1984

First published in Great Britain 1984
by Michael Russell (Publishing) Ltd,
The Chantry, Wilton, Salisbury, Wiltshire

Set in Sabon at The Spartan Press Ltd, Lymington
Printed and bound in Great Britain
by Biddles Ltd, Guildford and King's Lynn

All rights reserved
ISBN 0 85955 105 9

FOR RALEIGH TREVELYAN
WHOSE ENTHUSIASM AND ENCOURAGEMENT
INSPIRED THIS BOOK.
WITH TRUE REGARD

Contents

	Acknowledgements	xi
	Prelude	1
1	The Stewarts and the Mackenzies	4
2	The Lady of the Lake	11
3	From Richmond to Corfu	22
4	Friendships and Love	32
5	Blighted Hopes	40
6	An Artful Dodger	52
7	In Pursuit of Happiness	66
8	At The Grange and Bath House	74
9	Decline and Death	87
10	Patronage	101
11	Ripe for Heaven	117
12	Carlyle at Mentone	126
13	The Widower and the Widow	137
14	Schemes and Crises	150
15	Clutton and Nesfield Censured	161
16	The Last Adventure	173
	Bibliography	189
	Source Notes	192
	Index	203

List of Illustrations

John Ruskin and Louisa at Wallington Hall, from a drawing by W. Bell Scott, 1857. *Courtesy of the National Trust.*

Brahan Castle.

Louisa, c. 1859. *Permission of the Schlesinger Library, Radcliffe College.*

The Grange. *Permission of the Royal Commission on Historical Monuments (England).*

Louisa wearing mourning (perhaps for her mother), c. 1862. *Courtesy of the National Trust.*

Louisa, from a marble bust by Baron Marochetti, 1861. *Courtesy of the Marquess of Northampton.*

Louisa and Maysie, from a painting by Sir Edwin Landseer, 1862. *Courtesy of the Marquess of Northampton.*

Lord Ashburton, c. 1860.

Harriet Hosmer, c. late 1860s. *Permission of the Schlesinger Library, Radcliffe College.*

Thomas Carlyle, mid 1860s. *Permission of the National Portrait Gallery.*

Loch Luichart.

Robert Browning, probably reading from *The Ring and the Book*, from a drawing by W. W. Story made at Naworth Castle, September 1869. *Courtesy of the Pierpont Morgan Library.*

Melchet Court. *Permission of the Schlesinger Library, Radcliffe College.*

Louisa in old age. *Courtesy of Lord Loch.*

Acknowledgements

To Her Majesty The Queen for gracious permission to quote from a letter from Queen Victoria.

I am under a great debt to the Marquess of Northampton for having allowed me to make full use of the unpublished papers of his great-grandmother Louisa Lady Ashburton, and for enabling me to work at Compton Wynyates in surroundings of great beauty. This is a debt beyond my scope of thanks, which I can only record with all sincerity.

To Lord Loch, also a great-grandson, I wish to express my gratitude for his unfailing patience in answering my many inquiries and for the forbearance with which he has abstained from imposing his own views on my interpretation of facts and people in this story; and for permitting me to see over Loch Luichart, conducted there by Mrs Alick Matheson to whom manifold thanks are also due for guiding me around Brahan and beyond.

What I owe to Mr Raleigh Trevelyan I have attempted to set down on an earlier page of this book; he has also been generous with documents and photographs.

I have depended on the assistance of many and I should like to name those who have helped me most particularly: Professor K.J. Fielding, co-editor of *The Collected Letters of Thomas and Jane Welsh Carlyle*, whose knowledge of the Carlyles has carried me over several hurdles; the Lady Gladwyn, my cicerone at Kent House, Knightsbridge, where she had lived and grown up several years after Lady Ashburton's death, and whose vivid childhood recollections recaptured unrecorded details of the house as it had once been; Miss Ann Hyde and the staff of the Spencer Library, University of Kansas for the assistance they gave me during the time I worked there; the Hon. Betty Askwith who never failed with sound advice and sympathetic interest; Mr David Nunes Vaz, Hon. Genealogist of the Spanish and Portuguese Jews'

ACKNOWLEDGEMENTS

Congregation for information concerning Lady Ashburton's ancestry; Miss Jane Langton, Archivist of the Royal Archives, Windsor Castle, and Mrs Penelope Hunting for granting me access to her thesis on Henry Clutton.

The greater proportion of the holograph letters quoted here were sorted, and many notes made before her death, by the late Miss Helen Arbuthnot; I take this opportunity of emphasizing how her work has simplified my own in no small degree. I wish also to record my thanks to Vivien Noakes, author of *Edward Lear*, for the help her book has afforded me; to Dr William Witla whose *Browning and the Ashburton Affair*, published in the *Browning Society Journal*, 1972, crystallized my own views; and to Mrs Patricia Maxwell-Scott whose ready response to my use of Sir Walter Scott's unpublished letters has enabled me to present him as one of the chief heroes of this narrative.

Help in diverse ways has been afforded me by the Hon. Sir John Baring, Mr Morchard Bishop, Mr Wilfrid Blunt, Mr T.B. Brennan, Mrs Anthony Butler, Miss Margie Christian, the Revd Father Joseph L. Curran, Curator of the Hosmer Collection, Watertown, Mr Ian Donnachie, Mr Richard Dorment, Mrs Rowland Elzea, Miss Eileen Gainfort, Mrs John Gere, Mrs Ralph Grubb, Mrs Bert Harty, the Hon. Hubert Howard, Mr Evelyn Joll, Mr William Joll, Professor Cecil Y. Lang, the late Mr Peter McIntyre, Mrs John McKeogh, Mrs P.J. Macrory, Sir Torquhil Matheson of Matheson, Bt., Mr and Mrs Richard Ormond, Professor Clyde de L. Ryals, Miss Dorothy Stroud, Mr R.B. Stuart-Barker, Major-General Sir John Swinton, Dr Paul Thompson, Sir Anthony Wagner, Mr John Woolford; also the staffs of the Inverness Branch Library, Islington Local History Library, Marylebone History Museum, Mocatta Library.

As often before, copyright permission for use of unpublished material has been generously granted me by the following, and this I gratefully acknowledge: Mrs Pauline Dower for the Trevelyan Papers, John Murray Ltd. for letters of Elizabeth Barrett Browning and Robert Browning, Mrs Imogen Dennis for letters from D.G. Rossetti, the Ruskin Literary Trustees for those of John Ruskin, and the late Major-General C.G. Woolner for the use of the letters of Thomas Woolner. Also the Henry Bonham-Carter Trust for Florence Nightingale's letters, Mrs Katharine Macdonald for those of Alexander Munro, Mr Nicholas Mackenzie for Sir Edwin

ACKNOWLEDGEMENTS xiii

Landseer's, Mr Andrew Matheson for the use of the Seaforth Muniments, Rugby School for giving me permission to quote from the letters of Dr Arnold and James Prince Lee, Lord Stanley of Alderley for unpublished correspondence of his forbears, and the late Mrs Susan Stirling for the use of the diaries of Sir William Stirling-Maxwell, Bt. To any owners of copyright whom I have failed to trace or have inadvertently omitted I offer my apologies.

For making available to me material in their collections I wish to thank the Bodleian Library, British Library, Cheshire County Record Office, Glasgow City Archives, Houghton Library, Harvard University, Kenneth Spencer Research Library, University of Kansas, Trustees of the National Library of Scotland, Scottish Record Office, the Master and Fellows of Trinity College, Cambridge, Victoria and Albert Museum Library.

All quotations unidentified in the text are from the Northampton Papers. Original spelling has been retained, in most cases capitalization has been normalized, and in the letters of Sir Walter Scott punctuation has been silently inserted.

Prelude

England was mourning the Iron Duke. On 18 November 1852, under a forbidding sky, the London crowds thrust and pushed along the ceremonial way as the funeral carriage weighted with the burden of laurel wreaths, vases of burning incense, the pall and canopy of silver tissue and the trophy of swords and muskets, carried the first Duke of Wellington to his sepulchre in St Paul's Cathedral. Half England was said to be riding in the procession. As the hearse passed Bath House on the north side of Piccadilly, the plain yellow brick home of William Bingham, second Lord Ashburton, Thomas Carlyle watched it contemptuously from a second-floor window: 'Of all the objects I ever saw the abominably ugliest or nearly so. An incoherent huddle of expensive palls. . . this vile *ne plus ultra* of Cockneyism; but poor Wellington lay dead beneath it faring dumb to his long home.'[1]

In St Paul's itself, William Stirling of Keir, Member of Parliament for Perthshire, was seated in the bank of benches on the north side of the space under the dome. He noted in his diary that Lord Malmesbury, the Foreign Secretary, was observed reading *Punch* and many of the mourners had books and newspapers. Lord Douro, chief mourner, had just reached the great west door and was marshalling his supporters when he 'received a message from Prince Albert begging him to wait for half an hour as he was at lunch'. When eventually the coffin was in position and descended without further hindrance 'the effect was very impressive and Lord Douro, much affected, put his hand on the coffin with a sort of farewell motion as it disappeared – an action which would have been very touching had it not been absurdly aped by foolish Lord Londonderry who, covered with furs and frogs, pushed forward to do the same.'[2]

In the dome a twenty-five-year-old Scotswoman thought there could never be such a sight again. Thanks to her friendship with Henry Milman, Dean of St Paul's, Louisa Stewart-Mackenzie had

PRELUDE

been allowed to watch the procession from the pediment as it approached up Ludgate Hill, and now in the immense arched vault soaring above the 17,000 congregation she found the Dirge and the triumphant hymn 'Sleepers Wake' from Mendelssohn's 'St Paul' altogether most glorious. 'When all the hundred voices sang out the words "I am the Resurrection &c" it was like *Light* bursting in.'

In this swift succession of scenes the names of three men appear who in turn were the focus of Louisa's vehement emotions: William Stirling, the love of her youth but whose affections were placed elsewhere; Lord Ashburton whom – partly from ambition – she married as his second wife when her years of spinsterhood were marking her out for celibacy (though this by a last despairing throw she would have substituted for marriage to Sir Edwin Landseer, the aged, drunken artist and friend of many years); and Thomas Carlyle, once obsessed by the former Lady Ashburton, on whom when a widower Louisa was to lavish kindness upon kindness, an uncharacteristic patience and a wealth of unsolicited though not unacceptable solicitude. These were the human influences which were to determine in some degree the future of this impetuous, generous, inconsiderate and capricious creature. Robert Browning too, already an acquaintance, was to play a crucial part in the years ahead; also Harriet Hosmer, the American sculptress of some popularity in her time whose strongly masculine nature was revealed in a love for Louisa which was more than partly reciprocated.

Louisa was descended on both sides from ancient Scottish families and her affections were rooted in the Highlands from which she had sprung. Her interest lay in literature, in natural history, the Evangelical Church, but predominantly in the arts; and if her learning was not exactly extensive, her habitual eagerness for knowledge meant at least that she was well- informed. In appearance she was robust with strongly moulded features, a resolute jaw and beneath the firm line of her brows the brilliant dark eyes inherited from her Jewish grandmother. So arresting was the power and classical nobility of the head that Anna Jameson exclaimed at its resemblance to the celebrated head of Juno in Rome, the 'Ludovisi Goddess'.[3] Her voice was charming and musical, her smile illuminated her whole countenance. In effusiveness of language, spoken or written, she would have had few peers even in that effusive age, and both the flow and the warmth of her endearments were prompted as a rule by genuine feeling. Her slightly pushing manner was excused by her friends as vitality and a desire to worship at the feet of the illustrious. Many were enslaved by Louisa; and some were woefully infuriated.

I

The Stewarts and the Mackenzies

On 5 March 1827[4] a third daughter, their sixth and last child, was born to the Stewart-Mackenzies at Seaforth Lodge, Stornoway, on the Isle of Lewis. She was baptized in April in the small parish church, receiving the names of Louisa, after that formidable bluestocking Lady Louisa Stuart, her mother's friend, and Caroline, in memory of her mother's sister who had died a victim to the family curse said to have been laid on the Mackenzies at the outset of the seventeenth century.

Lewis, in the Outer Hebrides, had been a gift from the crown to the Mackenzies in 1611 and Loch Seaforth, on the south-east coast, had furnished the name of the earldom when their branch had been ennobled shortly afterwards. Mrs Stewart-Mackenzie had inherited the island from her father at his death in 1815, and she and her second husband James Alexander Stewart (who had obligingly added her name to his at their marriage in 1817) resided at Stornoway for several months of the year, granting it a charter in 1825, giving its first and only issue of banknotes and working hard to repair the neglect of generations so as to bring prosperity to the island. Both were dedicated Whigs and Liberals; among their efforts and achievements were concern for education and Church reform, the founding of a distillery to deter unlawful distilling, and a stern regard for Protestant religious observance.

A plot of rocky ground set slightly back and raised above the water was occupied by Seaforth Lodge. Facing the Minch, the narrow strip of sea between the Lews and the mainland of Ross-shire, open to every storm and buffet of wind, backed by low rolling hills, this isolated unpretentious eighteenth-century house in its grim windswept landscape of sea and moorland was the prelude to Louisa's life. Kent House, Knightsbridge, seventy-six years later, would see its close.

When her father died at Southampton in 1843 she seems scarcely to have mentioned his name again and his memory was

THE STEWARTS AND THE MACKENZIES

allowed to slip into oblivion. Perhaps there was little to recall, though his parentage alone should have promised something. Born in 1784, James was the second son of Admiral the Hon. Keith Stewart, of Glasserton in Wigtownshire, third son of the sixth Earl of Galloway. The Earls of Galloway could trace their family from Sir John Stewart who fell at Falkirk in 1298; from him descended the Stewarts and James VI of Scotland and I of England. Robert the Bruce had rewarded the Stewarts with land in recognition of services and an earldom had been granted by Charles I to whom the house of Stewart owned allegiance. In 1763, when Keith Stewart was twenty-four and a captain in the Royal Navy, his father made over to him the Glasserton property which lay just inland from the small village of Garlieston in Wigtown Bay. The parish church lay within the park; the house was surrounded by fine old trees. The young man left the sea and settled on his land, concerning himself with his farm and coal and iron mines, turnpike roads development and the improvement of the race of the Galloway black cattle. In 1787 he erected a new house on the foundations of the earlier one. It was designed by Adam[5] (who at the time was building Culzean Castle, also in the Lowlands) and built in grey granite.

Stewart's portrait ascribed to Batoni reveals a shrewd but amused countenance and a firm outline of nose and jaw which his granddaughter Louisa would inherit. Beloved in the country and a generous friend, from 1768 to 1784 he sat as a Member for Wigtonshire, combining his parliamentary duties with seafaring exploits – he saw service in the West Indies, in the North Sea and at the relief of Gibraltar. On vacating his seat in Parliament he was appointed Receiver General of Scotland, promoted to be a rear-admiral of the Blue in 1790 and vice-admiral in 1794.

This creditable career was enlivened by marriage in 1782 at the age of forty-three to Georgiana Simha d'Aguilar, a young Jewish woman twenty years his junior. The marriage, conducted by the Dean of Carlisle, took place 'at ye house of Miss d'Aguilar' in Manchester Square. The rate-book for that year shows eighteen houses already built in the square though none in the ownership of the bride. Perhaps she had rented No 5 for the occasion; it was owned by Captain Dalrymple, Member for Wigton Burghs and no doubt a friend of her husband.

THE STEWARTS AND THE MACKENZIES

A picture made of her at a slightly later time reveals an attractive face framed in curls falling to the shoulders. Her large dark eyes, long nose, short upper lip and rounded chin present no clue to her character, but Reynolds's painting of her when a child, holding flowers in her dress, has caught in the pensiveness of her gaze a gravity beyond her years. Her mother, Sarah Mendes da Costa, had died a few years after marriage and had settled her own private fortune upon Georgiana and her younger sister Caroline. Both daughters were therefore already well provided for, and now Georgiana, according to the marriage settlement,[6] was to receive in addition a jointure consisting of annuities, plate, jewels and china. Her very considerable personal estate and her husband's affection compensated for the brutality of her father, Ephraim d'Aguilar, and the misery he had inflicted on his unhappy family.

Ephraim Lopez Pereira, or Baron d'Aguilar of Highbury as he preferred to be called, was one of sixteen children of a Portuguese Sephardi, Moses Lopez Pereira, who had left Lisbon after the Spanish Wars of Succession and had settled in Vienna. There he ingratiated himself with the Empress Maria-Theresa and was granted monopoly of the sale of tobacco in Austria and Bohemia, drawing on experience he had gained in Portugal where he had farmed the tobacco monopoly. His financial transactions were of such magnitude and so successful that having lent money for the rebuilding of the palace of Schönbrunn he was created a Baron of the Holy Roman Empire in 1726 and assumed the name of d'Aguilar. He left Vienna for London in the middle of the century taking with him his children, his servants and his slaves and settled at Alderman's Walk, Bishopsgate. At his death ten years later his sons became naturalized British, Ephraim inheriting the title and £100,000. Six years after the death of his first wife Ephraim remarried, this time to the widow of an obscure member of his first wife's family. He continued to live on a princely and liberal scale in a house in Broad Street, with nearly thirty servants and carriages and horses in great number. But then, obsessed by the fear of losing money and claiming to have forfeited a fifteen-acre estate during the American War of Independence, he turned suddenly into the world's greatest miser. Selling his City house he closed up his country homes at Sydenham and Twickenham and two houses at Bethnal Green, and bought a house in Shaftesbury Place, Aldersgate, where he slept and kept prostitutes and the women he

THE STEWARTS AND THE MACKENZIES

had seduced; also their daughters. It was said to be 'an absolute chaos of household goods, merchandize and filth', and 'his habits were of the most unnatural, inhuman and degrading'. His name was a byword for bestiality. He leased a house and a large yard in Islington and there, in what was generally known as 'Starvation Farm', he kept some wretched animals, deliberately denying them sufficient food so that they expired of hunger, perished of cold on heaps of dung, or else fed upon each other.

Alienated from his legitimate daughters, who he said were 'too genteel' for him, and their husbands, he died in March 1802, supposedly cursing his daughter Caroline on his deathbed for having ventured to try to see him in his last illness. But as he died intestate, his fortune of £200,000, a valuable library, plate, jewels, bags of cochineal and of fine indigo were inherited by those very daughters whom he had so thoroughly disliked. It was said at his death that his life had been a combination of vice and virtue, of misanthropy and benevolence, of pride and humility and of cruelty compounded with kindness.[7]

Admiral Stewart did not live to witness the death of his father-in-law; he died at Glasserton in 1795. A few months later his eldest son, Keith, a midshipman on board *Queen Charlotte*, was drowned the day after the rout of the French fleet in the Channel by Lord Bridport. The boy was looking over the shipside watching the shot holes being stopped when he lost his hold and fell into the sea.[8] James Stewart therefore inherited at the age of eleven the lands and house at Glasserton and a rent roll of £16,000. His mother remarried two years later but was again widowed when her husband fell at the Battle of Waterloo.

These were Louisa's forbears on her paternal side. Her mother's lineage was less picturesque but of a more lasting influence. In the chronicle of this remarkable woman's fortunes may be traced the origin of much of Louisa's subsequent behaviour.

The consequences of the curse allegedly cast on the Clan Mackenzie in the seventeenth century had effect only very much later, by which time the family had acquired power through conquest and gift. According to tradition the first chief was a wanted murderer who, while taking refuge in the wild hills of Kintail in the south west of Ross-shire, saved the life of King Alexander III of Scotland when he was threatened by a stag. For recompense he was granted the lands of Kintail and took as a

THE STEWARTS AND THE MACKENZIES

device the stag's head (or 'caberfae' in Celtic) which became thenceforward the designation of the chief of the Clan Mackenzie and was to be adopted as the badge of the Seaforth Highlanders. The Mackenzies had fought for Robert the Bruce; in the fourteenth century they were made Barons of Kintail; battles, raids, risings, feuds had brought them territories so extensive that they stretched from the east coast of Ross-shire to the western seas. In 1623, when the earldom of Seaforth was created the Castle of Brahan was built as a fortified stronghold just south of Dingwall, in Ross-shire. It was here at the close of the century during the absence of the third earl that the family seer supposedly divined an incident distasteful to the earl's wife. For this he was charged and condemned to death. Before the sentence was carried out he delivered a curse on the Mackenzies, prophesying that in the far future the line would become extinct when the clan chief, both deaf and dumb, would survive his four sons and die without a male heir, and that a white-hooded woman from the East would inherit the remains of his possessions and would in turn kill her own sister.[9]

The fifth earl, a supporter of the Stuarts, had fled to France when his title was attainted and his lands forfeited after the first Jacobite rising in 1715. He left his factor, Donald Murchison, a man of lowly origin, to collect the rents of his vast estates and to forward them to him abroad – which Murchison managed to do, despite great difficulties. This loyalty, however, was ill requited for when, having received a pardon, Lord Seaforth returned to Scotland he forgot the man who had served him so devotedly. Only when he heard that Murchison was dying in poverty did he hurry to his side and offer what he could by way of reparation; but Murchison refusing to take his hand turned his face to the wall and died shortly after. (His great-grandson, Sir Roderick Murchison, the pre-eminent geologist, who became a valued friend of the Stewart-Mackenzies, commissioned Landseer to paint a picture of his forbear collecting the rents.)

Lord Seaforth had been obliged to sell most of his estates after his return from France. Though heavily encumbered by debt, they were in the main bought back into the family and were inherited by his son and grandson. Finally, in 1783, the lands passed to a kinsman, Francis Humberston Mackenzie, Louisa's grandfather, who in recognition of services to the Government

THE STEWARTS AND THE MACKENZIES

was made a peer in 1796 and given the titles of Lord Seaforth and Baron Mackenzie of Kintail.

This was a man greatly gifted, his taste tending towards a love of the arts and natural science. Walter Scott was his friend and it was said that when in his youth Sir Thomas Lawrence was financially embarrassed he turned to Lord Seaforth begging him to be 'the Antonio to a Bassanio', and on the loan of £1,000 promised to repay it in the manner most acceptable to his patron.[10] The subsequent full-length portrait of 1798 represents Lord Seaforth wearing the dress of the Seaforth Highlanders. Standing in a rocky landscape overshadowed by a menacing sky, with thistles springing up by his feet, this fine-looking chieftain holding an unsheathed sword appears to confront his world with the absolute confidence of his race. Yet the prophecy pronounced many generations earlier was to fall on him: not only was he the father of four sons whom he survived but he suffered the severe physical disability of being deaf and dumb. These defects seem not to have hampered a prosperous career which he faced with zest and enthusiasm. Before becoming a peer he was Member of Parliament for Ross-shire for a number of years and was then nominated Lord Lieutenant for the county. In 1801 he went as Governor to Barbados and served his term there until his return to Scotland in 1806. His governorship was not wholly successful owing partly to his inability as chief judge of the courts to hear the proceedings, and in part because his efforts to improve the conditions of slaves and the native population were criticized by the Barbadian-white ruling class and lacked encouragement from the Colonial Office at home. At the age of fifty-two he returned to his lands in Scotland, which though extensive in dimension were poor in revenue, and while living extravagantly he started to gamble and squander and was forced to sell part of his property. He had lost two sons before leaving for the West Indies and in 1813 a third son died; the next year saw the death of his only remaining son. This was indeed bitter anguish to the sorrowing father for here, with one final act still to be accomplished, was the tragic fulfilment of the ancient prophecy which Scott recorded in 'Lament for the Last of the Seaforths'.[11]

> In vain the bright course of thy talents to wrong
> Fate deaden'd thine ear and imprisoned thy tongue,
> For brighter o'er all her obstruction arose

THE STEWARTS AND THE MACKENZIES

The glow of the genius they could not oppose;
And who, in the land of the Saxon, or Gael,
Might match with Mackenzie, High Chief of Kintail?

Thy sons rose around thee in light and in love,
All a father could hope, all a friend could approve;
What 'vails it the tale of thy sorrows to tell?
In the spring time of youth and of promise they fell!
. . . . remains not a male,
To bear the proud name of the Chief of Kintail.

Lord Seaforth had been ill near Edinburgh for several months,
'all his fine faculties lost in paralytic imbecility';[12] Scott found it
'piteous to see such a wreck of what were once talents of a high
order'.[13] There was no chance of recovery 'and the conclusion of
the scene greatly to be wished for'.[14] Of his daughters when the end
came in 1815 one only, and that his eldest, Mary, had been married
and was now widowed. To her fell the heavy burden of inheritance.

And thou gentle dame, who must bear to thy grief,
For thy clan and thy country the cares of a Chief,
Whom brief rolling moons in six changes have left
Of thy husband, and father, and brethren bereft;
To thine ear of affection how sad is the hail
That salutes thee the heir of the line of Kintail.

2

The Lady of the Lake

Of the Hon. Maria Frederika Mackenzie's childhood (or Mary as she was always called) there is little to tell. She was born at Tarradale in the Black Isle on the Moray Firth in March 1783, the eldest of the Seaforths' ten children. Her mother, Mary Proby, daughter of the Dean of Lichfield, when not childbearing or active in the cares of motherhood, concerned herself with the poor and tried to improve their condition and education, so that the child grew up strong in her sense of affiliation to her own people and with a love of the Highlands which was perhaps the dominant feature of her life, as it was to be of Louisa's. Of its legends and histories and superstitions she could recount innumerable stories. On their own territory the Mackenzies were omnipotent and Mary retained and passed on to her daughter the quite unconscious tendency of expecting others to submit readily to her wishes, though in her this was tempered with a keen intelligence. She was of no striking beauty though of aristocratic bearing; her distinction as a young woman was enhanced by her wit and high spirits and an aptitude for enjoyment. Her youth was spent mostly at Brahan Castle and Stornoway, the homes of her ancestors, but when she entered London society her pleasure in balls and routs was that of any young girl and won her a host of friends. In Edinburgh she was acquainted with her father's friend Walter Scott, a friendship which ripened some years later into something more than admiration on his side, while she retained for him a lasting affection and a deep respect.

Life in Barbados with her parents presented a strange though not unexciting contrast to her Highland upbringing. Pilgrim House, the Governor's residence, was just outside Bridgetown whose white Georgian houses fronted the bay, stretching two miles. The great hurricane of 1780 had demolished the northern wing of Pilgrim House and it had never never been rebuilt, but with the arrival of so numerous a family the Assembly voted to restore it.

Two years after Lord Seaforth's arrival Commodore Samuel Hood was appointed Commander-in-Chief of the Leeward Islands and in October 1804 married Mary Mackenzie at Bridgetown in the presence of her parents, she being twenty-one and he twenty-one years her senior. Of Dorset stock, closely related to Viscounts Bridport and Hood, this doughty sailor had had an adventurous career. He had been with Nelson's squadron at Santa Cruz and was sent to assist him at the Battle of the Nile. From a Governorship of Trinidad in 1802 he moved to the Leeward Islands and there entered into a marriage which may have been contracted as one of convenience but which proved of great happiness to both.

It is possible that Mary saw it as a duty to her younger unmarried sisters for until she was led to the altar it was unlikely, in a nicely regulated society, that they would be asked in marriage. Something too of the romance of the great sailing ships, the skill of those who manned them, the brilliance of the uniforms, the first hand accounts given by 'Sam' (as he was called) of Lord Nelson, and other tales of valour, and perhaps a longing hope of an approaching return to the western seas and her homeland may have influenced an imaginative mind and affectionate heart. For Hood it must have seemed an obvious choice. There had been little leisure in the past to think of marriage and here was no ordinary girl but one of a superior mind, a happy disposition, cultivated tastes and an engaging eagerness for life. No doubt he was deeply attracted to her. It was time to marry and have a family but though, as Mary wrote later to a friend, 'we build castles about our picininis', there were to be none until her second marriage. Towards the end of 1804 Sam Hood was invested with a knighthood. 'The Commander is a Knight of the Bath', exclaimed Mary, 'perfectly unasked and in great measure unexpected.' Early in the following year Sir Sam and Lady Hood sailed for England.

This was the year of Trafalgar and Hood's career resumed its dramatic course. Soon at sea again he lost an arm and gained a pension of £500 for making a prize of four heavy French frigates off Rochefort. For this too he was presented with a sword by the City of London. Mary had spent a short time at Brahan but moved to London where she rented a house in Wimpole Street. She had many friends to welcome her, Lady Louisa Stuart, Mary

THE LADY OF THE LAKE

Berry, Lady Stafford, Lady Anne Barnard, Wellington's wife, and one evening she escorted the Princess of Wales to Covent Garden Theatre where she was introduced to the Duke of Cumberland.[15] When Sir Sam, her 'beloved creature', was at sea she suffered tortures of apprehension for his safety and victory, but for his sake prayed for action in battle and when nursing him after the loss of his arm exclaimed:

> My dear Soul what an unfeeling devil I was ever to think or wish him to have an action. You don't know how bitterly I reproach myself now. The dear creature has been more sweet tempered, amiable and delightful than you can imagine. I love him ten times better than ever and I think he has shown himself a greater hero in his sick chamber than ever he did on his quarter deck.

Mary herself had shown the makings of a heroine having been dropped between boat and ship in high seas and in darkness when he was brought into a home port, maimed and suffering. Uncomplaining she had sat all night by his cot in her wet stays.[16]

In 1807 Hood was elected Member of Parliament for Westminster and in the same year was at the bombardment of Copenhagen. Advanced to rear-admiral he later helped gain possession of the island of Madeira. When in May 1808 Mary heard he had a 'fever in the Baltic of a bad kind, sick and languid' she had a fright and feared she would find 'the poor fellow' much altered. He was to come home on sick leave and in July she went to Brahan to await him and hoped he would be pleased at her having obtained permission from the Admiralty for him to 'shift his flag into a small vessel on leaving the Baltic and come into Cromarty Bay'. No sooner recovered than he was off again and she was 'all in the dumps', until on 25 September 1808, heading her letter 'Great Victory for Sir Sam', she wrote excitedly of 'Sir Sam's most gallant action with the Russian fleet consisting of nine sail of the line whom he drove before him. Papa cried with joy when he heard the exploit of his boy'.

Walter Scott's friendship with Caberfae (as he called Lord Seaforth) was an old one, rooted in pride of their native land, but it was Mary Hood who captured a small corner of his heart. With mutual interests and friends and an affinity of tastes, they had met when Mary was in Edinburgh; when she was in London a delightful correspondence ensued, and if he too were in town they would

14 THE LADY OF THE LAKE

see each other constantly. In April 1809, having stayed on the way at Mainsforth in County Durham with his friend Robert Surtees, Walter Scott and his wife reached London. 'My friend Walter Scott is now in town,' Mary wrote, 'and I see him almost daily. He is by far the pleasantest Scotchman I see', and the one whose society pleased her most. She longed to introduce him to a friend of hers – 'You would be delighted with him, his letters are a perfect *treat*. Sir Sam says he is quite jealous and I assure you there is some cause.' He valued her knowledge of old Scottish lore, of 'plaided and plumed chiefs', half-forgotten customs and of tales lost in the mists of years. He countered her descriptions of the Highlands with his manifest love for his own Border country, urging her to stay with him and his family at their 'little farm called Ashestiel' overlooking the Tweed.

> I assure you this country, though it has neither the splendid luxuriousness of Kentish landscape nor the romantic dignity of your Highland mountains, possesses a very pleasing character peculiar to itself. If you were to say the English landscape resembled a modern beauty in full dress and that the Northern one was like an ancient amazon I think I would claim for our southern hills the character of a pretty barefooted Shepherdess with a milkpail upon her head.

During the London interlude Scott and his wife spent a few days at Tonbridge with the Hoods. Sir Sam, who had recently been given a baronetcy, was recruiting his health before a further spell at sea. It had been a happy time for Mary as was evident from her letter, thanking

> you and Mrs Scott for your visit which I feel as the greatest honour that could have been conferred upon us, and I shall look back to those three days as some of the most delightful of my life. I cannot help also thanking you for Marmion, to have the author call himself my friend and to feel at the same time that he is so, is a distinguishing [illegible] which however gratifying to the vanity of anyone is, believe me, far more so to my heart . . . there is no fear of me ever forgetting the friendship you have already honored me with.[17]

Scott's letters written during the many anxious months her husband was in sea-battle were filled with matters to entertain and comfort her; he was ever ready with his praise for 'the Knight of the

THE LADY OF THE LAKE

Sword' as he aptly called Sir Sam. He grieved – 'we who know and love both Sir Samuel and you' – that she would be deprived of her 'gallant knight' for so long. When his shore leave was cut short Scott observed that England was famous for thinking heroes had neither heart nor homes, and though Sir Sam's length of service in the Mediterranean was regrettable

> as a Briton I cannot but rejoice . . . there is no Man I would more depend upon, for the gentleness of his temper shows his fortitude as much as the bending of a sword blade proves the metal of the Steel.

The correspondence built on a perfect understanding gave him licence to tease her over her strongly Whig sympathies:

> I continue the incorrigible tory you left me and since your Ladyship has failed to make a Whig of me I need hardly add that I am likely to continue deaf to the voice of all future charmers, though they charm never so wisely.

He offered her bits of gossip; gave his opinion of the Prince and Princess of Wales and summed up: 'And so exeunt Prince and Princess for whom it is scarcely possible for anyone to have less anxiety than myself.' He discussed his political views – 'Oh thou most atrocious most incorrigible tory',[18] she gasped – news of friends, domestic matters, and begged her not to 'dismiss the Muses' during a *séjour* at Bath, for she ought not to neglect her poetical talent. When she told him she was learning Latin he was delighted:

> Knowledge itself can never be ridiculous – the affectation of it always is but you have not a particle of affectation in your possession so it cannot put a single ringlet of your locks out of order much less discompose the intelligent sensible head which these locks adorn.

(With the new fashion of short hair, Mary had cut hers, probably wearing short curls dressed in front. 'I have made a close crop, it is all the rage and becomes me without anything on my head, but build on the front.')

In spite of the 'sensible intelligent head' Scott was disturbed by the thought of Mary in London ('London is the devil's own drawingroom' he would later write), still in her twenties and unchaperoned in the corrupting influence of Regency society.

THE LADY OF THE LAKE

> There is something about her that makes me think of her with a mixture of affection and so anxiety [he wrote to his friend Morritt, of Rokeby]. Such a pure and excellent heart join'd to such native and fascinating manners cannot pass unprotected through your fashionable scenes without much hazard of a tinge at least, if not a stab. I remember we talked over this subject once while riding on the banks of the Tees and some-how (I cannot tell why) it falls like a death-bell on my ear. I would to God she were with us in Scotland. She is too artless for the people that she has to live amongst.[19]

And again two months later:

> I am vexd about Lady Hood and wish her here with all my heart and soul. I have not interested myself in anybody's happiness so much this long while and I feel very jealous of her unprotected state.[20]

In the autumn of 1809, when Mary was in London, she received news from Scott of a narrative poem just begun.

> I have bestowed much pains on the first canto of the poem which the public rather than I have called the Lady of the Lake, but I wish you could teach me to put a little spirit into my lover. I am reduced to despair by his intractability – in attempting to make him very good and amiable I have smoothed him into the merest walking gentleman that ever sauntered through six cantos. You fair pole stars of our eyes must certainly have some receipt to make us a little more interesting when we are under the influence of your rays. Pray teach me the secret; shall I make him jealous, or half mad or stark mad? I have made him swim through a loch already & he does not look a bit more respectable.

Provoked by no further news, Mary wrote from Bath in January 1810 remonstrating with Scott for having left her in the dark.

> Why do you tantalize me with promises of *extracts* and all sorts of fine things, when it is now three months since you have condescended to write me a line? I hear from report that you have written a most beautiful poem called the *Lady of the Lake*, and that it is to be forthwith published. But from you I have looked in vain for the samples I was promised.[21]

Robert Surtees was informed by Scott in March that the poem was

THE LADY OF THE LAKE 17

'a grand romance ambling on all fours like the palfrey of Queen Guenever'.[22]

In May when the poem was published Mary was sent a copy and after reading it a second time she wrote:

> My opinion is of no value otherwise than as the feelings of nature dictate to any one, but to say my mind it is the most exquisitely beautiful, the most original, and the most *inspired* performance that it is possible for the mind of man to give birth to.

She speculated as to whether she had been the prototype for Ellen, the Lady of the Lake. Scott's reply, written on 7 September 1810 and addressed to Sidmouth, opened by apologizing for the long delay in acknowledging her letter owing to the 'shifting state' of the family (though one always had time to write to 'friends one loves'). They had been journeying in the Highlands, he, his wife and little girl Sophia who had been no more trouble 'than a wax doll'. He gave her an account of their travels naming friends and places known also to her. Finally came the disclosure which must have given her supreme pleasure:

> *The Lady of the Lake* is very much indebted for your very *very* flattering approbation . . . it is very certain that I did very often think of that same Mary while attempting to draw a heroine of simple and natural and at the same time noble and generous feeling and manners, with something of the pride of high birth and a great deal of the kindly warmth of domestic affection. I should not have the vanity to think I had at all succeeded in the outline had not some thing of the resemblance occured to some of our mutual friends – which was paying my portrait or rather slight outline a very high compliment.

By the end of the year Mary had taken a house for eight months in Upper Grosvenor Street, 'close to the Park and is a very pretty little bijou'. From there, heading her letter 'Grosv St *Upper*, 22, My Birthday', she wrote to Scott in March 1811 asking if he had

> ever heard of the gallery that is being painted by Mrs Bruce for the Prince of Wales? It is to consist of thirty-five *Beauties* as they chuse to call them. They are miniatures drawn to the knees and really they are painted in the most beautiful style. For which reason I should have been selected for one I know not, but so it is.[23]

18 THE LADY OF THE LAKE

She was to wear the costume he had created for her as 'Ellen'. 'The picture to be taken at the moment she first appears with "locks flung back".'[24] She asked Scott for his opinion on the subject, in particular whether there was 'any impropriety in Ellen Douglas wearing the Mackenzie plaid & the branch of oak (the mark of our class)' at her breast. 'Also what is a satin snood?' she asked, 'and send me a drawing of a real old Highland brooch.'

Scott was quick to reply on 2 April with a sketch of the brooch which 'secured the folds of the plaid and was placed either on the breast or left shoulder', giving the effect of the whole plaid appearing to be attached by it. He continued:

> I have been trying everywhere to get a plaid and a patient damsel who will let me adjust it for her so as to procure an intelligible sketch but I begin to despair of success. In the meanwhile I must so express myself by negatives. It must *not* be thrown over one shoulder like the scarfs worn by shepherdesses in an opera and it must not be a complete mantle as an old wife wears it going to Kirk. If you can find a real plaid, I mean our shepherd properly, I think your Suivante if she has talents for the toilette will fall on a handsome mode of adjusting it. The *snood* was simply a fillet of a single colour drawn through the hair for the purpose of binding up the locks. It was the emblem of the maiden state & nothing else was ever worn by young Highland women or indeed Scotswomen of any province. All wedlock gave them was a right to cover their head with the Curch or cap. If a young woman lost the right to wear the snood without acquiring that of the curch it argued light and incorrect behaviour.

He had only to add that the brooch was described in the poem as of gold, but silver with glittering stones would look better on the tartan drapery in the painting. 'I think they cannot object to the Mackenzie oak or tartan.' He admired the power by which thirty-six beauties 'and Lady Hood of the number' could be assembled, thinking it most princely 'and it is one of the few exercises of the royal prerogative which I have ever felt prompted to envy.' He admired everything in the plan except 'cutting the figures short by the knees which is vile bad taste' and observed that in the character she was assuming she would be 'particularly injured by the circumstance, for it will be scarce possible to understand the attitude unless the figure had been at full length with a highland back

THE LADY OF THE LAKE

ground. Besides you should have had deer-skin buskins to complete the costume.' And unable to resist a dig at Lady Hertford, the Prince's mistress, he added for Mary's diversion: 'I hope the reigning Sultana has not bad ancles which is the only reason I can divise for the gusto.'

Wellington's successes in Portugal in May of this year were uppermost in Scott's mind, and his belief in 'my heroe Lord Wellington, I call him mine though he is now all the worlds'. He reported his attempt at writing

> a short poem on the affairs of the peninsular – it is to be called the Vision of Don Roderic and here am I and Mrs Scott in this solitary cabbin [Ashestiel], she sewing her silken seam and I meditating my sonerous verses with an old dairy man and footman for our attendance and cookery.

James Ballantyne, his Edinburgh printer, had given him 100 guineas for the poem – this he would send to the Committee for suffering Portuguese – and proposed to publish 'this precious rhapsody (for it is so to them if money can make it precious)' in the *Edinburgh Annual Register*.

> I intend to open my poem with a sort of address to Lord W – Do you know if he likes poetry? Pray ask Lady Wellington – Yet perhaps it is as well for me if he does not, for then he will accept of the compliment without criticizing it.

He promised to send her a copy as he was to have a few 'thrown off for my friends of which I need hardly say Lady Hood shall have an early one'. The poem was published in June, in which same month Scott wrote to Mary: 'Don Roderick has somehow acquired the *pas grave* of Castile and moves much more slowly than any legendary heroe I have yet brought on the carpet.'

The month of August was an agitating one for Mary. Sir Sam was promoted to vice-admiral of the White and appointed Commander-in-Chief of the East Indies. They were to sail to India in September on the frigate *Owen Glendower*, stopping at Madeira, Tenerife, Brazil and the Cape. Though pleased at going out 'to this fine country' she was full of anxiety at leaving her family and feared the term might be a long one. Some of these anxieties she confided to Scott, but he would not believe her 'evil-boding auguries'.

THE LADY OF THE LAKE

No, my dear Lady Hood; as you know that a poet and prophet were formerly synonimes I will prophecy and you shall believe. You shall go, since fate and duty will have it so, to the East Indies but you shall stay no longer than may be necessary for the Knight of the Sword to realise such a fortune as will enable him to retire from his profession and to purchase a huge highland estate where you will build collages, found Gaellic schools and reign a little queen during the fine months and enjoy your English friends when the weather of your Northern dominions grows too keen to be comfortable to their sovereigns. [As to the voyage he thought her] in far greater danger from the fiend Ennui than either from kelpies or mermaids; so pray make provision of good books and chuse them in those languages you understand less perfectly, because in that case you cannot read too fast and one book slowly read answers the purpose of three. In short, although I do not wonder at your present objection at leaving your native land and the best society in the world, I think you will find your residence in India with all the advantages afforded by your rank and situation too pleasant to need my correspondence as much as you anticipate.

He could not say how sorry he was for himself as this might only add to her regret. 'In short dear Lady Hood I love you dearly with all your very little failings pray make an effort and continue to like me as well as you can in spite of my great ones.' And finally he begged her to 'Keep a seat in your veranda and a cup of the wine Scheraz for the Border Minstrel for if he survives he will come to strike his harp.'

On the same day he acquainted a friend in Calcutta of the Hoods' impending departure. Of Mary he wrote that she was 'an ardent Scotswoman . . . generous and feeling and intelligent and has contrived to keep her heart and social affections vivid and awake amidst the chilling and benumbing atmosphere of London fashion.'[25] To Lady Stafford he observed:

If it is not quite the money-making place it once was, our eastern empire is considerably improved in point of society, and I hope Lady Hood will find many (at least among the gentlemen, for I dont anticipate highly of Indian ladies) whose conversation will interest and amuse her.[26]

THE LADY OF THE LAKE

He thought also that the 'dignity of the situation' was one 'which our friend will not dislike'. From India Mary sent him an oriental topaz seal, 'a very flattering token of her remembrance'. Scott was to see Mary Hood again but in altered circumstances and the friendship which had blossomed into affection would not regain the same old, unconstrained, intimacy.

There was much in India to satisfy Mary's curiosity. In 1812 she made a journey in a palanquin from Madras to Seringpatam and Mysore; great attention was paid her by native princes and some of the progresses were said to be marked by a sort of 'regal splendour'.[27] She was a good shot and could claim to have been the first Englishwoman in India to have shot a tiger. A journey taken along the Malabar coast and on to Poona brought her the acquaintance of the Resident, the Hon. Mountstuart Elphinstone, later Governor of Bombay. She had been spoken of 'in raptures by everybody'[28] before her arrival and he had formed the intention of joining her on her travels to Ellora. He had heard of her 'good sense, information, good looks, good temper, and vivacity'. At thirty-four he fell in love with this bewitching woman of thirty. He could not say enough of her. Furthermore she was familiar with French, Italian and English classics; these qualities made her 'the most agreeable companion I think I have ever met, and to see such a person at Poona had the air of a miracle.'[29] They studied Italian together and read Dante, but when it was time for Mary to leave for Ellora, though 'very desirous of accompanying her' he was prevented from doing so.[30] Yet his hopes were fixed on a journey with her to Baghdad and Persia the following year. When, after his death in 1859, a subscription was taken up to record his life and work in India by a marble statue to be raised at St Paul's Cathedral (now in the crypt), Lord Ashburton wrote to his mother-in-law, the former Lady Hood:

> Although you are so silent about your conquests the world is not so. I have therefore subscribed largely to the Elphinstone Memorial. Do you know why he never married? *I do* – perhaps *you* do too. You certainly should.

But 1814 brought an end to Mary's conquest of India. That 'beloved creature', Sir Sam, died at Madras in December and her happy years of marriage were over.

3
From Richmond to Corfu

Mary's homecoming in the early part of 1815 was a sorrowful and lonely one. Her husband and her remaining brother had recently died and in January of this year, before her return, her father had been buried. From Edinburgh on the 21st of the month Scott wrote to Morritt of having

> just seen Caberfae's hearse pass. I trust they will send it by sea for on land the journey must be fearful at this season. There is something very melancholy in seeing the body pass, poorly attended and in the midst of a snowstorm whitening all the sable ornaments of the undertaker and all corresponding with the decadence and misfortunes of the family.[31]

As he watched the sombre spectacle from his window at the Court of Session his thoughts lingered on Mary though news of Sir Sam's death had not yet reached Scotland. 'Our friend Lady Hood will now be Caberfae herself,' he wrote. 'She has the spirit of a chieftaness in every drop of her blood', and though the estate was terribly embarrassed he hoped that if Sir Sam had made 'a few tens of thousands in the east things may do better than I at present augur'. To Lady Stafford he wrote: 'All the Highlands ring with a prophecy that when there should be a deaf Caberfae the clan and chief shall go to wreck.'[32]

The ancient curse was not unfamiliar to Mary either, nor had it yet run its course. Had she not come from the East, from India, wearing her white coif, her widow's cap? It would have been a harrowing thought that she might yet be responsible for the death of one of her sisters. There were five of them, unmarried, and her mother and herself for whom provision had to be made from the involved state of the property. Brahan Castle was their home but at thirty-two, with undiminished vitality, she was not prepared to live quietly there with her six womenfolk. Now calling herself Lady Mackenzie she was often in Edinburgh seeing to her affairs.

FROM RICHMOND TO CORFU 23

The library at Brahan was to be sold in London and its shipment to be insured for about £3,500.[33] The letters of Charles II and Montrose were to go in a separate parcel. Towards the end of that unhappy year Scott reported her as 'shedding tears over her own family distresses'.[34] But earlier, in London in June, she had had the unparalleled experience, so she claimed, of acting to the Duchess of Wellington as the harbinger of the victory of Waterloo. One evening, seeing a dusty blood-stained chariot covered in laurels moving rapidly towards Downing Street drawn by four galloping horses, and two captured French eagles and banners at the windows, she guessed that this was the culmination which all England had been daily awaiting. As the Duke's aide-de-camp hurried on to lay the conquered eagles at the feet of the Regent, Mary quickly made her way with her tidings to Apsley House.

Her correspondence with Mountstuart Elphinstone at Poona reflected the renewal of her intercourse with Scott. This brought in reply a condemnation of one of Scott's works followed by an outburst of perhaps understandable pique: 'The child of fancy was flattered beyond measure by your recollection, in which I sympathized with him.'[35] If Mary ever considered the likelihood of marrying Elphinstone all such thoughts were dismissed by early 1817 when, signing herself 'Mary Mackenzie', she wrote to acquaint Walter Scott of her approaching marriage to James Alexander Stewart.

> I am going to be married to Mr Stewart of Glasserton. You may believe that no light attachment would incline me to give up the perfect liberty and independence I now enjoy. Indeed I am most deeply attached to Mr Stewart and as he is, I am certain, the same to me I look upon myself as certain of enjoying all the happiness which the kindest of your wishes could augur for me.[36]

The news engendered little enthusiasm, as was evident in the restraint of Scott's reply.

> My dear Lady Mackenzie, If words could express good wishes this letter would be a very long one, but as they cannot and as I know you will give me credit for hoping and wishing all that can add to your happiness, I will make my congratulations short. There are so many circumstances that must render the advice

24 FROM RICHMOND TO CORFU

and assistance of a man of honour and prudence especially useful to you that wisdom as well as affection seem to recommend a change of your condition. In every state my earnest and kindest wishes must attend you. I am ever most respectfully and truly yours, WALTER SCOTT.

James Stewart was a year younger than the wife he married at Edinburgh in May 1817 at her mother's house in Charlotte Square. A miniature made at about that time lends weight to the meagre account posterity has vouchsafed him. The dark expressive eyes seemingly apprehensive of what life was to hold in store overshadow the whole countenance, while a small mouth with tightly compressed lips beneath a long nose gives more than a hint of the 'peevish temper' which was recognized by others besides Scott. His chin is buried in the folds of his high neckcloth as fashion dictated; the tufted sidewhiskers contribute strength to the face which in other respects appears to show a lack of firmness. Scott's account of his first meeting with Stewart at the time of the marriage is contained in a letter to Morritt. He found him 'externally a pleasant and well-bred man' and the little he had seen of him he had liked. But there was a defect which 'bespeaks either no steadiness of principle or a peevish and discontented temper'; this failing was owing to having once been 'a keen Pittite, he has become a zealous Whig' – this no doubt under Mary's influence. It was also said that he had

> *gambled* and if he retains any itch of that kind I would as soon see a friend married to the Knave of Clubs – But our ladies' tongues in Edinburgh are not so well scraped as those of our sheep-heads and a single instance of thoughtlessness may be easily metamorphosed into a habitual vice. I wish her intended had less smile and plausible civility in his manner. I dont know what there is in that sort of politeness which always puts me on my guard – it often intimates a bad temper. But I will croak no longer for really I have nothing to say against the man and he is rather handsome polite and pleasant in conversation.[37]

Carlyle, who met him some years later, referred to the 'dark-complexioned Whig, lean, bilious, whose face consisted almost wholly of a long hook nose and two huge yellow eyes'.[38]

Mary's was certainly the guiding hand in that union. A man of

FROM RICHMOND TO CORFU

substance, Stewart eventually sold up his Glasserton estate to finance hers, and added her name to his. 'She married a very pleasant man, Mr Stewart of Glasserton who has a very good fortune,' wrote Sophia Scott ingenuously to her governess, 'and she has dropped her ladyship, and is now plain Mrs Stewart Mackenzie.'[39]

From the time of James Stewart's marriage in 1817 until he was elected Liberal Member of Parliament for Ross and Cromarty in 1830, husband and wife were jointly involved in management of their estates, those of Mary's being still heavily laden with debt. Six children were born within ten years, three sons and three daughters, Louisa being the youngest. Two years before her birth Mary had written to Walter Scott: 'My olive branches are now five in number three boys and two girls, the partiality of friends tell me they are all handsome and clever children.'[40] The boys on the whole proved unsatisfactory, though George, three years Loo's senior, was a much-loved brother. Frank, her elder by six years was expelled from Rugby School, moved on to Trinity College, Cambridge, ran up debts and died at Grenada where he was stationed with the Highland Light Infantry. Keith, the eldest of the family, also joined the army, went to India and China, married, and after the death of his father was little comfort to his mother, questioning the terms of his inheritance, overspending and causing grave trouble in the family.

Louisa's childhood was spent mostly at George Street, Edinburgh, on the Lews, and at Brahan where Gaelic was still more generally the tongue, where superstition, belief in the occult and in prophecies were rife and where she was allowed an unconstrained freedom which was to determine her behaviour in future years. Under a wide sky the castle, built of local grey stone very slightly shaded with pink, stood on a small eminence facing south and backed by wooded hills, its gaunt walls rising to three storeys pierced by tall narrow windows. (Writing to Scott from Brahan in 1822 Mary Stewart-Mackenzie had asked him to direct her how to make a bowling green at 'this strange ugly house'.)[41] In front, the ground, bordered by great oaks, fell away allowing the eye an unobstructed view towards the Conan river where fishing rights had been granted to the Mackenzies by Mary Queen of Scots. The gently undulating countryside contrasted strangely with the forbidding aspect of the house, but in the middle distance the

FROM RICHMOND TO CORFU

sweep of hills and moorland passes were reminders that the house, once fortified and crenellated, had been erected with shrewd knowledge of its acutely strategic position. Landseer, who knew the Highlands well, gave his opinion that Brahan – which he thought beautiful – was not his idea of the Highlands. 'There is a stern sincerity about Highland rocks,' he wrote, 'a sort of *unadorned* truth that you dont find in the *rich* combinations of the Banks of the Conan where everything is suggestive of comfort and tenderness.' At a short distance behind the castle and separated from it by a low stone wall stood (and still stands) an octagonal game larder, small and gracefully shaped, and beyond it in a line with the house, backing up against the hills, the eighteenth-century stables. Slightly to the east were the gardens enclosed within a wall; also the hot-houses and orchard. From there extended the three-mile-long drive to the main gates, their posts on either side each surmounted by a stag.

Scott had died in 1832, an occasion of sorrow to Mary. She had not seen much of him in these later years but she had received great pleasure from his acceptance of a little Highland terrier bred in Kintail and very scarce. Scott named him Ourisk (goblin); he was immortalized in Wilkie's portrait of the Scott family, peeping out from behind the figure of Charles Scott, Sir Walter's youngest son. In one of his last letters to his friend of twenty years he commented on its being a happy thing 'that in taking away much, advanced life leaves us the friendships which years have strengthened more valued and more valuable'.

During this time of retrenchment and childbearing for Mary, the ancient curse passed upon the Mackenzies had been played out. A Gothic monument on the side of the road marks the place of tragedy. One day, when Mary was driving her sister in a pony carriage, an accident occurred as the result of which Caroline died and Mary through a trick of fate had expiated the accursed prophecy.

By 1834 it was time for a migration to the south: Stewart-Mackenzie's duties at Westminster necessitated a more accessible home, his sons would soon be needing university education and his elder daughters husbands. He had applied for and had been refused the Governorship of Bombay. Trumpeters' House, Richmond, in Old Palace Yard next to Wardrobe Court, was purchased for £645. This was the third house to stand on part of

FROM RICHMOND TO CORFU

the site which had once formed the ten-acre stretch from Richmond Green to the river and had embraced Henry VII's Richmond Palace where Elizabeth I had died. Neglected and left in a near-ruined condition during the Civil War, the house had been rebuilt by James II in 1688. The back faces towards the Green but the two life-sized stone trumpeters on either side of the entrance, who gave the house its name, have perished. The front of this fine house, sometimes partly attributed to Wren, with its tall narrow windows and handsome portico of four Doric columns, commands a view across the wide lawn to the river. Louisa would have found a contrast to the grim fastness of beloved Brahan in the warmth of its red brick overlooking the great sweep of moving water below and the meadow banks beyond. The beautiful panelled library boasted a rococo ceiling introducing busts of Milton and Pope and it was here, when in the middle of the century Prince Metternich faced a two-year exile, that Disraeli on a visit to the statesman exclaimed '. . . the long library, the most charming house in the world'. (In this century Marconi, the inventor of wireless telegraphy, lived there for a year.) McCulloch, the gardener from home, had been sent for to work in the grounds; a room was found for him, his bed-furniture and cooking utensils, with a ton of coals annually. His terms would be fourteen shillings a week and board, and he was to take his passage on the Leith smack to Richmond. When in 1836 the Richmond enterprise proved too expensive and Loo and her sisters were packed back to Brahan and tenants sought for the house, McCulloch stayed on. Though they asked £50 per month rent, they secured only £40, for the gravel walks were in so bad a state that 'no lady can walk upon them'.[42]

In straitened circumstances, James had again applied for a post abroad and in 1837, when Loo was ten, her father was appointed Governor of Ceylon. She sailed with her parents and her second sister Caroline, Miss Price her governess, and John Carr their coachman, a native of Wigtownshire. The three brothers who remained behind to continue their education (Keith at Oxford, Frank and George at Rugby) were consigned to the charge of their Mackenzie maiden aunts at Leamington Spa.

Loo sustained the journey out very well despite the rough weather and seasickness; an elasticity of spirit, already pronounced, and an engaging curiosity made her an agreeable

28 FROM RICHMOND TO CORFU

travelling companion. If the two years at Richmond had opened her eyes to another world than Scotland, her three and a half in Ceylon gave her an insight to a life of which she could never have dreamed. It was a life of privilege, not by birthright as in Scotland, but inherent in an establishment where her father as Governor had control and influence, where ceremonials and homage were the rule rather than the exception, where native servants were ready to indulge every whim of a lively and intelligent girl. But her mother's strong commonsense was both influential and beneficial and she saw to it that Louisa remained largely unaffected (though hints of imperiousness were never entirely suppressed).

Queen's House, in the main thoroughfare of Colombo, was originally an old Dutch palace when the Dutch had been masters of the island, but since the British had taken possession at the beginning of the century it had become Crown property of the Government. It stood among shady trees and from a dilapidated state the house had recently been repaired to the frugal tune of £700, grudgingly approved by the Crown. Here Loo settled to her lessons; her interest in botany was kindled by the exotic flowers and vegetation of the East, and her youthful study of minerals was begun. The climate if unpleasant was not one to injure her, though her father when on a tour of the Eastern Province suffered sunstroke which affected his brain and his health never entirely recovered. Louisa's eldest sister joined her family in 1838 and married Philip Anstruther, Colonial Secretary to the Governor of Ceylon. This was a pleasant family concern and a much-needed antidote to the unpalatable news which had reached the Stewart-Mackenzies. Frank, their second son, had been expelled from Rugby for striking a praepostor and head of the house and refusing to apologize. A letter to the aunts from Mr Prince Lee, that great Rugby teacher, expressed his concern at what had occurred. Lamenting the spirit Frank had shown, the discipline of the school required 'immediate measures and I have been directed by Dr Arnold to send him home. Nothing can exceed the desire Dr Arnold has shown to bring him to a right state of feeling.'[43] The cause of Frank's intransigence is not now known; the head that bore the blow was that of Franklin Lushington to whom Edward Lear later became so devoted, and who as a distinguished barrister went out as judge to the Ionian Islands. Though only fifteen-and-a-half years of age he had gained his position through scholastic

FROM RICHMOND TO CORFU

ability, a system devised by Dr Arnold for running the school. Frank was close on eighteen and would have felt it beneath his dignity to apologize to one so much his junior in age. A postscript added that same evening to Prince Lee's letter explained that he had 'endeavoured to persuade your nephew to make the acknowledgement he is bound to do. I can do no more.'[44] Any boy at Rugby was expelled on the spot for a serious offence and sent home with his luggage by the end of the day. Thereafter Dr Arnold would in most cases do his utmost to ease the victim's path by recommending suitable tutors. In Frank's case, five days after his expulsion Dr Arnold wrote to the aunts telling them that a letter of apology from the miscreant had been received but that he could not accept him back. He had rarely written a letter 'with more Pain than I proceed now to write to you'.

> It has been an invariable rule with me – and a Rule which I have acted upon from the strongest conviction of its Benefits, – that a Boy once sent from this School must never return to it. The Time of Trial has ended and must end, when a Boy is once in the Chaise to leave Rugby. Feeling this I said to Mr Lee that up to the latest Moment of his Stay here, I would receive his apology – in Fact the Chaise was once sent away because he seemed disposed to comply.[45]

Rugby had been chosen with care by his parents. Arnold was known to be a supporter of the new Broad Church as well as being a great reformer; religious and moral principles took precedence over all other disciplines. Stewart-Mackenzie had been brought up a Presbyterian and Mary was to range herself with the Free Church of Scotland. Both were exponents of Evangelicalism. It was partly this proselytizing, particularly in schools, partly his disagreements with his superiors at home in matters of reform, also on grounds of ill health, that Stewart-Mackenzie was transferred to the Ionian Islands in the latter half of 1840. His wife had already left for England taking Caroline with her but leaving Loo with her father. The Richmond house needed a new tenant and Mary stayed there, completed the 1841 census[46] (which included the gardener McCulloch, four other servants and Pasquale, a foreign courier), and rejoined her husband at the end of the summer.

FROM RICHMOND TO CORFU

That same spring Louisa sailed to Corfu with her father. On the steamer between Ceylon and Bombay the cockroaches bit the skin of their fingers and ran over their faces in such numbers at night that driving them away was a hopeless task.[47] On arrival at Corfu in June James took up his appointment as Lord High Commissioner of the Ionian Islands; the Palace was being repainted and not ready for habitation. Writing in July to her mother still in England, Loo headed her paper: 'Pavilion, Corfu'; the writing shows a copperplate but fluent hand and the fourteen-year-old girl who had not seen her mother for nearly a year endeavoured to give some account of herself.

> I must tell you what you must expect to find me like; a great aukard, gauky girl; & outwardly I fear anything but pleasing; but dearest Mamma I hope you find my *mind* improved, purified, and more truthy. I hope you will find me fonder of intellectual pleasures for it is my wish and endeavour, to be dutiful, and good to you.

Miss Price had watched her 'during your absence with a *Mother's care*', and 'dear Papa' had also been 'very very kind' to her; they had the use of a 'yatch' and her mother was promised as much 'yatching' as ever she liked; they were living 'at the Pavilion, a little place adjoining the Palace'.[48] With her mother's arrival all this was changed. The Palace of St Michael and St George (the first seat of the Order) enjoyed a position above the cliff face to the north side of the town. Built twenty years earlier of white sandstone from Malta, weathered to a pale yellow, its wide front faced south across the dazzling blue waters of the channel widening to the open sea, and beyond to the Albanian snow-capped mountains. This frontage was enriched by a portico running the length of the house which in turn was supported by twenty Doric columns, affording some shade to the ground floor rooms. On the first floor, leading from the magnificent staircase, were the reception rooms newly decorated and furnished at a cost of £20,000 and hung with handsome tapestry, brocaded satin, and among the pictures a copy of Lawrence's portrait of George IV.[49]

The harbour of Corfu and its immediate surroundings presented a teeming though heterogeneous population as diverse in tongue as in trade and dress. Albanians engaged as armed police attired in shaggy capotes with pistols in their girdles, white petticoats and

FROM RICHMOND TO CORFU

embroidered jackets, mingled with Greek women in black mantillas, girls carrying water-pitchers on their head, Greek collegians wearing black gowns and cloaks.with long hair tied in a horsetail. Overriding all was the 'vulgar English speech' of the British garrison which made a 'very curious and striking contrast'.[50] On to the quayside and into this densely packed shifting crowd stepped Sir Walter and Lady Trevelyan, of Wallington Hall, Northumberland, on 4 April 1842.

4
Friendships and Love

When Pauline Trevelyan came ashore, looked about her, and that evening wrote in her journal that the woody hills, snowy mountains and a sea as blue as sapphires were 'quite like Bute', she was about to embark on an attachment which would afford her twenty-four years of devoted friendship. When she died Loo could exclaim with all sincerity: 'Except my child there is no one in all the world I loved as I loved *her*.'

The Trevelyans were seasoned travellers. Much of their seven married years had been spent journeying in Europe and they were now on their way to Athens. Sir Walter was a man of idiosyncratic tastes, impressively intellectual and deeply learned in natural history. An antiquarian, a dedicated teetotaler, he had found in his wife a woman of sharp intelligence, vital and compassionate, a fine linguist (also versed in Latin and Greek) and sharing many kindred interests, though hers were more generally disposed towards the fine arts of which she was an accomplished critic, writing periodically for the *Scotsman*. Her tiny stature presented a foil to her husband's height, her twenty-six years to his forty-five, her swift reactions to his more ponderous observations. An unflagging enthusiasm carried all before her. While both possessed unbounded energy they likewise both suffered from ill health – chronic gout on his part, on hers periods of agonizing pain ascribed to a tumour of which she characteristically made little. Sir Walter inherited two family properties, Nettlecombe Court in Somerset, where they made regular visits, and Wallington Hall, their home, the embellishment of which was the constant focus of their devoted care.

Through an earlier acquaintanceship with the Stewart-Mackenzies they were asked to stay at the Palace and Pauline quickly assimilated the outstanding facts: that the High Commissioner was in possession of a salary of £5,000, £500 allowed for wood, £250 for the gardens, besides servants, horses, boats; 'a very fine

FRIENDSHIPS AND LOVE

appointment' she thought it on the whole. She found her host a 'very quiet little man, shy at first but talks very sensibly when he does talk and seems desirous of doing good here'. Mary was a 'very agreeable and well informed person, much above the common run of ladies'. Louisa captivated her at once.

> One of the nicest girls I ever knew. She has more information and is a more agreeable companion than many girls of twenty. She is pretty and interesting looking and has very sweet and modest manners. I am becoming every day more fond of her.[51]

There was already some compelling element in this fifteen-year-old for Pauline to fall a victim to her artlessness, and though her own influence on Loo was to be incalculable – she guided her reading, inspired her with her own aptitude for drawing, curbed her impetuousness, forwarded her interests, unsparing of herself, emotionally devoted – she was yet shrewd enough never to lose sight of the genuine qualities of this warm-hearted creature. When the visit came to an end (indicated by Sir Walter's precise accounting of £1.18s.3d. for servants' tips)[52] they were calling each other 'sister', while Caroline the elder sister was judged 'not pretty but fat and amiable; not so clever as my favourite Louisa'.

The house was admired, also the shrubbery of geraniums, the catalpas and the may bushes in full blossom; in the countryside, where they were driven by an Albanian coachman 'all gold braiding and white kilt', the giant fennel, broom, aloes, the olive groves and orange trees all came under Pauline's approving eye. Recorded with lesser enthusiasm by this follower of Pusey were the Wednesday evening Baptist meetings (involving an early dinner) held in the house by Mr Lowndes, 'this missionary sort of man'. Two months earlier there had been riots, caused, it was rumoured, by unwonted proselytizing. He was said, in the judgement of others, to have great influence on the family for they 'have all an Evangelical twist – he sings psalms, expounds false doctrine, heresy and schism and makes extempore orations, by courtesy called prayers.'[53] Things were rather better when the Trevelyans were taken to a service in the fairly recently built garrison church of St George where they sat in a gallery pew. Another cause for discomforture was the presence

34   FRIENDSHIPS AND LOVE

of Lady Davy (Sir Humphry's widow) now 'haggard and dried-up', who long ago Walter Scott had thought 'a bit of a pretence'.

> She is one of those persons [he said] who aim at literary acquaintances and the reputation of knowing remarkable characters and seeing out of the way places not for their own value, nor for any pleasure she has at the time but because such hearing and seeing and being acquainted gives her a knowing air in the world.[54]

She was now living up to the reputation of talking everyone else into silence,

> never silent a minute and her talk all about lords and ladies and grand people who were her friends. At breakfast next day a new edition of Lady Davy, very provoking, prevents one from listening to interesting conversation of James Stewart-Mackenzie.[55]

But the High Commissioner was falling foul of authority at home, largely on account of his policies though his manic evangelizing and bad temper were also causes for friction. In the summer he and Louisa went to England for a short time probably to explain his case but on arrival he was dismissed his office. From London Miss Price wrote to Mary that Louisa was wearing a 'merino Union dress' against the cold, adding a tip in the fashion line:

> The last week's Paris fashion, and not much known yet, is velvet of *one* color but *two* shades, the outside dark violet, the lining almost lilac, trimming composed of both colored velvets, flowers or feathers to correspond, some are two greens, some two browns, and very pretty.[56]

Ruined professionally and financially (it was said of him that he was the only High Commissioner since 1815 whose revenue exceeded his expenditure),[57] Stewart-Mackenzie returned with his daughter to Corfu, there to await the arrival of his successor. He sailed home with his family in the spring of 1843; by September he was dead. He had suffered some injury on the homeward journey and at Messina where they had rested he had made his will, leaving his wife all he had and making her his sole executrix. He died shortly after arriving at Southampton; the coroner's report seemed

FRIENDSHIPS AND LOVE

to suggest chronic meningitis with, possibly, some history of tuberculosis. For the second time Mary was left a widow, with six children on her hands. Harassed by financial difficulties she was obliged to sell the island of Lewis and Trumpeters' House and to retrench wherever possible. Again Brahan provided the home and was the stable background for Louisa till she married; and later, whether at Bath House, Piccadilly, at Seaton in Devon, at Addiscombe or The Grange, in Rome, in Switzerland, taking the waters at Carlsruhe, at Mentone or at Melchet Court, Hampshire, or Kent House, it was the Highlands which afforded her a particular kind of homecoming and which drew her like a magnet. But though a most devoted and dutiful daughter she was mature for her age, eager for life and determined to ensure that it was led along her own chosen line. Her mother had moved in the aristocratic world, but partly through inclination, through circumstances, and the influence of Pauline Trevelyan whose interests were artistic and intellectual, Loo found her friends in that same environment and with few exceptions this was to be her course to the end. Religion, of the strongly Evangelical persuasion, was throughout her life an impetus of recurring degree, with occasional forays into the Anglican Church.

Soon after her return from Corfu she had met Florence Nightingale, who a few years earlier had received 'a call from God'. A friendship had been struck, infatuation had developed such as many romantically minded unmarried women entertained for each other at that time (a tendency to which Loo was never immune) and Florence, the 'beloved Zoë', signed herself 'Ever your dearest life, F. Nightingale', while Loo was 'your truly loving Bird'. This was also the time of her first acquaintance with Richard Monckton Milnes (Lord Houghton), for seven years the assiduous admirer of Florence; he was said to have told Benjamin Jowett very much later that when his proposal of marriage was finally rejected he had been 'on the point' of turning to Louisa with the same offer.[58] Madame Mohl, the Scottish almost dwarf-like figure, 'with its high antiquity and its supreme oddity',[59] luminary of Parisian intellectual society, taken up by Madame Récamier and Chateaubriand, and very devoted to Florence, also became a friend. Introduced by Parthenope Nightingale Loo was told: 'She knows a great deal about art, and would tell you all manner of books, and show you artists and help you in every way.' The

FRIENDSHIPS AND LOVE

Bracebridges, so intimately connected with Florence at the Crimea, were sufficient friends for Selina Bracebridge to warn Louisa over some now undefined issue. 'Dearest Loo Loo, watch over yourself not to let that demon jealousy get any entrance.' Mrs Jameson, the celebrated author of *Sacred and Legendary Art* and *The Diary of an Ennuyée* was another shaping influence. Though never Louisa's governess (as has been sometimes said, for Loo on her return from Corfu was sixteen and a half), she may occasionally have acted as chaperone in London, taking her charge to picture galleries and exhibitions. 'Flaming red hair, fierce eyes and square mouth' in youth, she was now about fifty, 'a rather short round and massive personage of benign and agreeable aspect'.[60] A friend of the Brownings, she had accompanied them to Italy on their honeymoon and most likely it was she who encouraged the introduction in Paris a few years later between them and Louisa, thus all unwittingly laying the stage for the still unresolved momentous declaration at Loch Luichart.

Louisa saw the Trevelyans whenever possible; if in London, sightseeing; a sail down the river to Blackwall to admire the *Great Britain*; to Dulwich, to Westminster Abbey. In the spring of 1849 she and her mother were guests at Nettlecombe Court where Sir Walter took her hunting for fossils; he 'found teeth and bones of a fish', also 'some good nautili'. In the late summer the Trevelyans paid a visit to Brahan, meeting there the Bishop of Norwich, his wife and two Misses Stanley. One of the daughters, Catherine, who married Dr Vaughan, headmaster of Harrow School, was a particular friend of Louisa, while the other, Mary, disgraced herself later by taking a band of nurses to the Crimea, unbidden and unwanted by Florence Nightingale. Furthermore she was wavering on the brink of Roman Catholicism. But in 1849 when they accompanied the Trevelyans and Loo on a four-day excursion 'boating down' to Balmacara and northwards to Loch Maree, the only hesitation shown by the sisters was whether to continue after the first day. They decided to return to Brahan, thereby missing a delightful row on the loch with a piper, blue and white gentians in profusion and a return home by moonlight. 'Too hurried [an excursion] to accommodate the Miss Stanleys,' Sir Walter thought. But the Bishop was ill with a 'complication of nerves, bile and determination of blood to the head';[61] he was soon insensible and died at Brahan on 7 September. The Trevelyans, tipping the

FRIENDSHIPS AND LOVE

servants £1, had wisely left the castle. Commissioned by Mary Stewart-Mackenzie to send her some fish, sixty herrings at the cost of seventeen shillings were dispatched from Fortrose.[62]

These years did not spare Louisa from family concerns. Her brother Frank died in Grenada, mourned perhaps only by his mother – certainly not by Keith, the eldest, who was said to have detested his brother and having married had come to live close by in a house on the Brahan estate, a constant irritant to his mother with his demands for money and arguments over property. Caroline, Loo's sister, married John Petre but lived a life of gentle discord and self-pity, and died early. George, to whom Louisa was devoted seemed at the age of sixteen to be heading for the Church. 'No profession' he thought, could 'be more glorious than that of a minister to proclaim the tidings to poor lost souls.'[63] However, by the following year he was at Woolwich from which he was temporarily discharged for lack of progress and ill health. A tutor, the Revd G.T. Warner, was found for him at Swansea, of true Evangelical worth, who contended that with regard to his amusements George 'should not go to any card parties from *my* house. These abound in Swansea but I can in no way direct or indirectly sanction them.'[64] By 1847 he had rejoined the army and sailed for Gibraltar to Louisa's grief. Signing herself 'Your ever loving wifie Lou Diddles' she wrote him a farewell letter full of anxious hope that 'the Work of Grace within both our hearts may progress nearer and nearer to perfection'.[65] She was on her own now, sometimes with her mother at Brahan where she taught at the nearby Dingwall village school, or else in London lodgings at Wilton Place. In April 1850 a cousin inquired if there was any truth that she was to become one of the Queen's maids of honour, and though she may have been considered there is no record of it.[66] Loo seems to have dramatized her apprehensions until Pauline, with forthright commonsense, asked: 'Why are you in a fright *now* about the maid of honour business? I thought Miss Seymour was appointed.'

Louisa was twenty-three and her thoughts must often have turned towards marriage. After leaving Brahan in 1849 Pauline had written to her from Arbroath of having met a friend coming out of chapel who

seized hold of me and whispered 'Oh my dear, he's here. Do talk

FRIENDSHIPS AND LOVE

to him about Brahan.' I asked who she meant. 'Why, Lord Reidhaven to be sure, dont you know him? Lord Reidhaven come here, come here directly', so up he came kilt and all. As soon as he was away: 'well dear – will he do?', so you must consider yourself engaged, darling. If you are to sell yourself, better do it for l.s.d. and besides he is young and well behaved and a gentleman. Dont cut me when you are a countess or I shall break my heart.[67]

When Mary Stewart-Mackenzie had sold the Lews it had been bought by Sir James Matheson, head of the famous mercantile firm of Jardine, Matheson & Co. His nephew, Alexander Matheson, a Member of Parliament for the Inverness district of burghs was now a widower and was eager to marry Louisa, his junior by almost twenty-five years. Furnished with an immense fortune he was buying Highland property on so vast a scale that in the late 1860s Louisa (then herself a widow), writing from Balmacara to Carlyle, could exclaim: 'The man who bought this great principality for many and many a year ardently desired that I would become the mistress of it.' With her energy and love for the Highlands this might have proved a successful match though to marry money arising from trade was not yet generally acceptable. The ardent lover finally took his dismissal and remarried in 1853, at which time Louisa met him ('there is always an awkwardness in the first meeting') and could truthfully say: 'I only had to see him to feel I did right and thank God I was enabled to do so', adding magnanimously that Mrs Matheson 'is very lovely and nice and he looks fat and as happy as possible'.

Louisa had felt no misgivings in turning down her suitor for she was herself in love – with William Stirling of Keir (later Sir William Stirling-Maxwell, Bt. of Pollok), art historian, author of *Annals of the Artists of Spain*, both dilettante and scholar and a notable collector of works of art. But while Loo lavished the love of a yearning heart on him (at the same time evincing an emotional tenderness for his aunt Jane) William Stirling was under the spell of the brilliant and captivating Caroline Norton. The daughter of Tom Sheridan, she had married the Hon. George Norton in the year of Louisa's birth and in 1836 her husband, naming Lord Melbourne, had brought an action

FRIENDSHIPS AND LOVE

for adultery, in which the Prime Minister had been acquitted. Reckless, beautiful and talented, with her hair 'raven-violet-black, the eyes very large, dark lashes as black as death', one could understand 'how she twisted men's heads off and their hearts out'.[68] Against so seductive a rival Louisa's chances admitted of little hope.

5
Blighted Hopes

In the early summer of 1850 Pauline wrote a teasing letter from Scotland to Loo who was in the toils of a London season: 'You heartless deceiver, there you are steeped to the lips in dissipation, never so much as thinking of writing to me.' But she recognized that her 'sister' was passing through a period of dissatisfaction. Her days held little purpose; idealistic, like most romantically inclined young women, and with a longing to improve the lot of mankind, there seemed no outlet for her exaggerated affections. She needed a saint to worship, a martyr to follow. Her aunt Mackenzie judged pretty accurately when she said:

> My belief is there is a thirst in your soul or your *heart*, that nothing earthly will ever satisfy. I do not believe there is any earthly possession, or position, that would not disappoint you, once it became yours. You may love an earthly object, till your love becomes oppressive to him and he might wish to fly from you.

In August her mother took her to Frankfurt and Bad Homburg (her first visit to a watering-place though the first of many) probably for a pain in her side which Pauline advised her 'to leech'. This was the beginning of her lifelong addiction to travel, but on her return to London, capriciously changing her plans from one day to the next ('you are a provoking monkey') she started on a period of restless activity which included a desire to learn Latin, to learn music, modelling, drawing; in short to improve her mind. Pauline persisted in pressing her

> to make friends with the Ruskins – you would do her good and I am sure you would delight in him. Can you call on her or is it her business to call on you? It is very kind of me to wish it, for there would be a great chance of your supplanting me in my master's affections.[69]

BLIGHTED HOPES

In 1851 the meeting was at last arranged and Pauline could write and tell Loo that Effie Ruskin ('so honest and true hearted and loving, her manner at first does her injustice') had been delighted with her, thought her a 'noble creature', 'such a repose and power and depth about her', and admired her 'fine head and calm expression'. John Ruskin's impression, if less pleasing, was of 'a romantic young lady – just on the edge of the turn down hill'.[70] They would meet often in the next few years but by September Loo was abroad, again with her mother, first in Switzerland, later settling in Paris where she stayed until the next summer. This was an important time for her. She met there the Brownings who were friends of Mme Mohl; and Lady Trotter, her mother's friend whose elderly daughter fell in love later with Loo, writing her love letters of the most nauseatingly sanctimonious kind. But to Loo the significance of the Paris sojourn was her fervent friendship with Jane Stirling who was connected through her family with Thomas Erskine of Linlathen, the saintly religious teacher to whose influence she was deeply committed. This woman of forty-seven, with an aura of invalidism about her, wealthy and restless, had lived in Paris for some years. She had been a pupil of Chopin after his return from Majorca with George Sand and had become his slave for life. Family legend maintained that he wrote one piece of music for her; two of his nocturnes he dedicated to her name. In 1848 she arranged concerts for him in Glasgow at the Merchants' Hall, and in the Hopetoun Rooms in Edinburgh. A Broadwood pianoforte had been supplied for his room and Jane's Pleyel for his salon at Calder House, where he stayed with her relations, twelve miles from Edinburgh. Notwithstanding these kindnesses and other considerable financial assistance, Chopin was irritated past bearing by her possessive devotion. He admitted that she bored him to such an extremity that he knew not 'which way to turn'.[71] When he died in 1849 Jane planted his grave at Père Lachaise with white rose bushes and forget-me-nots, but it was nevertheless a relief to her nephew William Stirling to be told by a relation that 'there is no impression made by his death of a character different from what might have been expected had *any old blind* clever man of genius been removed from her sight and admiration'.[72]

BLIGHTED HOPES

To Louisa this solitary individual with a background of religion and tinged with romance was somebody on whom to lavish inordinate affection. She signed herself 'Imp' to Jane's 'Lee' and offered her

> a little ring, my Dear Love, as a pledge of my true and deep affection. Will you wear it in memory of me? and believe *how much* I would be to you, if I could. This means constancy – it goes offered with my deep love and devotedness – for how good and kind my Dove is to me.

The admiration was reciprocal, for Loo captivated women far older than herself, and Jane's was of longer duration. A few years later, when on Louisa's side the friendship had lost its importance, a friend who had seen Jane Stirling ('she has the straightforwardness of a man, and I like that man's voice of hers') told Loo 'I am afraid she still admires you.' Together they visited picture galleries and artists' studios (Jane had once posed for a picture by Ary Scheffer); Robert Browning, unable to keep an earlier appointment being 'too late for the anticipated pleasure', accompanied them gladly to the Louvre on another morning; but most welcome to Loo was the opportunity to pour forth on Jane the forlorn hopes of her love for William Stirling. There had been some hopeful match-making on the part of Sir David Brewster, the natural philosopher, and Pauline, and Mary Stewart-Mackenzie had tried to inveigle him to Brahan on the pretext that she was cutting down some trees to open up a vista and needed a man of taste to advise her. With her impulsive nature and passionate heart Louisa left him in no doubt of her feelings and it had occasionally seemed to her that he showed some interest, but in reality his devotion to Caroline Norton though undemanding was all-consuming.

Returning to England in June 1852 Louisa was shattered by the appearance of George, her dying brother. She wrote to tell Mrs Browning of her fears, and to Jane she confided: 'George, so dreadfully altered, so weak, liver, stomach, circulation all wrong. So sweet and gentle such a blessed boy, so full of grace and truth'; of her love for William he had said that she was 'living in a delusion and nursing up to myself a misery'. Still in the army, George had married but having contracted some disease abroad was sent to Madeira to recuperate and was brought home to die at Southampton, as his father before him. Louisa, her mother, and his wife ('Mrs

BLIGHTED HOPES

George') were with him. Before she had time to hear of his death Elizabeth Barrett Browning had already replied in 'the tone caught from your letter'.

It touched me very much dearest Miss Mackenzie that you should have written to me in the midst of so absorbing an anxiety . . . As to Love we never love love, because it is divine as Himself . . . We go and come, but there is no farewell between those who love one another purely, naming Christ's name – only a short apparent parting, – and not a handsbreadth of distance, perhaps, if we could *see* . . . We have not it is true, met very often – but there are instincts are there not? – and when my instincts tell me, I am apt to be forward in love. My husband and I have felt a warm interest in you from the beginning, and shall to the end . . .

After George's death Pauline asked Loo to travel north immediately. 'Coming directly' was the reply, but having failed to arrive on the expected date and having then put off her journey for two days, Sir Walter fetched her at Newcastle and conveyed her to Whitby where they all walked to the little sandy bay, sat by the seashore, and Sir Walter read aloud from *Bleak House* which was being published in monthly parts. He and Loo went botanizing, bathing, went twice to church on Sunday, went to Seaton Delaval and after three days returned to Wallington where there was riding on the moors and Shakespeare read by Sir Walter. This was followed by a week at Roker on the Durham coast. Here Louisa did plenty of sketching, looked at chemical works and with Sir Walter went out in a salmon cable – and Sir Walter with indefatigable persistence read aloud from Carlyle. (He also calculated that with Loo and her maid, and 'groceries', the week had cost him £6.6s.3d.) On 1 September 'darling Loo went to Scotland'.[73]

This was a wretched time for Loo. The loss of her brother was a very real sorrow and her one-sided love affair was bringing her little happiness. She had no encouragement from William Stirling and she would admit again and again that he had never cared for her, yet she could not banish some vestige of hope. From Roker she had written to his aunt:

I am quite cheerful before people but in the night, and when I am quiet in the day I feel what I have lost though his name is so seldom on my lips it is never out of my heart. I can truly say my heart is not disloyal to him. He is ever there – and though the rushing tide of outward life goes on just the same, the inner life is *all* changed and solitary.

That autumn brought Louisa to London for Wellington's funeral but she was mostly in Scotland, and in December called on the Trevelyans in Edinburgh with Jane Stirling. At last Pauline was able to introduce her to Dr John Brown, the Edinburgh physician, who became a true and kind friend.

The year 1853 opened sadly for Loo, with her mother ill in Edinburgh after one of her 'attacks' – now unidentifiable, but severe and worrying for Louisa who loved her very much. Also she was eating out her heart. 'I have heard things of him which prove to me more and more how completely he has given me up.' A spiteful acquaintance

had said to a lady she should feel it her duty to *warn* anyone who she thought was getting fond of me as she felt what a fearful experiment it would be for them. Pray for me that all may work together for my good and that I may be made *holy* and a new creature.

By April she was in London, dining at Lansdowne House and among the guests were Monckton Milnes, Panizzi, librarian at the British Museum, and William Stirling. (Lord Lansdowne was a rather particular friend of the Stewart-Mackenzies and had most probably carefully contrived the invitation.) There was a violent altercation between Milnes and Panizzi as to the priority of giving Thomas Carlyle a private room for study at the British Museum. Panizzi insisted that it was not possible and that no favouritism should be allowed. Milnes replied that

Carlyle's great imminence ought to make him an exception. Panizzi retorted that he for one did not understand or value Carlyle as Milnes did, and he doubted whether the public agreed with him. Milnes got angry and said P was a foreigner and had no right to speak so contemptuously of one of the greatest literary men of England – instead of which it was his business to facilitate his studies. 'I know my duty perfectly well,' said P, 'and I will to the best of my powers fulfil it and facilitate Mr Carlyle's studies according to the means in my

BLIGHTED HOPES 45

hand—but for all that he shall not come into my study as a matter of right.'[74]

When she knew Carlyle several years later Louisa would have remembered that evening, perhaps for another reason as well. 'Saw William last night,' she wrote to Jane, 'and he was so nice and kind. He little knows how I worship him, nothing short of this could have stood his dreadful iciness.' He did indeed know of Louisa's passion and had been obliged to put a stop to her letters and to assume a distant manner when they met.

There were now visits and concerts with the Trevelyans to divert Louisa. An appointment with Claudet to have a stereoscope picture taken with Effie Ruskin was ill-managed owing to her keeping the others waiting. A 'lovely group of Effie and Loo' was unsuccessful and Pauline insisted on their sitting again. With the Trevelyans Louisa was taken to Herne Hill where Ruskin showed them much of interest; John Millais was also of the party. At another time Louisa and Pauline went to the ladies' gallery in the House of Commons to hear the debate on the Budget. William Stirling came up and talked to her and Loo's heart 'beat very fast' but that very day 'Mrs N[orton] came to town and I have never seen or heard of him since – if I can only call in enough *pride* I will put him out of my heart. I have never *sued* before and wont begin now.' Her churchgoing was not neglected and she took a melancholy pleasure in hearing F.D. Maurice preach 'such a beautiful sermon. He looked earnest and sorrowful and peaceful. There is a wonderful quiver in his voice – as if his spirit could not put itself forth in words.' Another Sunday found her writing to Jane from her lodgings in Wilton Place.

> Beloved one, I miss you *sadly* and feel so lost often without you. But my beloved I do feel that you are *always* with me – that I can never really be separated from you. I went twice to church today – once to St Paul's [Knightsbridge] opposite. I do *not* like the service chaunted, and the prayers intoned *at all*.

But the burden of her letters was her despair concerning William. While ardently wishing to see him, every meeting brought another stab to her heart. 'I hear *all* is at an end between Mrs N. and him – that they are quite separated now –but it does me no good as he is colder than ever when we meet so I believe he never did care for me.'

46 BLIGHTED HOPES

When she did not see him there were daydreams to resort to: 'I often think I will wait till I am old and he is old and see then what happens, she cant always last so beautiful and although I have no beauty at least he may be touched by ones tenderness and truth.' At twenty-six Louisa was not beautiful in the accepted sense but she was uncommonly handsome. Effie remarked on it, so did Pauline. The fashionable artist James Swinton had completed a chalk drawing of her; the price had been £36.15s.,[75] and her mother had been delighted by its likeness. (The previous year the Royal Academy had hung a portrait by the same artist of Caroline Norton and her sisters.) Dr Brown writing from Edinburgh hoped that her upper lip was 'as mobile and capricious' as he remembered it. 'You are I see, wild with the mad joys of London, out all day, out every night, run after doubtless by the men, fluttering and vexing the women.' He wondered, somewhat tactlessly, how it came about that 'you, with your inward graces are where you are and not the joyful mother of children, and the glad wife of a thankful husband'. Poor Louisa! – and doubly bitter for her to be told by someone 'that they heard I was going to marry him – but I denied it stoutly. I wish foolish idle people would hold their tongues.'

At the beginning of May Mrs Jameson took Louisa and the Trevelyans to see the pictures and sculpture at Bath House belonging to the second Lord Ashburton. Pauline thought the house 'very fine and magnificently furnished. It made one quite envious to see the great vases filled with dozens of quite forced roses and bunches of gardenias.'[76] The flowers would have come from The Grange, Lord Ashburton's house in Hampshire, the focus of all that was most brilliant in literature, science, the Church and society. These were represented in the large house parties, sometimes lasting the whole winter, where the guests, cradled in luxury dispensed by an immensely wealthy host, were subservient to one undefined rule only, that of shining in the art of conversation. This display of brilliance was directed by Harriet Ashburton, highly born and of a personality so compelling that she dominated the society of wits and scholars gathered under her husband's roof. Of these was Carlyle, cross-grained, disillusioned, dyspeptic, and so utterly obsessed by his magnificent hostess that to look 'into such eyes as yours, it is not possible always altogether to despair'. Though herself deficient in good looks he could still write to her: 'Of you I think as of the beautifullest creature in all this

BLIGHTED HOPES

world', for to him she was 'a Bird of Paradise' and when commanded with unconscious imperiousness to execute some trifling concern, he replied: 'Yes, I will, O *Principessa Nobilissima, carissima*, and love you all my days.'

Louisa would have known of this formidable lady, but for the present the valuable works of art at Bath House were probably of greater interest. She had recently gone, again with Mrs Jameson and the Trevelyans, to B.G. Windus's house on Tottenham Green to look at his collection of Turners and works by Millais which included *The Huguenot*; and before leaving for Wallington, where Loo and the Ruskins and Millais were shortly to forgather, Sir Walter had taken her to see some turquoise and Greek gold ornaments of great beauty.

When Loo reached Wallington towards the end of June she found the Ruskins and the Millais brothers already assembled; they were to stay a week before moving on to Glenfinlas, while she would again accompany the Trevelyans to Roker. Pauline thought Loo was looking very well, adding pointedly, 'also good-humoured'. That evening Effie 'looked lovely with stephanotis in her hair, William Millais sang beautifully' and 'Mr Ruskin' took over the occupation of reading from *The Tempest*. Loo had leisure to think of her longing for 'the idol who has so long filled my heart' and to write to Jane about him.

> There can never now be more than the sacred memory of its promise. It gilded my life — it made my past full of sweet recollections, my future bright with golden promise. I wonder if he will ever have such love again from woman.

She thought he had been kinder the last few times 'but I am really getting over it and he is curing me himself'. Expeditions filled up the following days, one of which nearly ended in disaster. Sir Walter, Ruskin and Loo had been climbing rocks, and on the way home Loo, who was driving, whipped up one of the horses, either out of devilry or from some wild outburst of pent-up feeling. Both horses tried to jump over a fence and they all had a narrow escape.

Effie was 'ill with a sick headache' for a couple of days, after which Millais started on his two pencil portraits of her; she praised Loo's drawings and 'encourages me by all means to go on, and I will yet do something'. Pauline had a serious talk with her which was reported to Jane.

48   BLIGHTED HOPES

> I felt my heart so tight today – when Pauline, telling me how much she regretted my not marrying said 'I never *can* understand about you and William Stirling for Sir David Brewster told me it was so evident he was excessively fond of you – and only wanted a little encouragement' – it made all my old feelings which I have been stamping on, jump up – oh! would I could tell him how truly and earnestly I have given him, and he still has, the only jewel I possess. A lady writes me word that in London it is again reported about me and him – but how vain and foolish I am. See him – do not let the few holy ties he has in life grow looser while that woman tightens the other kind.[77]

Coming from London, Effie Ruskin would have been aware of Louisa's painful circumstances but it is doubtful whether Loo, wrapt in her own melancholy concerns, was alive to the undercurrent of turbulent emotions affecting two of the party, to which Glenfinlas would contribute its own tragi-comical chapter. By the time Loo went to Roker it was clear she had renounced all hope.

> A note I have just received shows me beyond doubt the real state of things, so farewell to all my dreams. As you know he will have my prayers, always, always – you may tell him that the *real* love of my youth, the dream of my later years, was to be worthy of him.

November saw her in Edinburgh, joining the Trevelyans for the first of a series of lectures delivered by Ruskin, but characteristically they were made late by Loo getting into a great fuss about her ticket. Although she protested, Dr Brown assured her that 'in spite of you I intend to prefer you, a good deal, to Mrs John Ruskin. "Effie" is a butterfly, you are a dragon fly – and I prefer greatly the fly.'

In this same month an incident occurred which at the time passed almost unnoticed but which culminated four years later in Louisa's marriage vows. Lord Stanley of Alderley, nephew to the bishop who had died at Brahan, was staying with Lord Breadalbane at Black Mount in the Mar Forests and was given a piece of intelligence which he communicated to his wife:

> The Ashburtons have just bought a place in the Highlands in Ross-shire about fifty miles beyond Inverness. It is called Loch

BLIGHTED HOPES

Luichart and did belong to Sir Something [James] Mackenzie. They say it is pretty and some shooting, both deer and grouse.

Ten months later he was staying with the Ashburtons in their new shooting lodge and again wrote to his wife:

> The house is quite new and comfortable in the Italian style, liek a villa near Kensington. It is situated in the middle of a birch wood overlooking Loch Luichart a lake seven miles long. A great deal of it is very beautiful scenery.

He thought the mountains to be less fine than those towards the west, but it was 'within reach of civilized country being only seventeen miles from Dingwall in the neighbourhood of which there are a great many gentlemen living, all the Mackenzies of Ross seem to have pitched their tents there.'[78]

The year 1854 opened unexceptionally. Loo had spent the winter at Brahan, helping her mother to run the house, seeing to the poor and as usual teaching in the little school. But by the spring she was happy to escape to London where in May Pauline thought her looking very pretty 'considering her London dissipations'. They must have spoken together of the break-up of the Ruskin marriage a few weeks earlier, and towards the end of the month Pauline noted in her journal that

> Sir Walter had received a letter from Master explaining his affairs. There was little in it but what I knew before. He seems to have had a miserable time of it for a long while, indeed he had no real need of a wife, he only married for amusement, he would have been far happier with his father and his mother, and ought not to have married at all.[79]

Whether through Pauline's influence, her own regard for Ruskin, or disapprobation of Effie, Louisa preferred to be on friendly terms with Ruskin. Many years later Millais came to shoot at Loch Luichart – unaccompanied by his wife.

In London Pauline and Loo went to concerts and exhibitions. One day at Christie's they looked at drawings by John Martin and then went to the Museum of Practical Geology in Jermyn Street, 'the most interesting place in London'. Derby Day found Pauline unable to get a carriage, so making do with a cab she collected Loo and took her off to Little Holland House. She thought the grounds

BLIGHTED HOPES

and large old-fashioned garden beautiful and the house very pretty, 'all ups and downs and ins and outs. Mr Prinsep lives there and Watts lives with them.' Mrs Prinsep, whom they found charming, received them very kindly and showed them Watts's pictures and drawings. For Pauline the pencil drawings were 'the loveliest things I ever saw, 10 times more refined than Millais's —even — the oil pictures are grand and large in feeling as well as in actual size and execution'.[80] Loo would have remembered this day when in later years, and after Pauline was dead, she came to know Watts and owned some of his work.

In June when Loo went on one of her regular visits to Embley, the Nightingales' house on the edge of the New Forest, Florence was not at home. Since the previous year she had been Superintendent at the Harley Street Institution and now she had been approached by King's College Hospital to take up a post there as Superintendent of Nurses. Louisa helped to soothe Mrs Nightingale and Parthe; they would never come to terms with Florence's work and were as usual distraught. In the autumn Parthe told Louisa that her sister was sailing for the Crimea, and Selina Bracebridge, in a letter to her 'dearest Loo', announced that they had resolved to accompany 'the heroic Flo'. Samuel Smith, Florence's uncle, went as far as Marseilles with her and on his return gave Loo an account of his niece, observing that she had shown 'as much calm as if she were in Brahan library'. From Scutari Louisa received news from Selina that 'Flo is both general and soldier. I dont know in which part she shines most'; also that 'one of our Nuns, Sister Maria Gonzaga, has a voice perfectly like yours and something of your manner. She sets even the Nurses an example of humility and usefulness.' Louisa's voice was one of her most distinctive features, while her capacity for humility (alternating rapidly with arrogance) had obviously made its mark.

That summer, before war cast its shadow, Louisa and her mother had gone to Beulah Spa, for Mary Stewart-Mackenzie had had another 'attack' and the purgative saline waters had been recommended. Loo managed a day with the Trevelyans at Crystal Palace, only recently opened, but she was worried about her mother's health and by the middle of July they were home at Brahan. Before leaving London Mary had written from her Wilton Place lodgings to Lord Aberdeen, the Whig Prime Minister.

BLIGHTED HOPES

> I feel it a duty I owe to my family to lay our claim for some mark of distinction before your Lordship. In 1815, Lord Liverpool offered me in the kindest manner if I wished to recommend to the Crown the revival of my father's peerage in my person.[81]

At the time she had shrunk from the responsibility but now from personal inclination and possibly goaded on by her son Keith, and aware too that it might enhance Loo's prospects of marriage (for she was already twenty-seven), Mary hoped to recover what had been lost by her father's death. Lord Aberdeen, while not denying that her 'claim to a peerage might deserve favourable consideration', was 'unable to enter into any engagement to recommend to the Queen the creation of a new Peerage', and there the matter was allowed to rest.

6

An Artful Dodger

On their return to Brahan Sir Edwin Landseer was almost their first visitor. He was an old friend of both – twenty years younger than the mother and some twenty-four older than the daughter. As a celebrated artist he was much in demand as a companion and would travel every year from his house in St John's Wood to spend many weeks in the Highlands, moving from one aristocratic family to another, painting, and entertaining his hosts. Lady Eastlake said of him that he had 'a head of power and strength with that early grey hair which looks like the wisdom of age and the strength of youth mixed: he is in "very high society"'.[82] It had not always been so – he had achieved his success through hard work and ambition. Mrs Grote, wife of the historian, remembered him when he was about seventeen at a house where she often stayed: he had dined then in the housekeeper's room, 'not being thought fit company for the parlour'.[83] For close on thirty years he had loved the Duchess of Bedford and after her death in 1853 his health deteriorated and he drank too much. On his way to Balmoral after the Brahan visit he wrote that he was restored by its comfort and his wanderings with Louisa as a guide to 'the romantic and picturesque'. An ironical twist to this developing intimacy was that Landseer as a devoted friend had stood loyally by Caroline Norton after the Melbourne scandal, and she had written and inscribed a poem to him.

There had been some raillery concerning Swinton's portrait of Loo, a sketch of which Landseer had taken with him, and was now, on demand, returning. 'I fully intended it to become my Aladdin's Lamp – among my few treasures it would have been my kind star.' He sent for her acceptance three Highland subjects to hang in her Room of Rooms that they might 'remind you of your bright land'. From Landseer's letters over the next few years one can gauge the tone of Louisa's replies: flirtatious, provocative and

AN ARTFUL DODGER

bearing the inevitable pious tag. But by her command these were 'sent to a better world and I mourn over their ashes'. He wrote of his work, future plans and hopes, teasing letters strewn with gallantries, many of them illustrated with rapid sketches, sometimes of herself, of a dog strung up at her door masquerading as himself, her faithful servant. 'Which do you care for (in a Picture)' he asked, 'sadness or gladness?' His breaking health was often the central theme: 'I tell of my misfortunes tho' perhaps when I'm prostrate in the dust the best thing you can do is to put your foot on me as you did to the snail that invaded your garden.' Louisa's affection for animals of all kinds (despite the snail) is evident in these replies. 'Mrs Jameson tells me I am cruel in my subjects,' wrote Landseer, and she was probably echoing Louisa. As a young child Loo had acquired a goldfish in a bowl during the holidays on the west coast of Scotland and on returning to Brahan it had seemed to fall into a decline. Fearing that the water did not suit, the eight-year-old child began the long walk back to the sea carrying in her arms the fish in its bowl. In London recently, the death of her bird had upset her dreadfully. It had taken a bath in her dirty painting water and having gone into it a lovely thing with gorgeous bright plumage it emerged a thin dark London sparrow and died in convulsions, having probably drunk some of the water.[84]

Louisa was feeling the monotony of her life: there was no great cause, no great love to engage her feelings. After a long silence Pauline was gratified to hear from her at the beginning of 1855. 'I am glad to find that you are still alive, but you must be of a very great age. I gather this by adding together the enormous periods that elapse between each of your letters.' Besides telling her of the bullfinch named Loo which her maid, with misplaced gentility, always referred to as 'Miss Loo', Pauline added the news that a Mr Wooster, 'savant and litterateur by profession', had been engaged to put Sir Walter's museum in order and if Louisa had been there she would have had fine pickings as there were many duplicates. In May Louisa joined the Trevelyans at Spittal, on the coast south of Berwick-on-Tweed, and three events occurred to make her time there memorable. Having sent for the bathing woman she screwed up her courage and consented to venture into the water; but when in a great fright she went down to the beach the first thing she saw there was a drowned dog – 'which finished her', wrote Pauline. A note in Pauline's journal chronicled the second event: 'John Millais is to marry Effie Grey (!!) next month. I am sorry for him.' Finally in early June, Loo had news from her mother that her sister Caroline Petre was seriously ill with inflammation of the lungs and peritonitis, but Loo was forbidden to go; three days later 'in a sad state of misery' Sir Walter saw her off. The invalid had died and Loo was on her way home.[85]

Writing in the summer from Brahan Louisa urged Pauline to read *A Lost Love* (described in the *Athenaeum* as 'a little story full of grace and genius') and *Within and Without* by George MacDonald. To this Pauline replied that for Loo's sake she would read the first but the second she viewed with some distaste for Dr Henry Acland had judged it from reviews to be 'an excited (and exciting) unhealthy sort of book'. The *Athenaeum* on a first perusal could not pretend to fathom its profound meaning but being all pure poetry it was meant for 'the closet for quiet and reflective reading'.

In recognition of Florence's work in the Crimea a Nightingale Fund was being set up to establish an institute for training nurses. Louisa, eager to contribute, sent Parthenope a cameo brooch of her own to be sold. Mrs Gaskell undertook to see what she could do with 'some of our rich Manchestrians but, thank you, it is not "large" enough for them, and cutting and execution is nothing to size', so she would try elsewhere.[86]

Further illness on Mary Stewart-Mackenzie's side brought her and Loo to 43 Sussex Place, Brighton, to recuperate in the autumn of 1856. The Trevelyans were there too, which was conducive to constant visiting back and forth. One day when Pauline had gone to look at Loo's new microscope and to give her a drawing lesson she found Mary very nervous and 'in a queer sort of state. She fancied she couldnt speak and would talk on her fingers', but becoming interested she forgot her imagined complaint and spoke perfectly normally.

It had been a depressing year but, as winter gave place to spring, the auguries might have raised Louisa's spirits. Harriet Ashburton had died in Paris on 4 May 1857 and though her death had not been unexpected the loss caused sorrow among her friends. For the daughter of the Earl of Sandwich marriage with the Hon. William Bingham Baring, eldest son of the first Lord Ashburton, had not been a brilliant match in the hierarchical society of the 1820s in which she had held a leading position. After the early death of a son

AN ARTFUL DODGER

she had turned her talents to the management of great assemblies at The Grange which Maria Josepha, the Dowager Lady Stanley of Alderley thought 'a very bad style of house and a very disagreeable mistress, tho' she *is* so clever.'[87] Not a beautiful woman, and Lady Palmerston's telling observation probably carried a note of truth – that she knew of a man who 'makes chins and noses to order who might perhaps be useful to Lady Harriet and give her a better Nose, in exchange for her Redundancy of Chin'.[88] But where accomplishments, humour and a ready wit predominated, where the resplendence and self-assurance of the hostess supplied an intellectual and material contentment, her physical appearance was of no importance. Her unconscious imperiousness was disregarded by those who gathered at The Grange – Monckton Milnes, Clough, Tom Taylor, Samuel Wilberforce, Sydney Smith, and sometimes Thackeray, were numbered among her particular henchmen – for it fitted naturally into the order of the day that it was she who inspired, fascinated, stimulated; and directed the conversation which began at breakfast and ceased only when the guests after playing charades and the game of Bouts Rimés were lighted by candle to their bedchambers. Men were in preponderance since it was in them that the finest brains and wit would be found. Jane Brookfield (Thackeray's love of these years), the wife of the Revd W.H. Brookfield, a fashionable preacher, Inspector of schools, and himself an habitué of The Grange, was always welcome for herself, while Jane Carlyle, not unnaturally on the defensive, both admired and feared her hostess. At The Grange she was not the centre of conversation as she was at her tea table in Cheyne Row, telling her interminable stories. Partly repelled by her husband's adoration for Harriet, who she was bound to admit did nothing to encourage it, she would nevertheless accompany Carlyle on his visits, the 'Government Offices', as he morosely confided to Harriet, making the ultimate decision for them both. 'Bright Lady,' he wrote to his hostess after an invitation to the Highlands, 'believe me, if it stood with me the answer were not difficult.' The protestations with which Carlyle coloured his letters (but never spoke) left Harriet unmoved. Soon after Carlyle's death when J.A. Froude was collecting material for his *Life* he told Louisa that he had come upon Carlyle's letters to Harriet. 'Oh dear, I sometimes think Lady Harriet was an evil spirit. No malignant elf could have caused more misery, and yet I suppose it

AN ARTFUL DODGER

was to be.' The pain he had caused Jane was, however, of his own making. 'Was there ever in this world a man with such extraordinary power yet with no more power over himself than a crying baby.' Once, in talking to Jane Brookfield, Harriet had given an honest evaluation of what his friendship meant to her: '. . . my dear old Prophet Carlyle, and has anyone any right to more than one such friend in a lifetime?'[89] Of Jane she was tolerant, accepting her simply as Carlyle's wife, ready to offer country air when needed and bestowing presents which were not always acceptable, for Jane was on the lookout for slights. It was a strained relationship for both Carlyles, and unable and unwilling to do otherwise, he continued to write, sending 'Blessings on you, I have seen one royal woman, this too is something in one's life.' She was the 'one glow of radiancy that still looks of Heaven to me. Of you I think often, or indeed *always*.' On a summer's day he had seen her pass on Constitution Hill and, writing like a lover:

> I must make that serve for a week. It is the brightest star in all the week's firmament, perhaps the only star there . . . Goodnight. The Chelsea clock is striking midnight. The sun is right under our feet, and wet winds are blustering . . . Shall we ever have wings, think you? *Ach Gott!* I send you blessings as ever, and the best goodnight. Ewig, T.C.

Lord Ashburton had been an adoring husband, gentle, shy and generous, supporting his wife in all she did, and when on their honeymoon he admitted to Loo he had never been so loved in his life before as he was by her, Loo added courageously, 'Yet he *dotes* on HER memory.' Two days after Harriet's death he wrote to Carlyle:

> She has taken with her a part of the happiness she bestowed, but she has left me an inheritance of great price, the love of those who loved her. I claim that of you, in her name, and I am sure it will be rendered to me.

Perhaps when she died the blow fell heaviest upon Carlyle. From the first he had said: 'I dont think Lord Ashburton will marry again but I wont answer for his not *letting himself be married*',[90] but to himself it was 'the *loss* in several respects such as I need not hope to replace'. Later that summer Lord Ashburton had returned to Loch Luichart, surrounding himself with friends to dispel the solitude.

AN ARTFUL DODGER

Remembering his own visit, Carlyle wrote from Chelsea: 'But alas it is not the Loch Luichart of last year, nor ever will be again ... to me also it is a place sternly tho' beautifully *tragic* henceforth, beyond all other places', and despite Louisa pressing him, it would be fifteen years till he could bring himself to go there again. Three weeks later a reply from Chelsea to a further letter from Loch Luichart not only revealed what was threatening, but also the extent of Carlyle's jealousy for Harriet's memory.

> I am very glad to hear a word of tidings out of that memorable region again. Miss Stewart Mackenzie I have seen once or twice in late years: a bright vivacious damsel, struggling fitfully about, like a sweet-briar, and with hooks under her flowers, too, I understand; for they say she is much of a coquette, and fond of doing a stroke of 'artful dodging'; tho' I cannot testify to her ever trying the least particle of her skill in that way on my own poor self. If she turns up again, please give her my respects, and say nothing of the arts of dodging, whether she have them or not.

It is improbable that Carlyle would have noticed Louisa's partiality to 'artful dodging' had not Jane, staunch in her admiration of Harriet after her death, disclosed it. 'Louisa Mackenzie has been on the lookout for a great match these ten years', she snapped, and 'was notoriously "setting her cap" at Lord Ashburton six weeks after his wife's death.'[91]

A couple of years previously Louisa had met the Ashburtons at the house of cousins not far from Loch Luichart; now, in London, the role of helpmeet to a widower would have appealed to her even if she dared not look ahead to the material advances that might ensue. Her life was at a low ebb: she was now thirty and with every year that passed marriage became less likely, for despite her very obvious qualities of mind and heart, a restlessness perhaps born of frustration, her pious sentimentality, occasional arrogance, perhaps even her father's antecedents, did not attract the right suitors. There was also the lack of a substantial dowry.

Louisa was at Wallington in mid-July. It was the period of a great artistic enterprise in which W. Bell Scott had undertaken to paint eight large canvases for the central hall. Pleading

AN ARTFUL DODGER

poverty, Loo had not responded to the initial invitation, so that a more pressing one had followed.

> My love. I am sorry you have got into a financial crisis. I want Mr Scott to make a study of you to put you in one of his pictures. Dont say No to my request but come to me like a good old thing.

Pauline added that since she must exist somewhere Wallington would be more economical than most places and that she insisted on paying her journey. Ruskin was another guest at Wallington and helped Loo with her drawing in the evening, a scene perpetuated by Scott in a small conversation piece. Louisa had earlier asked Ruskin to recommend a drawing master; Lowes Dickinson from whom she would derive much benefit had been suggested. She had also asked Millais but 'good figure draughts-men being scarce', he had no one to suggest. Before leaving Wallington Louisa had borrowed £14 and was in haste to repay it. This brought a firm rejoinder from Pauline. 'I am not in the slightest want of £14 and so *pray* dont fidget about it.'

Pauline had not been acquainted with the impending improve-ment in Louisa's fortunes. In December she took Loo's jewellery to be valued at Reid's, in Jermyn Street, where very low prices were put on it. Nevertheless, being in need of money for the coming London season, and some 'understanding' existing between her and Lord Ashburton (which if brought to a happy conclusion would ensure her some very fine jewels indeed), Loo decided to take £50 for her diamonds. She still had little money, however, to repay the loan from Pauline who wrote rather irritably: 'Dont fidget so about paying me – it looks as if you wanted to pay me and then cut me and have done with me'. Letters from Loo were scarce that winter and Pauline was disturbed at not hearing from her. It was not till February (1858) that news reached Wallington of an intriguing nature, and then not through Loo herself but through a common friend who asked: 'How did they first meet? When is the marriage to be?' The Trevelyans were justly hurt at not having been taken into Louisa's confidence but it is legitimate to suppose that Loo was hesitant to tell them what steps she had taken to win a man she did not love but whom ambition, wealth, and common sense made it expedient to marry. In the new year of 1858 she found matters to write to him about from Scotland concerning a schoolmaster for the parish of Contin, a neighbouring village.

AN ARTFUL DODGER

Asking her advice for whom he should vote it enabled her to send Lord Ashburton a proxy voting paper and in reply he emphasized the need of avoiding 'bitterness between free church and establishment and put someone in the reading desk who would unite these children of both congregations'. However, the hope of success was so feeble as scarcely to deserve consideration. This had afforded Loo a motive for correspondence and ensured he would not forget his northern obligations. She was also writing to Parthenope Nightingale of a William Coltman who had asked for her hand in marriage; he was a friend of the Gaskells and the Nightingales, a Unitarian, a barrister with chambers in the Inner Temple. Parthe was instructed to ask Florence's advice on the matter but since she was near collapse and was seeing none of the family, Parthe shouldered the responsibility. In Loo she felt there was a 'spark of something very like genius, that you are an ingrained artist, a philanthropist and (a strange compound) a woman of the world'. Mr Coltman had little sympathy with these things though she commended his serene strength, his high-mindedness and his clear sense, qualities to appeal to Loo though it is doubtful whether she had any intention of listening to his suit, for her own hopes were shaping with startling rapidity in another quarter. Mr Coltman seems to have emerged heartwhole as by the next year Mrs Gaskell met his wife at a party and gave an exact account of her white dress, black velvet bow, sash, white feather, black pansies[92] – in short a toilette with which Louisa could never have competed.

Lord Ashburton was now fifty-nine and often so crippled with gout that he had to resort to crutches. His grandfather, Sir Francis Baring, had been the founder of the house of Baring Brothers; his father, the first Baron Ashburton of the second creation had, by marrying an American, added wealth to an existing fortune. In 1842 he had negotiated the treaty between Great Britain and the United States of America which had decided the demarcation line between Maine and Canada. His son had succeeded him in 1848, inheriting The Grange, property in Devon and Cornwall, and Bath House from his mother. To this he had added a villa at Addiscombe, another at Alverstoke and the shooting lodge at Loch Luichart. He had sat in the House of Commons for many years and had held government posts under the Tories but his innate shyness and modesty had not cut him out for public life. Five houses, money and position were a tempting proposition to any woman of

60 AN ARTFUL DODGER

Louisa's age; besides, her good-natured enthusiasm and sound intelligence combined with a 'locomotive energy' and a sense of mission would provide him with a capable wife, and perhaps an heir.

Writing to a friend after the previous summer Jane Carlyle had reported with prophetic insight that it was

> not so much sorrow that troubles him, one would say as *bewilderment* . . . I expect some scheming woman will marry him up – not because he is likely to care for anybody but because he does not know what to do with himself and would be glad that someone took the trouble of him off his hands.[93]

Gossip, largely adverse, was abroad and Pauline was deeply sympathetic.

> I am truly grieved my dearest love that you have such painful things to bear. Any sort of calumny must give one pain at the time, though one *knows* that one will live it down, that is sure at the end.

Louisa was at Brahan in September and among the party at Loch Luichart was the sharply observant W.H. Brookfield. To his wife he reported that Louisa had been invited for the first day she could leave Brahan, twenty miles distant, where her mother was ill and she had been fulfilling the duties of hostess. Expectancy among friends was at fever pitch. 'Is she to be Lady A? they would fit very well,' wrote one who thought Louisa a tonic in herself.[94]

But Louisa's course was an awkward one to steer. Landseer had been invited to Brahan and his visit needed to be handled with immense tact. 'I have become a timid old party living on *hope* and patience,' he wrote. Anxious to discredit any advice Ruskin may have given her with regard to her drawing, which was now showing real ability, he had written disparagingly of 'your friend Mr Ruskin the gt professor who guides the ignorant and leads public "taste", young men's *heads are turned*, and old ones insulted – the creature mistakes patience and stippling for truth.' She disagreed, but Landseer had not yet done. 'There is an unhealthy affectation in your friend J Ruskin's *nature* – that has done great *harm*. He now writes that English trees are vulgar and be d---d to him.' 'Chapters on commonsense' had been sent him by Loo, the 'value of each respected and appreciated', resolutions

AN ARTFUL DODGER

were made, but for how long, he asked. 'The Devil was ill, the Devil a monk would be, the Devil got well, the Devil a monk was he.'[95] To a probable homily from Loo regarding the necessity of adhering to the straight and narrow path he had sent in reply a sketch of herself facing towards an ultimate heaven at the end of a long stretch of road with her arms raised in a gesture of welcome, while to left and right disconsolate figures hurried furtively away down side paths. Beneath, Landseer had written 'How like you this horrid truth. Dont suppose that any of us can keep this path.' He spoke of himself as 'a silly harmless old paint brush' who should only be allowed to look at or associate with youth and beauty 'as one does with the cold chaste moon', adding two sketches of himself, one '25 years ago' with his arm round the waist of a young girl, and the other as an elderly white-haired man, alone, leaning on a stick: 'What has become my lot'. It seems probable that he expected to propose marriage, and, having had encouragement, to be accepted. Younger than Lord Ashburton and still possessing a captivating attraction for women, he had been shown enough affection by Loo for him to have been sure of his ground; so that when she attached herself to another the pain was the more profound for having been unexpected. 'She threw him over to marry Lord Ashburton, being all but engaged to him,' Lord Stanley of Alderley had written to his wife.[96] At the top of the profession which most interested Loo, she may have hoped to reclaim him from drink and to have set him upon a spiritual road; besides, Lord Ashburton had not yet formally proposed.

Matters were soon rectified, though it was perhaps in this context that a scene took place between Ashburton and Loo in which he may have taxed her with playing off one admirer against another. Whatever the cause he wrote her a letter of self-abnegation the next day.

> I will not deign to disavow the reproach, that I had conceived things disloyal or derogatory to your holy self. As for myself, I shall never forget it, for hateful as was the part I played you were so wise, so dignified so noble, that I would not forget your voice and words and looks. You must not discard me at once. I want to come back again as your suitor.

And as a suitor he was quickly accepted, Louisa offering him proof 'of that grace of mind and purity of heart which no other has as you

62   AN ARTFUL DODGER

have'. Originally he had not intended to marry for two years from Harriet's death and to keep their engagement secret until the autumn, but Mary Stewart-Mackenzie's ill health induced him to alter his mind so that he would have a right to comfort and assist Louisa. There remained only her mother's formal consent which must have been given willingly and thankfully, and a letter to be dispatched. This was most probably to the Dowager Lady Sandwich, Harriet's mother, of which Jane Carlyle's pen lost nothing in the telling.

> I have not recovered from the shock [she gasped in a letter of 1 November]. Lady Sandwich handing me a letter said 'Read that, I thought you would like best to hear it from *me*.' The letter was in Lord Ashburton's handwriting – first words caught my eye 'I have proposed to Miss Stewart-Mackenzie and she has accepted me.' No doubt of *that* if she had the chance. 'Marriage will take place as soon as *trousseau* and settlements can be got ready.' I shall never like the new Lady Ashburton – she is full of affectation and pretension if not pretence. Louisa M. who never saw Lady Sandwich has written asking her for 'her love' and blessing and so forth. Lord Ashburton wrote to Carlyle that he would not have married again if he had not found another of the same high nature. *That* aggravated me more than anything.[97]

According to Jane, Lady Sandwich, a woman of the world, took the news philosophically, her chief concern being that Louisa should make her husband happy. She wrote to that effect:

> You will I hope and believe be a very happy woman in marrying Ashburton – to a mind stored with knowledge he has the most loving and kindest heart – a heart that requires answering love and companionship – I am sure you will give him a cheerful and a happy home.

In London meanwhile Lord Ashburton's plans advanced for the wedding. It is not clear why this was not held in Scotland among the bride's own people. A possible, though unlikely, reason may have been some religious objection. Ashburton was opposed to Evangelicalism on too fervent a scale and had once written from Nice to Samuel Wilberforce, Bishop of Oxford, of a 'sanctified colony at Cannes . . . the low church in its full bloom. England can no longer afford such a picture of prayer meetings, holy ecstasies

AN ARTFUL DODGER 63

and the like.'[98] Three times he wrote to Brahan: 'If we have a Bishop [to marry us] my vote would be for Oxford. He is a good friend to me and mine. He will be so to you.' 'A kind letter from the Bishop of Oxford, offers to marry us. I like him and believe in him though not his politics.' 'Oxford awaits your decision. If you have no objection, nor entanglement I should like him to officiate.' Wilberforce had been a favoured guest at The Grange and perhaps for this reason Loo felt a certain hesitancy in agreeing; or it might have been that she suspected this son of a great Evangelical of holding advanced High Church views.

Letters went constantly to Brahan; there were the wedding presents to choose. He had found her a ring 'representing the emblem of eternity, a serpent with its tail in its mouth'; from her he asked for a watch guard of which he sent a pattern, convenient and light 'and never marks as dirty gold does, a white waistcoat', only it was to be in a more sober hue. But Loo's particular present was a bit of a startler to so modest and self-effacing a man, though he put a good face on it. 'The studs are beautiful, I should wear them proudly for your sake'. The buttons, however, were a bit showy. 'I rather shrink from them of my own taste, but they are beautiful, small, would go well with black, and do you know I have almost courage to wear them, worked up by thoughts of the donor.' Other letters, 'though scarce fit to offer up at your shrine', showed his devotion to her. 'I can recall you as you swam with quiet steps up the path at the falls; I can see you as you knelt at prayers.' She sent him extracts she had copied from devotional works.

> My reading has been in your extracts [he wrote]. I wish I could see you as you were when you wrote them. They partake a little of the mystical and I am so enamoured of the real that my nature revolts (not at the extracts at all but at the mystical). I may come to dream, as well as to know.

It was not mysteries that he found obnoxious, for things he could not understand he could take upon faith and instinct, but there were ideas which to him were no ideas at all but 'conglomerations of words. I try them by reason, and by instinct and they melt away into the unintelligible.'

Some obstacle, and it may have been this letter, caused Loo

AN ARTFUL DODGER

to wish to delay the marriage, but she gave no reason for it and he assured her he would not have to be censured again for 'indifference to sacred things'.

> It is enough [he wrote] that you should have been brought to this resolve by meditation and prayer. Let me not hurry you into an indeferrable engagement. My whole future will hang upon you. There is no shadow of turning in me. I am yours for ever.

This was followed by a short note. 'Come when you can but do not hurry or leave ought undone. You make sunshine, but for your sake I can bear the dark.' And looking ahead he exclaimed: 'Are we not happy ever to have a morrow brighter than to day?' When, having overcome whatever doubts assailed her, the date of the wedding, 18 November was settled, Ashburton wrote again asking if the Bishop might marry them at St George's, Hanover Square. To her trepidation of a wedding breakfast he assured her that there would be none 'but I cannot collect people together without feeding them enough to repair the excitement of witnessing so awful a ceremony, so fearful a sacrifice of youth and beauty too!' No cake, no favours and only family guests – his two brothers, the Hon. Francis and the Hon. and Revd Frederick Baring, and their wives, his niece, Lady Euston, and her husband, and two unmarried sisters, the Hon. Louisa and the Hon. Emily Baring. Another sister, the Dowager Lady Bath, could not be present. With all this Louisa agreed and after rearrangement and more change of her own plans her arrival with her mother in London was finally fixed upon. Rooms were engaged on the first floor of the highly respectable Thomas's Hotel, Berkeley Square, a resort of clergy and gentry: bedrooms, a dining room due north and a sitting room full south. Congratulations were arriving; Gladstone had paid a long visit to Ashburton on 7 November before leaving for a holiday on the Ionian Islands; his father had been a friend of Mary Stewart-Mackenzie, he had known Louisa all her life. The Bunsen family, friends of both sides, congratulated Lord Ashburton on the 'devoted affection of so transcendently a noble soul as Miss Mackenzie', while privately fearing the match would bring him 'many slightly insipid connections'. To Monckton Milnes Lady Palmerston wrote that to her the marriage seemed 'a great pity', believing Loo to be a great contrast to Harriet, though she thought her still handsome and wondered why

AN ARTFUL DODGER 65

nobody had married her before.[99] A letter of congratulation from Caroline Norton also contained regrets that she had not called upon Lord Ashburton that summer at Loch Luichart; he sent a draft of an imaginary reply to Louisa, to amuse her, asking her to burn it.

> My dear Mrs Norton, it is with pleasure that I accept your kind congratulations as an earnest of future interest. Your visit would have been most acceptable, as I might possibly then have made acquaintance with the real Mrs Norton which the world is always talking about. The Mrs Norton I know has mostly downcast eyes, speaks below her breath, and I am not quite sure that anything would melt in her mouth.

With Loo's arrival in London the pace accelerated. She arrived with a cold and found grapes from The Grange awaiting her. She paid a call on Lady Sandwich – a nervous moment for both of them – which passed off satisfactorily. Loo made a favourable impression on the older woman who found her 'pleasing and intelligent', with an amiable nature. 'I think you have secured a charming companion,' she wrote to Ashburton. There was the trousseau to be collected from Blackbourne's of South Audley Street, and Pauline to be introduced and taken to Bath House where the drawing room had been aired and decorated. (The Trevelyans' present to Loo had been a ring which Sir Walter's accounts show to have cost £4.18s.)[100] Bracelets were given to the four bridesmaids, Loo's Anstruther niece, and three cousins. The bridegroom had a severe attack of gout which necessitated the wedding service being held in the drawing room of Bath House; a 'carpet on rollers' had been arranged to carry Mary Stewart-Mackenzie from the carriage up the stairs and from there a wheelchair from which she need not stir 'until she goes into the next room to take leave of Loo'. It was a short drive that Louisa took with her mother on the wedding morning from Berkeley Square to Bath House on the corner of Bolton Street, and there, according to the *Morning Chronicle*, the service was performed in the most impressive manner by the Bishop, and the bride was 'most magnificently attired'.

7
In Pursuit of Happiness

On the morning of this happy bridal day Louisa had received a little note: 'To know how you are. The day is come when I am to take responsibility for your happiness, I do it with hope and confidence.' Louisa's sentiments may well have been otherwise. She was wretched at parting with her much-loved mother particularly now that she was ill and frail and needed her daughter's companionship, the more so as her son Keith was behaving with his customary perversity and his wife was spreading tales about Louisa. The elderly bridegroom, devoted and generous, was nevertheless so stricken with gout that the honeymoon abroad had been postponed for a month so that the next few weeks might be spent recuperating at The Grange and at Brighton. At Loo's entreaty demonstrations by tenants and villagers, to greet the couple as they drove through Northington and up the gentle slope to The Grange, had been declined. This was Louisa's first sight (and it may have been as daunting as it was exciting) of her palatial new home set in the undulating Hampshire countryside, which the Barings had acquired in 1817 from Henry Drummond, owner of the vast neo-classical building and one of the founders of the Irvingite Church. He had earlier made the Grand Tour in Greece and on coming home in 1804 had been fired with a desire to rebuild The Grange from the original seventeenth-century house into the likeness of a Greek temple. For this he had engaged as architect William Wilkins who had lived for two years in Greece and Asia Minor and who was said to have taken engravings of the Theseion Temple in Athens and the Thrassylic Monument as his models. Built on a podium this imposing house was magnificently sited, its portico of six great Doric columns facing east above a lake. The main building, which held the reception rooms and dominated the formal gardens to the south, was composed of nine bays flanked by giant pilasters; this extended to the west followed by a further slightly recessed

IN PURSUIT OF HAPPINESS

and less elaborate range of eight bays. On the north side was the entrance to the house at the end of a great avenue of limes. Additions which included a conservatory with a portico of four Ionic columns approached by a steep flight of steps were made by Charles Cockerell. The entire construction was unlike anything in Europe and unique in its conception.

The morning after her arrival, with her cold still upon her, Loo had made a round of the rooms. Her first letter was to her mother. 'Oh! it is such a beautiful place'; she hoped Mary would be 'spared to see it', and, in addition, how greatly delighted her husband had been by the Burmese bowl she had given him which he would have electrotyped for the centre of the table at Bath House to use with the gold service.

Loo's tour of her new domain would have led her into one of the handsomest rooms, the large dining room where Harriet had sat at the head of the table directing the never-ceasing flow of conversation. The chimneypiece by Flaxman was well set off by the six columns of tawny scagliola spaced against the walls under the vaulted ceiling which was coffered and coloured. In the drawing room the fireplace was ornamented by a frieze of relief portraits of the Bonaparte family; throughout, the paintings and works of art, mostly inherited though some more recently acquired, were of the highest quality. The week following the Ashburtons' arrival preparations were afoot for the marriage ball given to their and their neighbours' servants and to tradespeople. Loo was 'devoting her time to her new people and winning the hearts of all'. She inspected the village school and clothes were distributed to the poor, including 'six dozen charity hose'; Louisa and Emily Baring, her sisters-in-law, had been invited to stay. Harriet had never paid the least attention to any of the Barings, finding them uninteresting but recognizing their

> peculiar national importance and commercial dignity. They [Barings] are everywhere, they get everything. The only check upon them is, that they are all members of the Church of England; otherwise there is no saying what they would do.[101]

Jane Carlyle who had stayed with the sisters had found that 'the Baring manner is naturally so shy and cold' that she thought one might underrate the kindness of feeling, but that 'without seeming to take any *pains* to be kind' the Miss Barings made her feel quite at

68   IN PURSUIT OF HAPPINESS

home. 'What a deal of hearty laughing they *do* in a day.'[102] Loo and
Louisa Baring made friends from the start but Emily was not in
sympathy and was to be a sharp thorn in her side after Ashburton's
death.

A few days were snatched in London before a farewell visit to
Brighton where Mary Stewart-Mackenzie had rooms at 10 Lewes
Crescent. On 12 December the Ashburtons sailed from Folkestone
to spend a day in Paris and to continue by stages to Egypt, with the
Nile as their ultimate destination. Loo's last letters to her mother
spoke of her gratitude for 'love and tenderness all these years'.
'God grant that we may meet again in this world,' she prayed. 'I will
try more and more to make the Bible the rule of my life.' She
promised to make herself worthy of her husband in *all* ways,
adding how pleased he had been with his flannel nightgown. Snow
in Paris did not prevent the purchase of a peignoir for Loo's arrival
at hotels nor a long visit to Mme Camille, the dressmaker at the
head of fashion before the 'demi-monde Empress [Eugénie] took
the lead'. Her husband thought she could not be too much *'en
grande dame'* for his taste. Seasick on the way to Malta she
contrived to find with what Lord Ashburton called her 'usual
savoir faire' a chief officer to give her up his cabin – a great comfort
when they rolled heavily through a stormy sea into Valletta. It was
Christmas-time and all Malta was in the streets including Prince
Alfred, the Queen's second son, shopping for presents for his
mother. Lord Ashburton, sufficiently recovered and 'straight as a
drill serjeant' took Loo in her wideawake and without a crinoline
to the Christmas market, enjoying what she called the 'Dolce far
Niente' life. The Governor had them to dinner and a ball to meet
the fourteen-year-old Prince whom Loo thought 'a dear charming
boy, clever and intelligent with affable manners', but *The Times*
carried a leader at the end of the year deprecating his official
reception: 'We want him to learn his profession – not in a vapid,
half and half, Royal Highness, kind of way.' A friend of the
Ashburtons thought the whole proceeding was only fit for a Prince
Imperial. (Four years later, again at Malta, this same Prince was to
land himself in a thorough entanglement, but that was still in the
future.)

Loo now went down with rheumatism and was having trouble
with Clarke, the maid she had brought with her, who turned out a
bad maid, bad-tempered, and an infliction. She had insolently told

IN PURSUIT OF HAPPINESS

Loo that at Brighton the servants were sorry to see someone as respectable as herself working for a lady like Louisa. This must have been occasioned by Louisa's independent nature which had enabled her to go where she chose, as she chose, and un-chaperoned; to say forcibly what she pleased and to mix with artists, who except for a very few were not yet acceptable in society. Probably also her generally known and perfectly understood desire to secure a wealthy bachelor was made without the proper respect for form and delicacy. Having little interest in fashion she was unexacting in her dress nor was the arrangement of her hair particularly *soigné* (though 'Lord Ashburton is really particular about hairdressing'). To a lady's maid these matters would have been the antithesis of the refinements she would expect to find.

But the year closed on a note of relief. Loo was able to tell her mother that Ashburton was better, which made her happy, and he in turn wrote of Loo's 'genial unreserved nature.' But for another the weeks since Louisa's marriage had been a time of dejection. To Landseer it was mortifying that he could not overcome the pain of her defection, guilty though he said he had been of folly and weakness. To a close friend he admitted 'I really *do* try to forget and forgive . . . The Book I promised to close is not locked – hope plays the D--l with me.'[103] Loo also felt some shame for she continued to correspond; though what role she personified it would be imprudent to conjecture. 'Did you read her last letter? – it came open? I am afraid you think there is a dangerous flame in *her* mind? *she* is only rash – not bold *in* error.' It is possible that during the few days in London before the short stay in Brighton Louisa had gone to Landseer's studio in St John's Wood and had seen there his painting *Flood in the Highlands*, ready for the 1859 Royal Academy exhibition. 'I wish you could have seen poor Loo (and heard her sobs) when she saw it,'[104] Landseer wrote to the same correspondent in the new year. With her vivid memories of home but with her foot now set on a different path and the guilt of the trick she had played on the artist very present in her mind, Loo might well have been stirred emotionally.

From Alexandria she wrote excitedly, telling of their arrival at dawn and the five pasha's carriages to meet them and escort them to a palace prepared for them, and to give some idea of their magnificence: 'Fancy Clarke coming up all alone in state in a chaise and pair.' On arrival, giddy and sick, they had to smoke a pipe and

IN PURSUIT OF HAPPINESS

another on the arrival of the Governor, and bidden to make this their home and order all they wanted from the tribe of Nubian servants, Loo expressed herself realistically: 'Of course a great deal of Blarney'. The mosquitoes were a torment and the Ashburtons were glad to move on by special train to Cairo where husband and wife had much to retail to Mary on whom Lord Ashburton by an act of enormous generosity had settled many thousands of pounds, thus allaying all financial worries. To Louisa the pecuniary relief to her mother was everything.

> This act attaches me more to him than *anything* that he could possibly have done. I rejoice in his kindness to you – that *does* give me pleasure. He is so kind to me I am sure I ought to be happy and trust we shall each year we live together get happier.

There was plenty to occupy them in Cairo. The artists Goodall and Carl Haag were working there and either now or at a later date Loo acquired an oriental scene by Haag. Living in a constant state of royal representation there seemed to be strings of camels, steamboats, palaces and special trains on command. They had each procured a pipe which they smoked with enjoyment and Ashburton looked very handsome in a fez, though Loo had been unable to get an Arabian dress in time. Finally there were candles to purchase. Shortly before leaving England Loo had written to her 'dearest Zoë' (though they seldom met 'no one can ever occupy Zoë's niche in my heart') asking her to recommend books of Egyptian history, in particular anything helpful on hieroglyphics which her husband was specially anxious to study. Florence Nightingale when replying had reminded her to buy plenty of candles before leaving Cairo, for 'if you don't,' she had said, 'not all your money will get them for you afterwards unless you rob the Coptic church at Osgoot.' She urged her to keep clear of missionaries, 'they are the most awful charlatans I know.' She also sent to Bath House five volumes of Wilkinson's *Ancient Egyptians*, the first three volumes in German and two in English of Bunsen's work on Egyptian history, Arthur Clough's own copy of Rawlinson's *Herodotus*, Kingsley's *Alexandria*, besides six or seven further volumes. Louisa sent her affectionate thanks: 'I feel your kindness so much, dearest, may God bless you, and yet spare you to us all – and allow me to see you again in this world.'[105] It is doubtful whether the books were opened as Loo admitted to her

IN PURSUIT OF HAPPINESS 71

mother that her husband did not care about reading and 'he knows and cares nothing about antiquities so that we dont get the good we ought.'

Their boat was the admiration of the Nile and on it Lord Ashburton was 'as sound as a London Waterman', but as they drifted slowly towards the first cataract at Assuan Louisa had plenty of time to express her personal worries in her letters home. She had now been married two months. 'I wish there was any hope of a small chick, but that I much fear can *never* be, certainly quite impossible in the present state of things. But I have made my lot now so must be content.' Several weeks later she received her mother's reply and wrote in return: 'I am sorry about my depressed letter but I suppose all married people are unhappy *at first* and I confess it was a dreadful disappointment to me when I found I must in reason relinquish the fond hope of being a mother.' Lord Ashburton's state of health had taken her so much by surprise that she had '*no idea* how completely *unoccupied* his health has made him. I confess I felt all this keenly.' She had no one with whom she could talk and the insufferable Clarke was always saying things to show her 'how different was my lot to most young wives, indeed she is not a nice woman at all. But I have passed through all this now and we are *very happy* – he *deserves all* I can give him. I dont think now anything can come between us.' Lord Ashburton's gout was a great affliction but it seems clear that he was so debilitated that he was unable to have satisfactory sexual relations. Meanwhile Loo continued: 'We lead the most monotonous of lives, cup of coffee early, breakfast at 11.30, dinner at 7, between whiles Lord Ashburton sleeps mostly', but Loo herself missed Thebes on the way up because she was in bed. Assuan gave them some time ashore; the crew baked bread, Loo mounted a dromedary, sketched the hills black with granite in contrast to the valleys of golden sand, and the banks of the river lined with palms. They decided to dispense with maid, courier and appendages for the next part of the journey. 'Fancy Ld A and I being *alone* for a fortnight – *such* a thing! the most natural appears to me so strange but I *rejoice* at it.' She complained of her washing and the loss of collars which she could not stiffen with starch and which the wind blew away. But it was a happier time for them, loitering at Philae, and while Loo learned Arabic Ashburton was 'forking out baksheesh and between us we are the most popular European dignitaries. Loo says she never was so well in her whole life.' On the return journey they spent ten days at Thebes where Loo received news which saddened her. 'My heart mourns our dearest Jane Stirling, what a sweet and tender friend I have lost in her.' But she was able to write more contentedly to her mother. 'I have indeed a great deal to thank God for daily in giving me such a good dear husband and protector.' He had fallen asleep in the Tombs of the Kings and felt gout when he got back to the boat but the intense heat had slackened and Loo hoped to avoid a regular attack and she was now so fond of him that she would give up everything to nursing him. She realized that she was married to an invalid but she could agree to devote 'the best years of my life to nursing him, *dear* fellow'. For 'if ever a woman was married to a noble great-minded man it is me. He deserves all my love and *he has it*.' Nevertheless there was still the sadness of 'no thought of a piccaninny – oh how I wish there was – when I think of his health and my future days of nursing I feel what a little sunbeam it would be but I dont think this *great* happiness will ever be mine, indeed I dont see that it is possible.' To Ashburton Loo had become dearer every day; 'I do not know what right I have to such happiness.' He had given her a 'beautiful parure of scarabs, quite unique', and he had only to complain of her French genders, but she managed well and 'talks so prettily and makes herself so popular and gets her will'. The heat in their cabin was ninety-two degrees and they seemed to live on hot soup and hot champagne, and Loo had gained 'in her fair proportions'.

Back at Marseilles on the way home at the end of May Loo was thinking of a court dress and if there was to be a Drawing-room after their return 'who should present me, one of his people or one of mine?' If the former she would incline towards the Dowager Lady Bath who at the first meeting had seemed distant but Dr Brown told her she had 'won her beyond all chance of loss', and her husband explained that none of the Barings were demonstrative or carried their hearts on their lips 'to be exaled in a kiss or a fair word', but kept it safe for those they loved, and were Loo to look into his he would be found all hers. He was on crutches again and 'still no prospect of a chick, but it may be my fault as he is much better. Perhaps some day God will give us this great blessing but I doubt it.' Nevertheless they were happy together. 'We moon about all day in the fresh air; we read nothing, do nothing but moon' and

IN PURSUIT OF HAPPINESS

they were in the 'most Elysian state of cooing worthy of the second day of honeymoon'.

From Biarritz Lord Ashburton wrote to his mother-in-law that Loo was triumphant for she had at last discovered her vocation. If she could only dress her hair, make gowns, prove obedient, she could make an excellent lady's maid. She had always packed her own trunk and carpet bag and breakfasted in full time. They had slept two nights at San Sebastian where Loo 'must needs bathe' though bathing was forbidden, the Governor of the Province holding that the water was too cold. The Ashburtons represented to him that the 'Highland blood was hotter even than the Spanish and that courtesy should not forbid in the land of chivalry what was free as air in our land of churls'. So an order was given that one bathing machine should be advanced into the sea and an official in uniform arrived to say that the pernicious and immoral practice of allowing ladies to be bathed by men could in no case be permitted, so for two days Loo was hand in hand with a female, knocked over by each successive wave.

8
At The Grange and Bath House

It was exciting to be home and from Bath House in the middle of July Louisa made what she called her married debut at Lansdowne House and was 'mobbed'. Catherine Stanley, widow of the Bishop, took a different view.

> Lady Ashburton made her first public appearance and was not very favourably received by the fashionable world for she was uncommonly ill dressed and had put on the Ashburton jewels on a rough head of hair, however she was very glad to see her old friends and so delighted with her Nile travels that I think she really forgot the conventionalities of less crinoline and all.[106]

She may have been wearing on her forehead what has been described as 'a raspberry tart of diamonds'[107] and worth seeing; it had belonged to her husband's mother. Conversely, Dr Brown at Edinburgh had heard that Loo had amazed London with her beauty – not surprisingly, 'for in these degenerate days she is a wonder'.

Now that her position in society was assured Loo's eccentricities had become more pronounced and though Lord Stanley of Alderley in his usual offensive manner found her 'full of bad taste, ostentatious and courting publicity'[108] there were plenty who admired her and to a friend she appeared 'a brilliant and shining vision'. There is no doubt that she held for many a very compelling power; and one can only admire her desire to do well and her concern for her doting husband. Her first care had been to ensure that he put himself into the hands of Dr Richard Quain (later created a baronet), a man of charm and ability in whom she and her mother had great faith, having been his patients for several years.

There was no pausing now at The Grange. A day at Strawberry Hill had to be fitted in though Lord Ashburton went there reluctantly; he 'hated the hostess', the renowned Lady Waldegrave, considering her a *maîtresse femme*, charitable though she

AT THE GRANGE AND BATH HOUSE 75

might be, who was so ambitious to succeed that she would stop at nothing. Writing in confidence, Lady Sandwich told Mrs Carlyle that the Ashburtons had been to her every day after their arrival, but as they always came together she had not been able to see Ashburton alone. He seemed very happy and very submissive, *'but this is only for you and Mr Carlyle'*.[109] Loo was all kindness and amiability. A visit to Ashburton farm properties in Somerset and on the Wye had to be undertaken before the journey north to Wallington, to Castle Fraser, and, most longed for of all, to Brahan and Loch Luichart. From Wallington in early August Ashburton wrote that he liked Loo's friends and could easily fall into their ways and live their kind of lives: 'a learned leisure', holding great charm for an idler like himself. But there was no likelihood of restless and energetic Loo allowing this and from Brahan he wrote to Carlyle: 'For nine months I have been struggling on and on. I cannot yet feel that I shall ever be at rest again, so unsettled have I become' (to Carlyle this statement was decidedly 'an unwholesome item'), yet he was in better health than he had ever been. Of Mary he said it would have gladdened Carlyle's heart to have seen this 'noble relic of better times'. Brahan was of course Loo's bourne of earth and there, again according to Lord Stanley, they had a great public reception with Lord Ashburton making 'a most absurd speech and seems more devoted and less in awe of his present Lady than of the past'.[110] To a friend it seemed that they were as happy as people ought to be who were still gathering 'matrimonial honey' and that Loo seemed perfectly contented with her lottery ticket – 'it certainly is not an o!'[111] Their time was divided between Louisa's old home and her new one at Loch Luichart. Harriet had liked it of all things and had commended the comfortable small house, the beautiful walks through the birch woods and down through the terraced garden to the lake, and the country town of Dingwall where one could get nothing but 'a Finnan Haddie and a Shandredan'.[112] Louisa would later add a turret, portico and gargoyles, throw out two bow windows, and enlarge the house to include fourteen bedrooms, one bathroom, main rooms on the ground floor, servants' quarters, a coachhouse, stables, harness room, gun room, peat house, slaughter house, and out-of-door rustic larders for venison and game. On the tower above the front door she inscribed the couplet: 'Watch and pray, Time hasteth away.'

76 AT THE GRANGE AND BATH HOUSE

Careless of gossip Loo was pressing Landseer to join them but he was not to be manipulated again and acquainted with her character he was armed against small talk and gossip. 'Loo has everything at her feet. Once when I was talking *grave* nonsense to her she said "remember you are God's child" – and so good came out of Humbug.' He had no time to discuss her pictures and sketches (probably her alleged motive for inviting him) but sent her a message that she had 'better things of his than she could find at any imposters'.[113]

By the late autumn the Ashburtons were back at The Grange and the house parties were resumed. This was a testing time for Louisa who may have felt that her predecessor's brilliance overshadowed her own less sophisticated manner and that all eyes, whether of friend or stranger, were upon her. Although Lord Stanley of Alderley thought that none of Harriet's friends seemed to have 'any feelings but those of distaste to the present lady',[114] this was not so. The Brookfields who had been on intimate terms with Harriet were there for Christmas and Mrs Carlyle was the first to hear that except for some minor shifting of pictures the caravanserai was little altered, though he would not write of the greater changes which that Eastern word implied. There had been a dazzling Christmas tree with costly presents for everyone, while for Loo, the crowning triumph to her marriage, 'an embryo possibility'.[115] Brookfield was conscious of being a very superior person: his ambition and vanity had made him many enemies, as when he arrived to preach 'adorned in starched bands and rich ribbed silk ... in glum silence with a condescending nod ... arranged his flowing locks before a looking glass'.[116] To others he was a clergyman of cultivated tastes, a born actor who played his part upon the stage rather than in the pulpit.[117] His wife was greatly admired for her looks and charm of manner but on arrival at The Grange (perhaps wearing her new bonnet with large blue flowers, praised by Mrs Carlyle) she was disconcerted to be asked by Loo if the servants were treating her correctly since it was likely that they thought they need not trouble themselves about looking after a clergyman's wife.[118]

The parties were smaller than in former days but with a new 'particular cachet, for Louisa had a sparkle and geniality all her own'.[119] It pleased Mary Stewart-Mackenzie to hear from Brookfield that her daughter filled the functions of her place with

AT THE GRANGE AND BATH HOUSE 77

grace and energy, though all who knew her were aware that whatever she undertook she would do well. It also seemed to indicate that Lord Ashburton must always have been a principal but so quiet and unassuming that one had been inclined to overlook it. He appeared younger and jollier and in prodigious contentment.

The new year of 1860 brought the Monckton Milneses and Carlyles to The Grange. At the time of Ashburton's engagement Carlyle had written of his thankfulness that a remedy 'beyond our expectation' had been found to counter the widower's solitude, but husband and wife returned after three years with some foreboding. Ashburton had read the first two volumes of Carlyle's *Frederick the Great* with eager relish. Uncouth as was its style he found the wisdom of selection, the vigour of expression and the rigid fidelity of statement beyond any other historian, but Carlyle cared little for eulogy and was sunk in perpetual gloom. Jane, meanwhile, was in a serious fidget over her asthmatic little dog Nero (whose name had provided Harriet with the acid jest of calling his owner Agrippina)[120] but was determined to keep her head, feeling it would be a sort of infidelity and disloyalty ever to care for another Lady Ashburton. Louisa was equally resolved to enrol her as a friend, knowing she had been slighted by her predecessor. With 'a noble frankness' she presented herself as an unworthy substitute and 'Even I,' Jane said, 'who had set my mind against liking her could not resist the pains she took to make me.' As to Lord Ashburton: 'Oh No! he shows no sign of regret. His devotion to the new lady is perfect, and really, he never was so *made* of before.'[121] Out of doors the keepers were dressed in shooting liveries with tall, gold-laced, cockaded livery hats;[122] on Sunday evenings thirty-eight servants knelt for prayers in the dining room, the men on one side and the women on the other. The house was choke-full with twenty-four visitors; nothing, Jane thought, could exceed their magnificence and the indoor warm water-pipes made it feel like summer. In the evening the women, including four young newly-weds, were all 'viing with each other who should be the finest. The blaze of diamonds every day at dinner quite took the shine out of the chandeliers.'[123] How different a story it was now from the days when, writing of Bath House and its occupant, Jane would exclaim:

78 AT THE GRANGE AND BATH HOUSE

When I first noticed that heavy yellow house without knowing or caring to know, who it belonged to, how far was I from dreaming that through the years and years I should carry every stone's weight of it on my heart.[124]

Her letter to Loo after The Grange visit was in bright contrast. She wrote of it as an 'Arabian Nights Entertainment sort of thing' and that her ordinary life thereby gained immeasurably in dinginess and dullness. But she had come home with 'loving and trusting feelings towards *you*, my Lady, which are a pleasant wonder to myself'. Another letter telling of Nero's death brought a warmly sympathetic reply starting with a reprimand to Jane for being a bad correspondent 'and so unkind not to give me *ever so small* a place in your hearts'. She was glad to hear that Mr Carlyle had shed human tears over Nero, 'but he is made up of *tenderness*, *that* is what I felt most in his nature', and though they had scarcely exchanged twenty words she hoped some day he would let her know him 'for I am a good deal in love'. Later she wrote of the value she put on any expression of regard from them for she had chosen them out from the time they first met. 'I hope you will let me look on you as friends for Life – indeed I feel you are so – quite enshrined in my heart – so different from the passing shadows of a day.' Impulse and exaggeration were to be the keynotes of this frenetic friendship. But for Jane the spell was already at work. Her defences were no match for that Highland strength.

Louisa had good reason to be satisfied with her parties, one lot staying on until squeezed out by newcomers. She had her own friends to invite; among them was Parthe, married now to Sir Harry Verney, the Evangelical who had earlier wished to marry Florence. He was stunningly handsome, but according to Ashburton Parthe made up in intelligence for his dullness. With the dispersal of guests Louisa was able, on a Sunday evening, to have a quiet coze and read the evening service followed by the last sermons in Job with her husband, with whom she said she spent a life of deep happiness and hoped to spend an eternity in heaven. Her pregnancy, four months advanced, was the fulfilment of her prayers, while the house and its treasures provided a perpetual occupation. There were alterations and improvements to be made; the drawing room was repapered in a rich brown showing off the pictures to perfection, with the Van Dyck group of the children of

AT THE GRANGE AND BATH HOUSE

Charles I as a centrepiece. The music room in a delicate green with a pleasing arrangement of portraits was equally satisfying. Loo's boudoir, with walls covered in Chinese paper and curtains matching, was partly turned into a museum and Sir Walter Trevelyan allowed Mr Wooster to come south to catalogue the natural history, minerals and aquariums. But Pauline warned her that he worked very slowly. 'Remember that, my impetuous young woman.'

Nothing was wanting now but more room and shortly a new house. When writing to Brahan Lord Ashburton spoke of the change Loo had made in what was once a desolate place – there was not a soul in the establishment that did not feel the vivifying influence of her presence. The place, the poor, the schools and the clergy and all that surrounded her 'smiles and responds to her gorgeous presence'. Out of doors she 'cuts and she plants and makes vistas' and was busily directing a working party to make the new walk to the church. Here too she had plans which stretched over a couple of years. The architect William Butterfield was brought in to redesign part of the village church of Northington (entirely rebuilt at the end of the century). Designs for modifications to the east elevation included new roofs to vestry and tower, new copings, crosses to the gables and alteration in the east window.[125] Inside, the pulpit was to be placed against the north wall and the Westmacott family monument raised to stand clear of the altar rails. Four texts were to be inserted into niches, there was to be new paving, new glass for the west window. Piers and gates for the churchyard were also under way. In the schoolhouse a stove was needed and the addition of a soup kitchen to the nurse's house. All came under Butterfield's direction.

> Your Presbyterian daughter [wrote Ashburton] is to decorate us after the latest patristic purity of architectural doctrine. She has lost her heart to Mr Butterfield and Mr B. to her.

Louisa hoped he would go to Loch Luichart as well but time did not allow. Later, after Ashburton's death, she required from him a monumental red Aberdeen grave cross but Butterfield feared there would be a difficulty in putting a legible inscription on granite.

The culmination of the Ashburtons' happiness was the birth of a daughter, with a complete head of hair, at Bath House on 26 June 1860. The unspoken disappointment of its not being a son was

80 AT THE GRANGE AND BATH HOUSE

accentuated for Loo by her invalid husband having but a short lease of life, thus placing her own future and that of her daughter in jeopardy by the haunting spectre of primogeniture. 'This much loved place which on the birth of an heir will become a thousand times more loved,' Ashburton had written, but the little girl was only four years old when The Grange ceased to be her home and the watering-places of Bohemia and Baden, the Swiss Alps, the Roman Campagna and the French Riviera became even more familiar to her than her mother's house in Ross-shire. Her birth had not been a difficult one, only a few weeks overdue. Loo had become very unwieldy 'carrying her treasure in front of her' as Victorian decorum so aptly reported, or, as Lord Ashburton more trenchantly observed, 'waddling like a fisher's wife'. They had lived quietly at The Grange, watching the advance of spring which told of 'precious times gone by spent with those who are gone where all the Immortals go' and there they remained till well after Easter 'and the Resurrection is completed'.

The child was delicate and her parents had wished for a christening at Bath House but Arthur Stanley who was to conduct the service insisted that it should be held in a church of the parish. A brother of the Stanley girls who at Brahan in 1849 had hesitated to accompany Louisa and the Trevelyans to Loch Maree, he would before many years be installed as Dean of Westminster. Now he was a canon of Canterbury, and of Christ Church, Oxford and examining chaplain to Tait, Bishop of London, later Archbishop of Canterbury, that thorough evangelizer of Aberdeen stock and friend of Louisa. At St George's, Hanover Square, at the end of July, the baby was baptized Mary (though always called Maysie) for her grandmother, and Florence after the Lady of the Lamp. 'If you wish to call your daughter after me', Florence had written, 'as a token of my affection for her, as your child, and of yours for me, it cannot but be *very* grateful to me.' Pauline thought the names ran very softly and pleasantly and were very nice even if she wondered silently at the exclusion of a closer friend and longer friendship.

Jane Carlyle was so eager to see the baby that her enthusiasm bordered on the delirious. 'I saw her all over, lying like a pearl in an oyster shell', she wrote effusively, probably more anxious to please the mother than for love of the child. Her unrestrained attachment to Loo was a measure of her own loneliness and emotional starvation, and she blossomed in the warmth of Louisa's kindness

AT THE GRANGE AND BATH HOUSE 81

and demonstrativeness. In the years that followed Jane's letters were couched in terms of increasing devotion (though to close friends there were occasional tart remarks about Louisa) opening with 'Oh my darling! my darling', alternating sometimes with 'Dearest, sweetest, beautifullest', and continuing with exaggerated fervour. Sometimes it was the effect of a letter from Loo which 'makes me long to take you in my arms and hush you to sleep, as if you were a tired wee child, and kiss off all tears from your eyes'; and sometimes Jane was almost frightened to think how indispensable Loo had become.

> If you were to tire of me now, and if you were to die before me! and if you were anyhow taken out of my life! Why I should fall into as great trouble as I ever was in when young and excitable about a 'lost love'.

But to her husband, though grateful for Louisa's kindness to Jane and later to himself, the past remained a poignant sorrow. One day at The Grange he went round his old walks 'a *Shadow* very sad and beautiful escorting me', he wrote to Harriet's mother. Inside the Northington church he read the little tablet bearing the date of Harriet's death 'which will be memorable to me all the days of my life . . . there is no forgetting possible.'[126]

As in the previous year the Carlyles were again at The Grange at the beginning of 1861. Jane had had some azure blue moiré given to her by Lady Sandwich made up into a dress for the visit, and had received from the same source a seal-fur pelisse, a luxury long sighed for but at twenty guineas not to be thought of. It was one of the coldest winters for many years and at home in London Jane wrote to tell of the Serpentine quite frozen over, at night thronged with skaters holding torches, a band playing, stalls, little canvas booths dotting the ice with flags flying selling 'roast taties', wine, porter and ginger beer. She thought Londoners beat the world for being able to do nothing without 'refreshment'. Even Carlyle, walking past the festive scene at midnight, expressed a strong desire to be taught to skate.

Louisa's activities were now directed towards the arts. Baron Marochetti, the fashionable and successful Piedmontese sculptor, was at work upon portrait busts of the Ashburtons. Alexander Munro had executed one of Lord Ashburton, exhibited at the Royal Academy in 1860, and Loo had seen the marble medallions

82 AT THE GRANGE AND BATH HOUSE

at Wallington he had made of the Trevelyans – and must have admired them since her mother too had sat to Munro. Jane Carlyle went to Marochetti's studio in Onslow Square to meet Loo there, but as was not unusual Loo failed to put in an appearance and Jane poured out on paper an account of the sculptor's admiration: Lady Ashburton was 'a beautiful woman – amazingly beautiful, and her eyes – there is in them such goodness and a *something wild* that is very beautiful'. She thought the clay model a goodish likeness though evidently not flattering, but the tinting of the marble head gave the impression of a sickly Madame Tussaud waxwork. Sir Walter Trevelyan noted in his diary that he had seen the bust at the Royal Academy (1861) but made no comment.

Richard (Dickie) Doyle had long been a visitor to The Grange and over the years Louisa would acquire several of his drawings. In 1862 she paid £200 for a pair of drawings by Noel Paton (whose Presbyterian father had turned Methodist, afterwards Quaker and finally Swedenborgian, beliefs perhaps not altogether inimical to Loo). When Pauline met him in Edinburgh she thought him 'heavenly', and passed on a message that he had not completed the pictures from his *Morte d'Arthur* sketches as he was waiting for the summer to do the backgrounds from nature. W.W. Leitch, the Queen's drawing master, who for some years before Loo's marriage had given her drawing lessons, was not forgotten; in 1861 Louisa bought seventeen of his watercolours, many of them Highland landscapes, and some copies of works at Bath House which she knew she might never inherit. Her almost manic collecting and expenditure included two Rubens sketches of great beauty besides a first impression of the *Raising of Lazarus* by Rembrandt.

Indoors, Bath House was now to be given a new face. The exterior of this modest-looking Piccadilly house on the corner of Bolton Street, partly obscured by a wall, had been built in 1829 on the site of the old Pulteney Hotel, the resort of foreign royalties, in particular of Tzar Alexander I in 1814 at the time of the victory celebrations. Three-storeyed, bow-fronted in the middle, and of yellow brick, the house faced towards the Green Park; the entrance from a courtyard was at the back as were also the stables. Louisa supervised the lighting, the arrangement of furniture, the servants (she had lynx eyes to detect an omission) and the food. The Carlyles had made her a present of a small Persian prayer-rug of fine texture,

AT THE GRANGE AND BATH HOUSE   83

given to them by Lewis Pelly, secretary of the British Legation in Teheran, and bought at a bazaar at Herat. It had lain by the side of Jane's dressing-table but 'was quite out of harmony with our plain furniture'.[127] Told by Lord Ashburton that Loo was to repaint some of the rooms where the paintings hung, Pauline had 'asked Mr Ruskin what colour he thought generally agreed best with those sort of pictures'. He suggested for the walls 'a *quiet* crimson', or a 'soft subdued green – not so blue as duck's egg but very soft and retiring' on which many pictures looked lovely. Pauline thought this would 'agree charmingly with Rubens', having in mind his three famous paintings at Bath House, one measuring six feet by nine. Landseer, also appealed to for advice, replied that to do justice to the Old Masters one sacrificed beauty and fashion; he disliked 'those *feeble* tints which were supposed to light well' and could not recommend 'primitive hue that might *tyrannize* over ones Eye and take the energy from the painter's combinations'. Above all, he begged for caution in the final decision.

Large parties were held at Bath House in the early summer of 1861 with Lord Ashburton commending his wife's selection of guests and her 'loving easy' manner of receiving them. The Gladstones were among those in May, coming from a dinner at Baron Rothschild; the Trevelyans were often there in June, Sir Walter noting with admiration the house and its objects, and the soirée for the Geographical Society of which Lord Ashburton was President.[128] Loo went to the Derby day races at Epsom and was scandalized by the behaviour of some well-dressed women who between them drank one hundred bottles of champagne without glasses or tumblers, given them by two men in a carriage; and two men and women were observed to empty eleven bottles of champagne. To Loo's consternation, on the way back, 'the Clapham saints distinguished themselves by throwing stones' – presumably at the inebriated. Pauline had a lace stall at the South Kensington Museum that month for the School of Design Bazaar, of which Loo was also a patroness. She was receiving many demands for charitable causes: one from Fulham Palace recommending the Highgate Penitentiary; and later in the year Mrs Gladsone was collecting for a kitchen in Lancashire for the 'poor afflicted people' suffering from the cotton famine, where happily her Irish stew was proving acceptable. Louisa had offered financial assistance to an East End clergyman (reliable to preach an

84 AT THE GRANGE AND BATH HOUSE

Evangelical gospel) and one Jeffcock was selected whose work was 'of a missionary kind'. Tom Taylor, barrister and writer for *Punch*, had formed a committee with Mark Lemon, *Punch*'s first editor, and others to raise money on behalf of Mrs Stirling, the accomplished 'artiste' who had recently been robbed of every article of valuable jewellery. Long as she had been on the stage she had never yet taken a benefit night and her friends and admirers wished to replace the ornaments. There is nothing to show that Louisa frequented the theatre, but Tom Taylor having been a Grange visitor during Harriet's reign she may have felt called upon to contribute. Grisi and Jenny Lind, however, she admired greatly and spoke of as friends – the latter having such a '*true* look' and 'singing like a *great* artist, full of genius'. On being asked by Loo if she could recommend a nurse for Maysie she had one to suggest, excellent for a babe in arms, but not where moral training would be required, for 'like most of that class of governess (alas!) more like a heathen than a Christian'. A letter from Florence Nightingale, written in April 1861 from her sofa in Burlington Hotel after nearly a year's silence, was of a different nature. Opening with less than usual warmth ('My dear friend') she requested Loo to return by railway parcel any letters she might have of hers. 'One of those female ink-bottles, who are my dread and despair is collecting material for a life of me', and she wished to burn every letter written in her own hand. Nervously she inquired: 'You have not left any such maiden stores at Brahan, have you?' That passionate friendship was long ago at an end though affection and respect remained.

Pauline writing to 'My darling' from Wallington in July to confirm the Ashburtons' visit the following month lamented the death of Elizabeth Barrett Browning. She had been so ill so long one never thought she would die. Thinking of their son Pen, with the golden hair, and how his mother worshipped him and what it must have been to her to leave him behind, Pauline hoped Browning would listen to advice and send Pen to school. The journey to Wallington was accomplished by train and the travellers left Bath House for the railway station with a wagon containing baby's iron crib, baby's bath, sundry luggage, and the butler to arrange the cot and swing it in the family railway carriage. Next, a cab with maid, man, and nurserymaid; then baby and nurse in the state chariot driven by the coachman and attended by their tallest footman; and

AT THE GRANGE AND BATH HOUSE 85

finally the parents in a carefully chosen hansom, stuffed to extinction of life, fearful to look at, painful to emerge from. There was a short stay at Brahan where Loo's widowed sister-in-law, 'Mrs George', was living and caring for Mary Stewart-Mackenzie, now an elderly invalid; and then on to Loch Luichart with constant visits back to Brahan. On one of these, wishing to help Loo 'in this curious state of things', Mrs George thought it best to warn Landseer who was staying there that Louisa would be arriving. But by then embarrassment and sorrow had faded and he was induced to stay at Loch Luichart. Perhaps it was on this occasion that annoyed at not finding Loo on his return from a day's stalking, when he and another guest had gone their several ways into the forest, pitted against each other, he made a collage on one of the windows from the brown wrapping of a parcel and tissue paper, on which he made a sketch of a deer and a stalking party.

Francis Grant, the accomplished and fashionable portrait painter who had so effectively portrayed Landseer in 1852, had recently completed a portrait of Lord Ashburton for the sum of £420. Although the sitter had 'bored on and slept standing' to have the picture finished he found the result wholly successful and flattering and meant all future photographs of him to be taken from it. 'I may now rest for ever unless I grow still younger with still blushier tints and brighter eyes.' The portrait showed him standing full-length in forester's dress, his looks belying his sixty-two years and his infirmities. Landseer was now engaged to paint Louisa and Maysie together but it was slow work; though a start was made, Landseer's bouts of depression and drink slowed its progress while Louisa's unpredictable migrations made sittings difficult to obtain. That Christmas of 1861, while Brookfield read aloud from *Othello* in the evenings at The Grange, Landseer wrote a letter illustrating it with a sketch of himself asleep, slouched across a table, a bottle in his hand.

> I have become the Bottle imp to drown pain. When I am fit for service in any form I shall pack up my all (Mother and Child) and hope you will receive me with a fixed intention of aiding the completion of the poor ill-used canvas.

Louisa thought herself misrepresented in the portrait and at a previous sitting had suggested being made more of a 'fine lady'. 'Shall I have to make such a promotion in the Picture?' he asked,

86 AT THE GRANGE AND BATH HOUSE.

ending on a faint note of reproach: 'This is Xmas day, I am alone. How would you stand being alone in the world.' In the small half-length portrait the artist has caught the forceful character of the subject, who stands with her back turned, her head in profile looking at the child in her arms. The features are almost masculine in strength, the hair roughly dressed, and the impression of energetic purposefulness faithfully recorded. Shortly before her marriage Landseer had sketched out her future career and his appreciation of her character and nature was very exact; these he transmitted unerringly onto the canvas. To please her he made her a present of a portrait of her husband in the summer of 1862 as a pendant of that of herself, finished in one sitting of four-and-a-half hours – pronounced by Loo to be divine, a wonderful likeness, and in painting worthy of any gallery.

9
Decline and Death

Gout and general debility made it advisable for the sake of Lord Ashburton's health to winter again in Egypt in the first months of 1862 and the Trevelyans were invited to join them. This they were unable to do and when the scheme foundered Ashburton was thankful to escape the infliction of so long a journey. Instead, a congenial party of friends gathered at The Grange in January: the Carlyles, Bishop Wilberforce, the Charles Kingsleys, the Argylls; only Thackeray had been prevented from coming through ill health. Loo sat down to write to her mother but Monckton Milnes, Louisa Baring and Carlyle were talking so loudly that she found it difficult to write; Kingsley, the Duke of Argyll and the Bishop of Oxford were discussing Darwin and his *Origin of Species*. The Prince Consort had not been dead many weeks and Louisa lamented the loss of such precious talent; Maysie − 'if her little life is spared' − was recovering from some childish stomach complaint, but her father had suffered acutely, seized by a sudden oppression of heart and lungs. In this fearful emergency Loo had acted with great presence of mind, had done what was necessary and then sent for Quain. 'I am alive and owing to Loo,' he said. 'She does not belie the race she sprang from and rises above the heroic.'

Aware that if he died without a male heir The Grange would revert to his brother, the Hon. Francis Baring, Ashburton decided to buy for Louisa the property of Melchet Court, bordering on the New Forest some fifteen miles from Romsey, belonging to his youngest brother Frederick, rector of Itchenstoke, who had inherited it from their father. The house stood on rising ground in a park of some 700 acres, commanding extensive views south to the Isle of Wight, and rich in rare specimens of foreign trees and ancient oaks, cedars and beeches. But the classical red brick house did not agree with Louisa's

DECLINE AND DEATH

taste and was to be rebuilt; tenders were put out and the architect Henry Clutton chosen to make designs for the new building.

Meanwhile, in the spring of 1862, Louisa found herself again pregnant; hopes were centred on a son and much advice on 'guarding the hope' was proffered by solicitous friends and Pauline wrote 'God be with you in your joy to come'. In April the Ashburtons were in London; they dined with Dean Milman where, after an interval of eleven years, Loo met again Robert Browning, now a widower; they looked at the gigantic building for the International Exhibition at South Kensington, but the access was almost impassable from the triple line of waggons unloading. The exterior was by no means promising, but when Ashburton went to its opening on 1 May he thought the problem of building picture galleries had been solved for ever, the lighting was perfect and no matter where one stood a picture could be seen in all its details – his own *Judgement of Solomon* by B. R. Haydon (once Landseer's), though high up, had never been seen to greater advantage. From The Grange Loo wrote an emotional letter to Bath House reiterating her love and reverence for him. 'Oh! my darling, your dear presence is my life, may we be permitted to meet again, I am more and more your own devoted Wife.' Their hopes were checked by a miscarriage and Loo sobbed on her husband's shoulder in an agony of grief, not at her own loss, which was great, but at her mother's disappointment.

At the end of June, with Lord Ashburton in the grip of an attack of gout and Loo convalescing, they took rooms at the Westcliffe Hotel, Folkestone. Here Jane Carlyle who had been suffering from 'sleeplessness' joined them. 'I think we *ought* to try and meet oftener,' Loo had written earlier and had been sending weekly hampers of fresh butter, eggs and cream to Cheyne Row from the farm at Addiscombe. Heading her paper 'Foxton' Jane told her husband that on her arrival Loo had asked '*Did* I think you would come?' and although she had given the impression of having expected Carlyle to accompany his wife, Jane did not think he had really been expected 'or exactly meaning you to come at this moment'. It was an astonishingly quiet house to be a hotel but she feared Carlyle would take exception to the amount of light in the bedroom; the window was large and had only a white muslin blind and curtain to cover it. Of course he could pin up his travelling rug

DECLINE AND DEATH   89

as so often in the past. He need bring only such clothes as would fit into his carpet bag, and the constant loins of roast mutton and boiled chicken, though objected to as all too English, would exactly suit him. But Louisa's eccentricities and curious lack of consideration prevailed and Jane was bewildered to know what were her wishes. 'I havent a notion whether she expects *me* to stay two days or two weeks!' A few days later Lord Ashburton had laid aside his crutches and was able to go out in a Bath chair with Loo, so that Jane had no opportunity of seeing her alone and had not been able to come to any conclusion regarding the length of the visit, though '*en revanche* there is much celebration of your book *Frederick* [iii], and your genius and your "poetic language"'. However, a sudden thought had struck Lord Ashburton that he must go up to town. 'He is knocked on the head by "sudden thoughts" every hour, now,' Jane told her husband, and 'My Lady too talks of going up next week for a concert.' In short,' she continued, 'there is a general confused movement as of Bees about to skepp!'[129] Dr Quain from Harley Street was in attendance and Jane thought him not only a 'slippery Irishman' and a humbug but a 'silly wheedling' creature as well, with whom the Ashburtons were infatuated. Louisa missed Jane excessively when she left and was tempted to sit down and write her a 'romantic outpouring'.

A few days before the stay at Folkestone Louisa had been on an exciting expedition. Pauline made a brief entry in her journal on 24 June: 'Rossettis. Red Lion. Loo etc.' The Morris Firm at 8 Red Lion Square had opened its doors in April and the two friends were sharing the interest of being introduced to the new establishment. To Pauline the work of the members of the firm was familiar for she had carefully examined their exhibits at South Kensington, had studied the murals at the Oxford Union in 1857 and had more recently commissioned a watercolour from Dante Gabriel Rossetti. His designs for glass would have been available for inspection and this was to lead Louisa into more than one commission within a few years. Pauline paid a second visit in July but by then Loo was at Brahan; writing of her mother to Mrs Monckton Milnes she thought there was 'more of Eternity than of Time about her'. Mother and daughter had such a perfect understanding of one another that 'we were, all my life long, such *dear friends*'. The Ashburtons had taken

DECLINE AND DEATH

the Villa Jaune at Nice for the winter and Loo felt apprehensive at saying goodbye to her mother for several months.

At The Grange that autumn before the departure to France there was a smaller house-party than usual. The Carlyles had come for a week; he found it 'somewhat mournful . . . so many changes done by fleeting Time'. But Jane enjoyed it. 'Helpmate seems to like it better than I! We go home tomorrow, positive as per bargain.' Nevertheless Carlyle had taken pleasure in an argument with the Bishop of Oxford in which he had put him right in two Scripture quotations;[130] and there had been the occasion when everyone returned to the dining room after dinner 'and the Bishop read the evening prayers, and then addressed the party, including the clustered domestics, an army, who had been busy clearing the board, on the virtue of self-sacrifice'.[131] A photographer was on hand at what Jane called 'an easy rate of 5 guineas a day' and photographed her seated with Loo standing beside her, and Carlyle and Ashburton sitting on a bench under the portico overlooking the lake.[132] The American sculptor Story and his family were also among the party. William Wetmore Story was in his mid-forties, a New Englander by birth, Roman by adoption. Versatile, brilliant and cultivated, before the age of thirty he had won acclaim as a barrister with a treatise which became the standard work in American courts. Lacking any formal training he had turned seriously to sculpture and had made this his life's work, though he also sought expression in poetry and Jane Carlyle recorded that he sang like an angel.[133] His first visit to Italy had been in 1847 and thereafter he quickly settled his studio and family on the third floor of the north wing of the Palazzo Barberini in Rome where he and his wife entertained extensively. He had been an intimate of the Brownings and Robert's departure to England did nothing to weaken this friendship. At the International Exhibition he showed the first version of his tremendously popular *Cleopatra* (eloquently described by Hawthorne in the *Marble Faun*) and his no less successful *Libyan Sibyl*. Louisa's attention may have been attracted at the same time to two works by Harriet Hosmer, an American sculptress living also in Rome, whose passionate friendship was to shape her middle years.

The Ashburtons arrived in Paris in late October on their way south and put up at the Hotel Bristol in the rue du Faubourg St Honoré. Their departure from Bath House had held all the chaotic

DECLINE AND DEATH

91

ingredients of what to Loo had become a normal removal and of which Jane Carlyle sent a description to a friend.

I found a wonderful complication at Bath House and only the baby starts tomorrow! of course accompanied by two nurses, men servants and Lady Ashburton's sister-in-law [Mrs George]. Lord Ashburton should follow on Saturday. And as for Lady Ashburton she has suddenly taken a notion she is in the family way again!

Her doctor declared she must not stir from the sofa (on which she was lying) the whole winter, while Ashburton was unable to stand another one in England. 'What a pretty mess!' concluded Jane.[134] But there was worse to follow. Louisa's pregnancy was imagined and Lord Ashburton fell ill within a few days of their arrival in Paris and remained seriously so for eight months, first at the hotel where they occupied the greater part of the *entresol* ('rain, rain, and always this dreadful entresol'), and in the new year at a rented house at Chaillot. Louisa, tortured by an anxiety that veered between despair and hope, mourned that she had not 'gone my nine months' and so remained in England to have been confined there at about this time. 'It is now that I regret that mishap of the summer,' she said. The supposed cause of his illness was damp sheets. 'Could such things as happen to immensely rich people' ever happen to themselves, Jane Carlyle wondered. Maysie was sent to Nice in Mrs George's devoted care with the footman Bailey, Sedille the cook (who had been in Harriet's employ and disliked the new mistress), Corbett the nurse and Jeannie, nurserymaid, who pronounced her native tongue so unaffectedly that Lord Ashburton dreaded his child acquiring a broad Scottish accent. His travelling physician, Dr Christison, a valet, Loo's two maids, and their cook remained in Paris. Daily letters went to Mrs George concerning Maysie's health, Maysie's clothes, Maysie's diet, Maysie's teeth, her prayers and her liver.

In the middle of November death was apparently close at hand. 'He is dying, I see it now and I am broken hearted. I love him so much,' and Francis Baring, his brother and heir to the title, hurried to Paris thinking to find him a corpse. Writing to his wife on 15 November Lord Stanley of Alderley told her that 'Francis Baring set off to see his brother – if it should end fatally their alarms at Lady Ashburton's frequent mishaps will be relieved.'[135] Loo's

DECLINE AND DEATH

relations with the Barings were precarious. Emily came but her presence proved such a trial that Loo felt 'so *crushed*, so *broken*'. She seemed to care little for her brother's recovery – though coming from a reserved family it was probably more reticence than lack of feeling – and she was also out of sympathy with Loo, saying that the people who were liked by her on Monday were loathed on Tuesday and that she behaved thus with the servants also. 'Dry as a stick' and 'ill-natured' Loo thought her and Emily seems to have surpassed herself by saying that instead of acquiring Melchet her brother should have just bought a piece of ground in Kent and built on it. When she left Louisa admitted to having behaved shamefully to her and 'she *hates* me'. Ashburton's illness was very grave – dropsy, lungs and kidneys affected, 'gout all over' (Jane thought him so broken in constitution and no stamina to hold out long), and Loo already saw herself a grieving widow. 'Oh, I feel so lonely, so *sad*, the widow's life without the widow's liberty'. 'Life looks *so* bleak, so dreary without him who was its crown and joy', and when Francis returned with his wife, a daughter of the duc de Bassano, Loo, who had spent sometimes thirteen hours by the invalid's bed, could not avoid a sigh of exasperation.

> She is so *full* of triumphant happenings she always makes me discontented – with all her prosperity and a picture of health – and I who am young enough to be her daughter leading the life *she* ought to lead.

Stricken and overwrought, Loo was unprepared for a further blow which fell on 28 November. A laconic telegram from the butler at Brahan told her: 'The lady died here this morning.' Loo's desolation was complete. 'Never was love for me like hers,' she cried. 'If I had only had one look more.' Lord Ashburton, who had looked at death across the bodies of his first wife and their son and was now worn by illness, did not show sufficient anguish to please Loo who felt he

> does not know what grief is. But I am sure he means all that is kind and we are bound together now so I must make the best of things. But oh! for one word of genuine tender sorrow. 'The last of the Mackenzies gone,' he said.

Unable to leave his bedside Louisa could not attend one of the last great Highland funerals to take place. As the five-mile column of

DECLINE AND DEATH 93

mourners headed by pipers playing the lament of their clan wound its twenty-mile way to Fortrose Cathedral where Mary was to lie with her ancestors, people from all parts joined the procession and followed the hearse on foot. All Louisa could do was to put herself, Maysie, and her servants in Paris and Nice into mourning. 'It must be done as handsomely as possible that I may show every mark of respect to her Beloved memory.' As for the two-and-a-half-year old Maysie, for three months she should wear *deep* mourning: a black silk dress with white flounces, a black cashmere, and a white cashmere trimmed with black were appropriate; on no account the brown gaiters but one of her many white pairs, and since her chest was thought to be weak her new dresses were to be made 'high – not with a loose Garibaldi shirt body', but tight-fitting. Louisa had seen a child in the Champs Elysées wearing an ermine long cloak; this too was considered though Lord Ashburton thought it would be too hot for Nice. Seven pounds was to be spent on the servants' mourning: a suit of black for Sedille, and for Bailey a black livery. Meanwhile, Keith Stewart-Mackenzie, clothed in hypocrisy and deceit, was telling lies about his sister all over London and was behaving odiously with regard to his mother's possessions; but Louisa was determined to make a fight to retain all family papers.

The move from the hotel to the house in the rue des Bassins brought relief from noise and from exceptionally high bills. Their accounts were handled by R.O. Maugham, solicitor, who for some twelve years had managed all legal affairs for the British Embassy. (He married in 1863 and was the father of Somerset Maugham.) Lord Ashburton was no better and Loo felt the move was only 'to die more quietly *here* than *there*'. Mingled with grief for her mother and fears for her husband was concern for her child. She had seen Sir Charles Locock, the Queen's physician and *accoucheur*, who had been in Nice; he had reported that Maysie was self-willed and spoiled, also constipated (for which he prescribed asses' milk), and unnaturally precocious. The daily letters to Mrs George contained suggestions of arrowroot, sago, semolina, tapioca, for puddings; a piece of tender beef; a 'few grains of Turkey rhubarb of a morning'; a 'fish dinner' once a week and if she peaked then to give her more meat; a 'pastry bread in the shape of a Half

94 DECLINE AND DEATH

Moon' would be more wholesome if a day old; 'convulsions with her teeth' threatened.

At Christmas when Ruskin passed through Paris he thought there was little hope for Lord Ashburton and Carlyle sent Louisa a message, if Lord Ashburton were still alive to receive it.

> God go with you, guileless, brave and valiant man, who have accompanied me in my Pilgrimage so far, and been friendly to me like a Brother; whom I shall soon follow. Farewell! . . . Yours and his, faithful till I also die.

Queen Victoria had sent him a copy of a book relating to the late Prince Consort (possibly the volume of his *Principal Speeches and Addresses*) with an autograph inscription in the royal hand, and in the new year came a message from the Queen expressing her sympathy and asking for news. To counter the unrelieved oppression of such gloomy communications was the arrival in England of Princess Alexandra of Denmark for her marriage to the Prince of Wales and Louisa had invited many friends to watch the wedding procession from the windows of Bath House. Jane Carlyle could not bring herself to go to 'an *empty* sorrow-struck house', she felt she would do nothing but cry; 'When will you come back? Oh, when will you come back?' The Brookfields were among the guests and Sir Charles Locock enjoyed his excellent view but was disappointed that all the pictures in Bath House were closely covered up. There was general praise for the Princess and Lady Palmerston liked the connexion of all things. 'We have had too much of Germany and Berlin and Coburgs and this is returning to our old friends,' she wrote to Monckton Milnes.[136] It was said that the Princess 'sits on the floor and takes hold of the Queen's hand and puts her head on the Queen's lap and says "lets talk of Bertie".' And from the Revd Richard Chenevix Trench, Dean of Westminster, Louisa heard that after the wedding reception the passage of the Prince and Princess of Wales 'hand in hand through the company was like a fairy view of grace and beauty'.

Her husband's health progressed and Louisa made a lightning visit south in March to see her child. Jane Carlyle had heard of the 'sensation' Maysie had made at Nice: two doctors to see her every day and all proceedings so royal that people talked of nothing else. On returning to Paris Loo found the Monckton Milneses at

DECLINE AND DEATH 95

the Hotel Meurice; this created a diversion and one evening, laying aside Trollope's *Orley Farm* which she had been reading to the invalid, she accompanied them to the Théâtre des Variétés in the Boulevard Montmartre where the Emperor had lent his box. On the following night Louisa had Mrs Francis Baring's box at the opera. She was getting on well with her now and she also found Mrs Frederick Baring affectionate and friendly. Ashburton's niece, Lady Euston, had been on her way to Paris when at Boulogne, hearing of the death of her father-in-law, the Duke of Grafton, she 'turned back to become a Duchess'. Carlyle's Fritz had fallen and cut his knee and Loo presented him with a young Arab horse, to be called Noggs (from *Nicholas Nickleby*). 'Nothing in him but loyalty, elasticity, dexterity,' wrote Carlyle in thanking her. 'Strong as a little dromedary, swift as a roe.' Earlier in the winter, thinking he would die, Lord Ashburton made a present of a new velvet dressing-gown to Carlyle and after the Ashburtons' return to England that summer Dr Christison took it to Cheyne Row where both Carlyles tried it on to show it off to the other. It was unanimously voted the 'ne plus ultra of dressing gowns', though the one Carlyle wore most continuously was the grey camel's-hair sent from Persia with the prayer-rug, which he was still wearing when he sat for Boehm's statuette in 1874.

A friend, Charlotte Davenport Bromley, arrived to cheer Louisa – 'such a darling woman' Jane had thought, though conceding that those whom she disliked found her odious. Miss Trotter, who lived at St Germain-en-Laye, was an acquaintance from Loo's earlier Paris days and this renewed friendship would burn with an intensity second only to that with Harriet Hosmer. The one visit Loo made was to an aged friend of her mother, the widow of Auguste de Staël, eldest son of the celebrated Madame de Staël. On their way to England from the Auvergne, where Pauline had hoped to recruit her health, the Trevelyans stopped at Paris and during this happy reunion Louisa took the decision to build herself a house on the Devon coast at Seaton on land held by Sir Walter; the Trevelyans too were erecting a house there and would be immediate neighbours. This was a pleasant thought because reluctantly, during the dark days, she had agreed to let Loch Luichart for £1,800 a year for five years: though it was 'pain and grief to me' the future had seemed to hold little likelihood of Lord Ashburton's ever going again to the property he had made

96 DECLINE AND DEATH

over to her. The lessee was the notorious Laura Bell, once a demi-mondaine known as the 'Queen of London whoredom'[137] but now Mrs Thistlethwayte, who had experienced a spiritual conversion and held revivalist meetings. Mr Gladstone compared her to Tennyson's Guinevere and a close friendship developed between them.[138]

Now Louisa's own health fluctuated and leeches were impending but Monckton Milnes considered that 'these Scotch women have enormous strength, nothing can knock them up'. Lord Ashburton was convalescing and Dr Quain's visits from England were less frequent; these, to Jane's utter disgust, had cost £1,200. 'Little beast,' she added. 'Young Christison is worth a dozen of him.' Meanwhile her zest for picture buying returned and the Revd Frederick Harford, a friend from Malta at the time of her honeymoon, then chaplain to the Bishop of Gibraltar and now a minor canon of Westminster Abbey, was consulted about pictures for sale at Christie's in July. His criticisms were confirmed by the sale prices, though Landseer's *Attachment* which he was inclined to disparage was sold for over 1,000 guineas. Louisa had bought Turner's watercolour *Tivoli* through an agent for 1,800 guineas from Christie's on 18 June and was now regretting the immense sum paid and wished to resell it. Dr Quain doubted she would find a customer at the price given and Landseer whom he had seen did not speak very highly of Turner, 'but somehow he is very chary of his praises'. Ruskin, however, thought the *Tivoli* 'quite above and *beyond* all price'. 'Things do not often occur to give me pleasure' and it was a strange sensation for Ruskin to hear of something that delighted him.

He urged her to beware of damp – 'once mildewed its old paper will perish like dust' – and to avoid a strong light; 'properly cared for it will last for ever.' Mr Harford wished her to keep it a year or the public would suppose some 'unapparent queerness' had been detected. It was hung in Bath House where Sir Walter Trevelyan went to see it in July and when a year later Louisa disposed of it the sale price was fifty guineas more than she had given. Before leaving Paris she was investigating the purchase of a Daubigny river landscape at 5,000 francs.

With unparalleled relief the Ashburtons returned to The Grange at the end of July. In the early part of the month W. W. Story had been in London to make arrangements for the publication of his

DECLINE AND DEATH 97

two-volume *Roba di Roma* and had with him a parcel of family photographs for the Ashburtons (possibly also of his studio works) – no doubt invited to do so by Loo, with a view to a purchase or the giving of a commission. Not finding them in London he had left the parcel with Robert Browning bidding him deliver it on their return. By November Browning informed him that he had done so and followed it with a second, amused, letter in reply to a newly arrived communication from Story which must have held an account of Loo's characteristically hectic acknowledgement of the photographs. 'Most capital is your description of Ly. A whom I fancy,' wrote Browning on 26 November 1863, and since he liked them both he could rejoice that Lord Ashburton had got the masterful wife he desired. 'He *would* have it so, and has got it.'[139]

Browning had settled in London with Pen after his wife's death and would shortly begin the great memorial poem to their time in Italy. To Henry James he was a man of double identity, the poet and the 'member of society'.[140] Many were to enlarge on his worldliness, his loud voice and cheerful demeanour, the dapper dress and alert manner which might indicate a financier, a politician or diplomatist[141] – 'more like a stockbroker than a bard';[142] but others detected the genius in the formidable intellect and wide knowledge of classical history, of literature, music and of art, and his profound insight into human nature.[143] But these topics he would never discuss though his conversation was vigorous and unaffected, 'the effervescence of a bright and powerful mind'.[144] He spoke constantly of his wife, with admiration and devotion, and with courage faced the years ahead dedicated to the education of his son and to his own work. After that ' – my end of life . . . one day – years hence – to just go back to Italy – to Rome and die as I lived, when I used really to live.'[145]

On her return to England Louisa threw herself strenuously into multitudinous activities. The building of Melchet was in progress and shaping into a large red brick Jacobean house; the one at Seaton was not forgotten. Thomas Woolner, one of the original Pre-Raphaelite Brethren and now a successful sculptor, known to Loo either through Pauline or the Carlyles, was invited to Bath House to see the pictures. Through the good offices of Alexander Munro, Rossetti sent Louisa two unfinished watercolour drawings of *The Salutation of Beatrice* which she agreed to take upon completion, and from a large number of his sketches and

98 DECLINE AND DEATH

studies bound in an album she enthusiastically selected thirty-four. These Rossetti undertook to have mounted and to add some slight additional work to the composition sketches to explain them fully, but as with so many of the eccentric gestures which governed much of Loo's behaviour neither the album nor its contents were ever mentioned by her again. At the turn of the year, however, Rossetti forwarded to The Grange her pair of watercolours apologizing for the delay in completing them but believing that the intervening time had given him 'a thoroughly fresh insight of it on taking it up again'. He thought he had particularly improved the 'glow of light' in the second one, but there was no admission of his assistant, W. J. Knewstub, having had a hand in the colouring.

In her fondness for the illustrious Loo had been consistent in her wish to have Ruskin as a guest at The Grange and had at last secured him for dinner at Bath House. 'You are too severe on me in saying I have resisted your hospitality', he wrote, 'I have only resisted your enticements into that depressing condition of things which in England is called countryside.' The Carlyles came to The Grange in the early autumn but Jane was ill with a painful arm and could take no pleasure in her visit. Soon after she fell heavily in a London street and for many months underwent such suffering that while she thought she would go out of her mind it seemed best to keep from her two deaths which occurred at the beginning and end of the winter. Thackeray died on Christmas Eve. As a friend of Harriet, and often at The Grange, he had dedicated *Henry Esmond* to Lord Ashburton in 1852; Louisa had known him before her marriage and had been a great favourite of his.[146] Dr John Brown wrote from Edinburgh that 'he was essentially great in thought and feeling, grand and kind and tenderhearted'.

Except to those close to him, the death of Lord Ashburton was not so deeply felt. He was taken ill in March and Pauline who was at Seaton went by train to Winchester and on by fly to The Grange to be a support to Louisa. It was her first visit there and she was delighted by the 'very fine place', the lodges and the cottages on the estate and the high, chalky, hilly country, abounding in juniper trees and firwood. On Palm Sunday they attended service in Northington Church and the next day before returning to Seaton she looked over a quantity of prints, drawings, engravings and photographs of all sorts of degrees of merit. Some were indeed beautiful things, and she admired the 'very pretty Daubigny

DECLINE AND DEATH 99

picture'[147] in the conservatory which was most likely the one acquired for Loo in Paris. On 23 March Lord Ashburton died 'of a sudden attack in the heart' following on pneumonia, 'with no suffering but deadly faintings'. It was a dreadful grief and shock and Pauline wrote to her 'beloved Loo':

> If any love can comfort you now that nearest and closest and best of love is hidden from you (though for certain it is all about you still) you must believe that we are as closely bound to you by the ties of old, loving friendship as we could be by ties of blood.

Dr Christison was with him at his death and sent a description to Lord Houghton (Monckton Milnes had been ennobled the previous year). Louisa had reached her husband's side immediately after his heart attack had come on. 'She is sadly distressed by this sudden termination to her unremitting care.' Loo followed this up with a letter of her own to Lord Houghton.

> Everyone, however distantly associated with my Beloved one, is *dear to me*, how dear. . . . Gratefully shall I cling to you, for his sake – his sake, who was all the world to me – my own ideal Knight, so pure, so brave, so loving.

She hoped she would find 'high and holy duties' to perform in his name.[148]

Carlyle felt the loss acutely; it had been an enduring friendship for close on twenty years. Jane, when she was given the news, was lying ill 'with a cruel malady that I believe will be fatal', and though her letter was full of eulogy for the dear departed ('if ever there was a man ready to pass from this sorrowful earth to be an angel in Heaven it was he!') it was of her own love for Loo that her letter chiefly spoke. 'My spirit flies to your dear side. . . . Oh! do not forget me', but when she heard of Lord Ashburton's generous bequest of £2,000 to Carlyle, she ungraciously exclaimed to him: '"The wished for come too late", *Money* can do nothing for us now.'[149] Dr Brown wrote of the spiritual and eternal good which husband and wife had received from each other 'during these strange long years of watching and nursing and dying – for it has been little else. You were a nurse as soon as you were a wife.' The matron of Bethany Convent at Brentwood, one of those to benefit from the great range of Loo's charitable concerns, had heard of 'the Home-call of your Beloved one', but Florence Nightingale who

DECLINE AND DEATH

had also heard had left it to Louisa to take the first step by asking if she had been remembered in her desolation. Back came the reply:

> May 15.
> My poor dearest, I have indeed thought of you in your great loneliness. . . . Your happiness so short, but it was full while it lasted.
>
> Yours overflowingly
> F. NIGHTINGALE

On receipt of this letter Louisa went at once to Park Street to see Florence and the next day there was a further letter. 'Dearest, very Dearest. It did one good to see you bearing that intense loss with real seconding of the will of God'; she trusted that they might 'meet again even before another world'. To comfort Loo's sense of loss Carlyle bade her reflect that

> This is sore, sore while it lasts; but one gradually rallies, finds that in new duties, a life still full of such, and which can be done (in a measure) as still under the old dear banner, and in the name and as if for the sake of them that are away. Courage, courage!

Louisa was uncommonly swift in rallying.

IO

Patronage

Louisa Lady Ashburton was now thirty-seven, with a young child and a very considerable fortune. She had few obligations or responsibilities, she was free to indulge her tastes with no one to restrain disbursements which, made often on a momentary whim, were inclined to be as rash as they were exorbitant. Her heavily built frame and commanding demeanour lent an additional appearance of authority to what Brookfield called 'this too wandering meteor', as she pursued her mercurial path through the remaining forty years of her life. A woman of impulse and contradiction, she had to be accepted on her own terms; but where she offended she would exert herself to humour and conciliate. 'Generous, violent, rash and impulsive, ever swayed by the impression of the moment';[150] what was inconvenient she chose to ignore and her indifference to anything approaching exactitude was a reflection of an inherited vein of arrogance which in youth had not been disciplined and which with maturity tended to become emphasized. In her building and collecting extravagances she was particularly known for her disputes, and among those who suffered from her intractability were Munro, Woolner, W. W. Story, Nesfield and Henry Clutton, as well as lesser men. Of the great names, Ruskin had tolerated her because of the Trevelyans' affection but when that tie was loosened by death his path and Louisa's rarely coincided. Only Carlyle, owing to age and a wearied determination, and, not without some bruising, Browning, through a justifiable want of tact and the tenacity of an abiding love, escaped her manipulations.

All her pent-up energy was channelled into completing Melchet Court and adorning it with a craftsman's skill. On the day of Lord Ashburton's death, in a reply to Loo, Thomas Woolner wrote of his delight and pride in her commission of a marble chimneypiece for Melchet drawing room. The number of figures, depth of relief, the size and expenditure had still to be determined,

and would she suggest 'a lovely poetic subject'. An exchange of
some fifty letters and visits continued throughout the year. In May
came her order for an Asiatic and a sleeping lion, a lioness, an eagle,
a group of leopards, and a stag – probably all for the new pleasure
grounds. In August an 'Enoch' was ordered (Woolner had given
Tennyson the subject for *Enoch Arden*); in December she paid
£126 for a marble slab for the chimneypiece. A letter to Woolner
from Rossetti written in May was perhaps the germ of the
sculptor's posthumous portrait bust of Lord Ashburton. 'I am
asked to ask you', wrote Rossetti, 'what is your price for a bust of a
gentleman, and whether you would have any prospect of sufficient
leisure to do one shortly.'[151] The work was begun in October and
on its completion a year later Woolner could confidently say that it
was one of the most delicately finished works he had done. Never
having known Ashburton, though he had stayed at The Grange
after his death during the period of his hostess's great surge of
enthusiasm, he had been obliged to work from photographs.
Landseer had lent him his portrait of the sitter; Pauline had wished
Woolner had known 'the exquisite sweetness of the expression and
the quiet thoughtfulness and mixture of the gentleness and
intellect'. She thought however that he would do more than
anyone else could. Jane had had a further relapse and had been sent
to Scotland to recuperate. 'I should give much to kiss your dear face
again. Ever your loving your dying Jane Carlyle', she had written to
Loo. But home in Chelsea in October, with Woolner on his knees
by her sofa showing his relief at her recovery as he kissed her over
and over 'with a most stupendous beard! and a face wet with tears',
she summoned up strength to go to his studio in Welbeck Street to
look at the bust. She could honestly say she thought it very like.

> I am *sure* it is good for I recognize in the brow and upper part of
> the face the same look of my Father which first attracted me to
> Lord Ashburton, and gave him a fascination for my eyes such as
> no other man's face ever had.

Compared to it she thought Munro's earlier bust 'quite
contemptible'.

W. W. Story had spent the winter of 1863 remodelling his
Cleopatra which was considered a great advance on the first and a
few days after Lord Ashburton's death he wrote to Loo from Rome
to thank her for photographs of herself for which he had asked.

PATRONAGE

'The fact was that I wanted your head to use for my new Cleopatra' and he hoped she would consider this a compliment for Cleopatra was 'the most charming woman of her age'. Perhaps he was seeking a purchaser but he would have trouble enough with Louisa in the years ahead. One of Loo's first acts as a widow was to have various of the Bath House paintings copied for herself and she appealed to Rossetti to recommend a copyist. Both Legros and Fantin-Latour were in England and available for the work and after a dispute, in which the former was struck across the face by Whistler (whom Rossetti had consulted), he was engaged and immediately set up his easel, so that Rossetti writing to Loo in September was able to assure her that Legros was at work on the Giorgione and was delighted with his task. The Frenchman, with a Titian half finished, had completed a Murillo copy in January 1865 at 200 guineas and was preparing to undertake Rubens's *Wolf-Hunt* for which he must ask 500 'guinées', its dimensions being so great. Photographs were taken of paintings at two guineas a picture, a proceeding much hampered by the housekeeper, and ill requited too, for Loo did not settle the account for fully two years.

Rossetti also was prospering in some degree by Louisa's indefatigable liberality. (His aunt Charlotte Polidori had been governess and companion in the Bath family for many years and Loo's sister-in-law had owned one of his major early works.) She was at his studio in October (1864) and though undecided between two drawings 'as usual seemed kindly desirous to have all I showed her',[152] but 'Lady Ashburton has not gone fasting through the fact of my artistic provender here being all bespoke.'[153] She ordered 'another big Venus and a small duplicate "Joan of Arc"'. 'Also,' he told Munro, 'she has bought up Chapman whole. Also she proposes to give endless work to the shop. She is a regular stunner.'[154] George Chapman, a portrait painter, kept his canvases at Rossetti's house and stayed there himself when down on his luck. Loo seems to have left this whole output in Chapman's charge; in 1866 she received a message that he had a gallery of pictures belonging to her. The *Joan of Arc* was speedily despatched but the *Venus Verticordia*, a preparatory study for which she would have seen in Rossetti's studio, found another home. He was invited to The Grange, but disliking the country excessively he

PATRONAGE

found such a web of work to finish and begin that if I went
to the country I should find

Oil in the running brooks
Varnish on stones, and *paint* in everything.

Louisa's building requirements in Devonshire were now
formulated and gathering momentum. A fortnight after Ashburton's death Pauline sent her an estimate for £700 for the
concrete and timber house and a further £100 for the stable
and coach house. The site on a field of cowslips and a forest of
daffodils was already marked out according to Loo's wishes
and in early May the Trevelyans with their architect went to
Seaton station to meet Loo who with characteristic unconcern
failed to arrive. From Bath, where she was obliged to take the
waters for rheumatism, she made a descent upon Seaton in
June with her architect, Henry Clutton. That she was dis-
pleased with what she found is evident from a ten-page letter
from Sir Walter Trevelyan in which with infinite courtesy and
no small impatience he explained that she was at fault in
peremptorily demanding some of his adjoining land which he
was not prepared to grant to anyone. But the misunderstand-
ings were only temporary and by engaging London workmen
Seaforth Lodge was ready by the end of the year – though the
roof slates blew off at every gale and the north wind created
unforeseen draughts. Loo set about its decoration with renewed energy. Writing to Madox Brown in October Rossetti
recounted her delight at what she had seen at the Morris Firm's
shop; that she had ordered several tiles and pieces of glass and
had seemed disposed to put a good deal of the decoration into
Morris's own hands. Shortly after, writing at 9.30 in the evening, Rossetti again exclaimed to Madox Brown: 'I've been kept
until this blessed hour, chiefly by incomprehensible messages
from the miraculous Lady A.'[155] William Morris fell ill and
Loo's order got delayed; Rossetti's help was enlisted and
Morris & Co. retaliated with a letter from Red Lion Square
noting that they had not yet received the dimensions of the
space in which the tiles were to be fixed. Burne-Jones's account
book for June of the following year refers to a '"Small design
of Paradise" for Lady Ashburton, £1.10.0',[156] presumably
glass for Seaforth Lodge.

During a second stay at Bath, still full of rheumatism and immeasurably depressed, she earned a line of sympathy from Carlyle. 'Oh dear, oh dear, the ebullient and effulgent Highland heart crushed down. . . . Courage, courage, dear Friend better days *are* coming'; and in a second letter he bade her not to give way to black thoughts. 'The Future *is* still yours; and noble victories lying in it, if you yourself be noble.' Louisa needed just such advice if the terms of her husband's will were to be fought and won.

Her unwearying activities kept her a good deal in London that autumn of 1864. A visit to the Carlyles whom she had not yet seen was promised and Jane was transported:

> I wonder if you have any adequate conception how your coming has been watched and waited for. . . . Oh my darling, my darling; who that comes near to you, and is cared for by you can help loving you with a whole heartful of love!

And after the visit had been paid: 'You have really been in this room with your dear sweet eyes, and musical voice and adorable ways!' Her mourning figure on the stairs had been so beautiful in the 'absurd whirlwind of coat-confusion around you'. In November the welcome was less rapturous; Jane told a friend that Loo had kept her out of bed till near twelve. Moncure Conway, the American Unitarian minister at Finsbury, mentioned having seen Loo and Louisa Baring at Cheyne Row one evening after tea, on which occasion Carlyle told them it was his habit to drink five cups at that hour.[157] Louisa's kindness to the Carlyles continued undiminished. Hampers of vegetables, cream and eggs arrived almost daily from the farm at Addiscombe, and, a special present for Jane, a fine grey for her brougham. Before long his owner found him insufficiently vigorous for a carriage and was bent on sending him for the winter to one of Loo's straw yards at Addiscombe. 'How rich people are imposed on! Lady A's coachman gave an enormous price for this horse of mine and she fancied it a treasure.' In January the horse had gone for some months and Jane was discontented to find she had to hire one in its place. Loo's own chariot and barouche went to be cleaned at Burkin & Co., Chandos Street, and the sociable and landau needed some adjustment.

Aware that Loo's generosity extended to many philanthropic causes Pauline had enlisted her support for another bazaar in

106   PATRONAGE

London. She hoped to make stags' antlers a source of great
profit. 'People like them for lobbies, they are so picturesque', she
wrote from Nettlecombe. But neither their own nor Sir Thomas
Acland's keepers had any left. Could Loo send any? 'Either
fallen off horns or heads with horns?' The latter would fetch
two shillings and sixpence, and one shilling for a good pair of
fallen off horns. Pauline wished she had thought of it sooner so
as to have had a good stock in hand.

But overhanging Loo's numerous pursuits lay the haunting
prospect of her impending removal from The Grange to Melchet
which was insufficiently advanced to do more than provide her
with a home in one wing. Pauline understood how it would feel
to abandon her 'beautiful and happy home'. Many blessings
would follow her for all the good and kind things she had done
there, and Pauline believed that in time she would have none but
happy memories 'of those dear days'. But to Loo, and to those
immediately concerned, the 'dear days' were lost in a warfare of
altercation and a clash of misunderstanding; The Grange was a
house divided against itself. The ground for quarrel were the
terms of her husband's will and codicil.

Lord Ashburton, in his will of July 1862, had left Bath House
and its pictures to Louisa for two years, after which they were to
revert to the holder of the title. In December 1863 he added a
codicil to the existing will in which he left the leasehold of Bath
House, its pictures, busts and chattels to his wife absolutely;
also all the pictures at The Grange without exception, whether
usually belonging there or not. His executors were his cousin the
Hon. Thomas Baring, shortly to succeed as second Baron, and
later Earl of Northbrook, and George Stovin Venables, barrister
of the Inner Temple, owner of Llysidinam, a considerable place
on the Wye, contributor to the *Saturday Review*, a friend of
Tennyson, of Thackeray, Monckton Milnes and Brookfield.
Witty, articulate and rich, he had been a member of the
Apostles, the society founded at Cambridge for discussions of
serious subjects, and here his particular friend had been Henry
Lushington with whose sister, according to Jane Carlyle, he had
had a 'life long engagement . . . never carried out for reasons
known only to themselves'. One of the Stanleys of Alderley had
thought Venables a disagreeable man,[158] but he had stayed
often at The Grange in Harriet's day, though during the time the

PATRONAGE 107

family had wished him to marry Emily Baring he had felt obliged to absent himself.

Thus, through her husband's declared wishes, Louisa was in command of Melchet Court, of the villa and farm at Addiscombe, all his American stocks and shares and securities, Bath House, its pictures and other valuables and all the pictures at The Grange; Loch Luichart and Seaforth Lodge were already hers. And for Maysie she held land, real estate, manors, farms in Devon, Cornwall, Somerset, Herefordshire, in the Isle of Wight and Hampshire. She insisted that the furniture at The Grange was hers also. Writing to Lord Houghton from there she explained that her husband had wished Melchet to be furnished from The Grange so as to save her spending capital on furniture which would cost at least £10,000. He had given his brother Frederick £2,000 for the furniture in the old house at the time of purchase, though this had been mostly removed later by its previous owner. As Ashburton had left

> such a large income *quite free of debt*, to his *very rich* successor, and as *they* have no associations with this place (neither in the first Lord's or in my darling's time) I shall take as he desired 'all that will save you having to buy for Melchet'.

Within three months of Ashburton's death a list was drawn up by Johnson & Ravey, braziers and ironmongers, of Conduit Street, consisting of 108 kitchen items removed from Bath House and stored with them, of which 39 were stew pans varying in dimensions. (Presumably Loo left behind at The Grange the 230 copper kitchen utensils belonging there.)

On the day of her husband's funeral the Revd Frederick Baring had gone to Louisa's room at The Grange and had started to talk about the will and codicil and had spoken most unkindly of his late brother, and from something she had said and he had misunderstood he had gone to London and told the family that Loo had begged him to inform them that her husband was not to blame for anything they objected to as she had herself made the will and codicil in her favour. (Not ten days after Ashburton's death Loo had seen in a letter from Frederick Baring to the Agent: 'Nothing can be done at The Grange till that woman and child are cleared off the premises.')

108   PATRONAGE

To the charge that she had been responsible for the codicil Loo had no answer to make but a simple denial, but to Lord Houghton she wrote:

> I am as innocent of all action of making the codicil as *you* are. Thank God I was brought up by parents who would have regarded such conduct as *scarcely honest*.[159]

In May, Waterhouse, the solicitor who had made the will and codicil, chanced to hear of the slander and sent Loo the instructions for the codicil given him by Lord Ashburton, every word written in her husband's own hand. It was the first she had ever seen of it.

Intimacy between Louisa and the Barings had never been close; it was now non-existent except for the loyalty of Louisa Baring, always a friend of Loo who had, Jane Carlyle was told, expressed herself forcibly: 'Whom should a man leave his property to but his own child, and whom so fit to entrust that child to as the woman who had been everything to him?' The family had disliked Louisa from the beginning, aware that she had contrived the marriage for position and wealth. They were probably jealous too, of the ascendancy she had held over Lord Ashburton, while the knowledge that she had brought few assets with her and that the bestowing had been all on his side added to their resentment. The fact that she had given him a child probably told against her; that he had loved her deeply and had found great happiness was ignored. His brother and successor, Francis Baring, now third Lord Ashburton, detached himself as far as possible and left the settling of the estate to the executors and his own solicitor, Mr Marx. His health was bad and he died four years later following a stroke.

It was Frederick Baring who did his best to undermine the legality of the codicil and who thus almost provoked Louisa into obtaining legal address, so anxious was she that 'no stain should be put on his [Lord Ashburton's] spotless honour'. Venables, 'an honest old dish' as Jane called him, in agreeing that she was justified in her indignation, hoped she would give up the scheme which would be inconsistent with her dignity and 'by repudiating the supposition that you influenced the form of the will you might seem to countenance Mr F. Baring's unreasonable notion that the will was in itself unjust'. He thought that there could 'scarcely be two opinions' that the will would have been perfectly correct if

PATRONAGE 109

everything without exception had been left away from collateral heirs – as it would have been in the majority of cases where there was an only child. Thomas Baring, his co-executor, regarded the will as being 'almost unnecessarily liberal where the family were concerned'. In September Frederick Baring was circulating some 'new legend'. To Venables it appeared 'useless to damn up the stream of scandalous gossip when it was through so porous a mind'. He believed the world, so far as it discussed Louisa's affairs at all, had generally come round to the right and natural view that it was a mistake to mention any of the family in the will and that they ought to be much more satisfied. Louisa decided to adhere to the wishes expressed in her husband's will and resolved to hand back Bath House and some of its treasures after the term of two years.

Her final departure from The Grange took place in the late summer of 1864. Writing to Lord Houghton she wondered how her life would be, cut off from all outward ties with her husband, 'but it cannot be more desolate and drear than it has been to me ever since that day of March when the Light of my Life went down.'[160] Later, when she had leisure to take stock of all that had come with her from The Grange, she wrote to her brother-in-law, Francis Ashburton, telling him that she had intended leaving certain items at The Grange and referred to family busts, including those of his father and mother. These she proposed returning to him. On reflection they were refused, but Emily Baring who held a particular grudge against Louisa, seeing The Grange stripped bare and ignorant of Louisa's offer, could bridle her tongue no longer.

My dear Louisa,
    It is with much reluctance I write on a most painful subject – The Grange – but one effort I must make to induce you to restore the family busts and Lawrence's picture of my Father to the family. It is not generous nor kind towards Francis to remove any memorial of past days. . . . Forgive me for saying it, had you ever known him it would have been impossible to have so acted in despoiling the house made by my father which to us is desecration. He put them there; dont suppose, we any of us repine at the largest provision for you and little Mary, it was quite right to do so, it is only at seeing destroyed what we venerated as being done by my Father. . . . I have long been unhappy but consoled myself with the idea that it [The Grange]

PATRONAGE

would not be as bad as was said, but alas it could not be much worse.

She would also have liked to have seen returned the Munro bust of her late brother 'and I think it ought to remain but at the same time own, you and little Mary have the prior claim.' Loo's rejoinder went to Venables.

Yesterday's post brought me the enclosed. It is quite impossible for me to communicate with Miss Emily Baring on the subject. Before now she knows I suppose that she might well have spared herself the trouble of writing and me the pain of reading such a letter.

The things she asked for had been offered back, all but the bust of her own husband 'which nothing would induce me to part with.' She was ready to let the Lawrence painting go instead of the bust, 'but I never can see on what grounds Miss Emily Baring thinks that [Maysie] ought to have neither bust or picture of her grandfather.' To Venables, any association with Emily Baring was an embarrassment but he replied on Louisa's behalf, informing her that he considered Loo in the right on the question itself and that it was scarcely possible for her to answer a letter in which such terms as 'spoliation' and 'desecration' had been used. The miseries of a family feud dragged on: a further altercation concerned Loo's removal of certain items from the grounds of The Grange, namely lights in the Pinery, a fowl house, iron hurdles, and some young plants, and after it might have been supposed that every possible ground for complaint had been exhausted Mr Marx charged Louisa with being about to remove the furniture of the Northington schoolhouse. Matters were resolved but the will left an indelible mark and except for Louisa Baring Loo saw none of the family until her daughter was grown up. As a final thrust she inserted in *The Times* of 26 March 1866 the following notice, exactly two years after her husband's death when her own term at Bath House had expired:

THE ASHBURTON FAMILY. Bath House, Piccadilly, has just passed into the hands of the present Lord Ashburton. The house and its splendid collection of works of art were bequeathed as a free gift to the title by W. Bingham, Lord Ashburton, whose private property they were.

PATRONAGE

If the Barings lost no opportunity in condemning Louisa she was hardly reticent herself – at least on paper. Letters flew to her friends. Carlyle wisely urged her 'to *be off* with all the people, and their afflicting ideas; to retire into cold politeness and *silence*'; but she was so 'headlong, hasty, the wild Highland heart!' Brookfield, writing on Privy Council paper from 30 Brompton Square, the house which had lodged so many actors, had not heard a whisper of any 'adverse demeanour' at which she hinted, but could only remotely conjecture the estrangement to be based on such untiring devotion to her late husband 'as to elicit evidences of gratitude and reciprocal affection not so palatable to every body'. To Dr Brown the Barings' behaviour seemed so strange 'after what they knew you were to – and did and suffered for their brother – and after the sacrifices you have made for their benefit'. Jane Carlyle delivered herself more vehemently:

> Oh my beautiful Darling! I do love you with all my heart and more than all my strength, *that* being small! And, to keep up a wholesome balance of feelings, I hate the Barings in the same degree! all except Louisa, who I believe is true to you. All that was good and noble in the Baring family belonged to you, heart and soul – belongs to you still under new conditions – sweep the rest out of your life.

By December Loo was ready to establish herself at Seaton having settled her outstanding affairs with regard to a very temporary residence at Melchet, examined Woolner's bust of her husband and commissioned Leitch to do some 'Grange subjects', views of and from the house. This work was sadly held up by his being summoned to Windsor Castle to attend upon the Queen and Princess Helena. He had also been directed to make further sketches of some pictures at Bath House 'endeavouring to give as faithful and general an interpretation of the originals' as he could, knowing how devoted Loo was to them. Mounted and in folios it was now possible for them to be carried around. The mounting of his own drawings he felt eagerly about, preferring a white mount to Louisa's wish for gold; their framing by Vokins he also considered a matter of importance but Loo effectively by-passed it by not replying to his inquiry.

PATRONAGE

Seaforth Lodge, though of no great architectural merit, was comfortable, with ample room for guests and commanding a fine view of the sea. Although the Trevelyans' delightful Venetian Gothic house close by was not yet finished when Loo and Maysie arrived at Seaton for Christmas at the end of 1864 they were there to welcome Loo to her new domain. Pauline was enthusiastic, admiring all the things from The Grange, Leitch's drawings, a Dürer etching, Rossetti's *Joan of Arc*, some good china and fifteen etchings by Whistler for which Loo had given £60. 'Very fine but quite beyond me,' Pauline sighed into her journal.[161] A number of guests came to stay during the next months, Henry Clutton and his wife, Louisa Baring, Miss Davenport Bromley, Miss Price the governess of far-off Ceylon and Corfu days, Venables, and Loo's sister Mary Anstruther, now a widow. But Louisa did not remain continuously at Seaton; Addiscombe claimed her, the garden at Melchet, Sidmouth, Exeter, the letting of Bath House from mid-April, and all the many arrangements which kept her in a perfect turmoil of activity. On 8 March 1865 the Carlyles arrived for four weeks and the following evening he read Tacitus on the Jews, with a running commentary. 'Most delightful' Pauline found it.[162]

> The dear Carlyles are here [Loo wrote to Lord Houghton on 17 March]. He is like my beloved one in so many ways – loved him so truly – that I cling to him. I know you will believe how much I feel having *him* here, as the day comes round, which took from me that husband who was my stay and comfort.[163]

Lord Houghton would not have known that two days after the Carlyles' arrival she had left for Cornwall for three days leaving Maysie in Pauline's care and asking Carlyle to escort her, which he refused to do. Jane exclaimed over the 'lovely and lovable Hostess', adding that 'truly the latter end of that woman was better than the beginning.'[164]

While Loo was away Mrs Carlyle drove with Pauline and talked of the Leigh Hunts who had lived close at hand in Upper Cheyne Row, and how they used to be always borrowing money and scorning them for being thrifty. With the arrival of Woolner and his wife they made an expedition to (?Ottery) 'St Mary's' to see a house being sold cheaply. The women drove in a carriage, Woolner, Sir Walter and Carlyle riding. Jane was tempted by the beautiful situation of the house, the sitting rooms, and good

PATRONAGE

113

though small bedrooms. They had a picnic luncheon on the handsome garden steps and since the Carlyles were not seriously interested in acquiring it Louisa earnestly entreated Woolner to buy, ready to advance him whatever sum he wished. With the Woolners' departure only the Carlyles and Trevelyans remained; Pauline walked with Loo to fields where the daffodils grew as thick as grass; forced roses arrived from Melchet; and on the evening of the dreaded anniversary, 24 March, Carlyle read from his *French Revolution*.[165] Two days later a letter reached Louisa from Bailey, now promoted to butler, informing her that twenty loads of goods, including five large furniture vans, had reached Melchet from Bath House. The bookcases and marble slabs were so heavy that the bill had amounted to £150. All movable cupboards had been brought as well, but Bath House had been left perfectly clean, while at Melchet the stone corridors in the servants' offices were filled with about 150 cases – not all of them in the way of the workmen.

On 3 April Loo left with the Carlyles, resolute in driving Jane about London, looking at pictures and arranging Carlyle's sittings for the bust she had commissioned from Woolner. Jane thought it a trying business for both sitter and sculptor and declared it would never be worth the 100 guineas Loo would pay for it. Photographers were engaged as Carlyle was driving Woolner to despair 'by the different aspects he presents. But certainly,' Jane continued, 'Mr C never has a post-chaise face like what Mr Woolner had given him last week.' She thought it was as 'hollowed out' as were the faces of William Macready, the great actor, and the American Charlotte Cushman, whose resemblance in manner, voice, and countenance the *Spectator* had noted when they had acted together in *Macbeth*.

Once more at Seaton, Loo promptly wrote to tell Jane how she was 'revelling in Fredk [the final volumes just printed] the most readable book of this age – so universal in its intellectual food'. She missed both Carlyles. 'Amidst the many "confusions" that obscure my intellectual vision, there is one fact that stands out clearly, viz. that I want you both back hungrily.' She asked for a few words of consolation which she so longed for and signed herself 'Yours ever gratefully and tenderly'. Meanwhile, a stark entry in Pauline's journal on 26 April conveyed the 'news of Lincoln's assassination'. Lord Houghton arrived to stay and read aloud his article on Cardinal Wiseman (recently dead) which was incorpo-

PATRONAGE

rated in *Monographs*, his recollections of friends published in 1873 and dedicated to Venables. This was of special interest to Pauline who had known Wiseman in Rome in 1838 and 1842 at the time that she had entertained thoughts of being received into the Roman Church. A selection from Swinburne's poems (most certainly *Atalanta in Calydon*, newly published) was also declaimed and may have been Louisa's first introduction to the poet's work though she would have heard Pauline talk of her friendship for him. That summer one of the Stanley sisters wrote of staying with Lord Houghton where they met the Gaskells and F. D. Maurice and 'little Swinburne – the rising Poet. A most hateful little object with a large head of flaming red hair that stands on end.' They were condemned to sit for four hours in a circle listening to him 'spout out his new tragedy of Mary Queen of Scots. It was *so improper*.'[166]

Louisa was making preparations for escape to Wiesbaden in the summer and had decided to take Maysie with her. Jane expressed herself with a wail of desolation.

> Oh my Darling! It is not fair to speak in that way of going, and staying abroad indefinitely because you are not needed and cared for here!. . . . You can not but know in your heart that not one woman of a thousand has as much love laid at her feet as you have.

Loo's circumstances were such that a period abroad offered a welcome refuge. Melchet was not yet habitable, no London home existed, family slander was not entirely stifled, the Civil War had interrupted her American income, and she was suffering from rheumatic disorders. But there was still a great deal to encompass before her departure.

Edward Lear was holding an exhibition at the beginning of May and Loo was among the enthusiastic crowd.

> Lady Ashburton as handsome as ever [Lear entered in his diary], enchanted with the drawings and Cedars – which she absolutely thinks of buying. Tomorrow I am to have her determination.[167]

His *Cedars of Lebanon* was a large oil painting conceived in 1858 when Lear was in the Lebanon and originally intended, as he wrote to Woolner from Rome, to be painted from 'the big seeders at Sir John Simon's [President of the Royal College of

PATRONAGE 115

Surgeons]'.[168] But the Oatlands Park Hotel at Walton-on-Thames had proved a better locality than Blackheath and Lear worked on the picture there in the latter part of 1860, finishing in the following spring. It was shown at Liverpool in 1861 and again at the International Exhibition of 1862, where it was badly hung and won little praise. Lear had studied under Holman Hunt but this was his first major work executed without assistance. He proposed asking 700 guineas for it since Millais, whom he despised for having dropped Pre-Raphaelite principles, had recently received a large sum for an inferior work.[169] The day following his diary entry there was 'No notice of Lady Ashburton by call or letter', and the next day,

> 4 May: Horrid to relate Lady Ashburton writes 'her means cannot allow of her purchasing the Cedars etc.' which she might methinx have known earlier.[170]

Woolner took his last sitting from Carlyle in mid-May, profoundly thankful to have finished his task; the difficulty had been so great that it had made him ill and depressed from the constant strain. Predictably, he thought it the best thing he had ever achieved – 'It is certainly the most strange and mighty looking.' Carlyle, who had never been sanguine, allowed that it looked 'a most impressive thing'. Triumphantly Jane wrote to her husband from Tooting where she was staying that Froude 'cannot bear your bust – the only person who has sense to think of it as I do'.[171] J. A. Froude, the historian, who was to be Carlyle's great biographer, had met him in 1849 but had not gained the Carlyles' friendship until he moved to London in 1861, and thereafter, particularly following Jane's death, he would be one of Carlyle's closest intimates. With the bust in its final stages, Woolner was reminded of the marble chimneypiece which was yet to be executed for Melchet, and as further ornaments for her house Loo commissioned from him a figure of Puck, to be cast in bronze, and a large high-relief carved in marble of *Virgilia Bewailing the Banishment of Coriolanus*.

Louisa was at Seaton by the middle of May. Pauline spent an evening looking over her collection of Leitch drawings and the next day was shown a fine sketch of William Dyce's *Madonna and Child* which Loo had acquired at Christie's on 5 May from his studio sale. Back in London there was shopping at Swears and

Wells in Regent Street for six pairs of pearl spun hose and fourteen pairs of thread gloves, and red and blue striped hose. Cross, the Melchet gardener, had sent a hamper to London per passenger train containing six bundles of asparagus, twelve broccoli, tarragon, rhubarb, spinach, onions, and other garden produce. Departure for Wiesbaden was fixed for the last day of July; Jane was at Bath House on the 26th (though let, perhaps not yet occupied) 'and found the Lady looking lovely in a spruce little half *mourning* bonnet!' She insisted on going to see Jane that evening, appearing at half past eleven and staying till nearly one o'clock. 'Taking such great slaps out of my time', Jane grumbled to a friend, 'as nobody else does or would be suffered to do.' There was still time to ask Woolner to be on the look-out for a work by Holman Hunt, though as Hunt was taken up with 'courting and dining out generally' Woolner thought it more probable that he could do Loo a little picture when he got to the Holy Land. Finally, she agreed to meet Lord Houghton and go together to the British Museum to look at the acquisitions which the Keeper of Greek and Roman antiquities had himself excavated. She would be 'delighted to go and see Mr Newton's new wonders. It is my favourite haunt – that dear old Museum.'

11

Ripe for Heaven

Unhampered by restrictions, Louisa's life now assumed something of the character of a rolling stone. Her friends had expected her home in the winter but the delights of travel, fostered by the unrealistic fear that her husband's will was to be disputed, kept her abroad two years. But they were not years of inactivity. Wiesbaden, where she stayed with Maysie, was her immediate destination but the handsome town of Carlsruhe with its fine art gallery was more to her taste for there also lived the evangelical de Bunsen family, the widow bereft now of the Chevalier de Bunsen who had been Prussian Ambassador in London for many years and had died in 1860. Before settling herself there in a rented house Loo went for a little dissipation to Italy with Miss Emily de Bunsen (another deeply sentimental friendship) and hurt her arm and shoulder when the carriage overturned near Aosta. Landseer came to hear of the accident and wrote asking to be enlightened and hoped the damage was exaggerated. He had had a letter from Wiesbaden in which she had told him of the tales circulating concerning her husband's will. 'I have a right to be trusted as an old friend – not heeding gossip or the *bosh* of what is called good society.' He reported unvarying industry on his part; her portrait he had back for 'improvement'; 'the Lions are to find their resting place in Trafalgar square in a year or fourteen months from this time', but that rather depended on Marochetti as Landseer's part of the undertaking was done. He thought highly of Marochetti, to Woolner's annoyance, but Woolner, known for his professional jealousies, was one who could seldom resist a thrust in the right quarter. When Landseer had seen him at Professor Tyndall's lecture at the Royal Institution he asked to come and look at Carlyle's bust. 'It amused me the tone in which he spoke of Marochetti, as if he were a really great artist,' wrote Woolner. 'This struck me as something quite odd from a man unusually able in his own line.' Nor could he resist a further gibe at the time of the Royal Academy summer exhibition of 1866: 'Our friend Marochetti seems to have distinguished himself by sending a number of busts of such portentous ugliness – and he has painted them all a red lead colour!' Pauline had long ago assessed him: 'Just as bright and just as overbearing as usual',[172] and Loo would not have been deceived, but it was in her nature to pursue the renowned and to distinguish them with her patronage.

There was a great if uneven, exchange of correspondence in the first part of 1866 – uneven because Woolner had difficulty in obtaining replies to his letters. *Puck* was completed, *Virgilia* proceeded with, but the burning question was whether Loo would agree to the Carlyle bust being exhibited at the Royal Scottish Academy in the spring when Carlyle was installed as Rector of Edinburgh University. That being settled, it fell to Alice Woolner – for there were signs of her husband tiring of the inattention of his benefactress – to inquire whether, should such a proposal arise, the bust might be kept in Edinburgh and Louisa have a copy, to be ready for her return. The Carlyle bust and that of Lord Ashburton had both gone north 'and have been treated in a very honourable way. They have put them each on separate pedestals, a distinction hitherto only granted to royal persons.' (There had been a suggestion of Gladstone's bust standing as a pendant to that of Carlyle – past and present Rectors – and the question arises why, and on what grounds, Lord Ashburton's was selected to be shown.) A prompt though negative reply to the matter of accepting a copy of the original bust was received and Woolner wrote Loo his approbation, thinking that 'the feeling of its [the bust] being the first is an important matter in itself if you have it at all'. Watchful on her behalf for pictures to add to her already sizeable collection (and Reynolds's *Mrs Thrale and Her Daughter* was an acquisition of this year also), Woolner was able to tell her of a sale of Old Master drawings at Sotheby's in June which included fifty to sixty Titians. Were she interested, would she give him 'some kind of notion of what your resolution reaches', for several men of immense wealth, the British Museum with its large grant, and rich dealers, were expected to be bidding. Louisa promptly sent him her limit – £100 – and Woolner secured for her an example from Claude, from Fra Bartolomeo, Correggio, Cuyp, Van Dyck

RIPE FOR HEAVEN

and three from Titian, all for £50.10s.6d. A suspicion of trouble to come arose in a reference to his *Virgilia* which was demanding hard and long work to make an impression on so large an object.

Other news caught up with Loo as she moved backwards and forwards from Nice to Mentone in the early part of 1866, and back to Carlsruhe in April, with Maysie always by her side. Pauline, once again at Seaton, frail and ill, wrote of Loo's flourishing rhododendrons, of the donkey walking through her shrubbery and of a shoal of great black porpoises at play in the water. She spoke of the prospect of their going to Lake Maggiore in May, Ruskin accompanying them, and 'to meet you would be worth anything to me'. From the Brookfields, living now at 6 Sydney Place, Onslow Square, when a curate could be found to officiate at Somerby, Lincolnshire, where Brookfield held the incumbency, came a description of a party at 10 Downing Street a few months before the Prime Minister, Lord Russell, resigned.

> Great, high and handsomely proportioned rooms – utterly undecorated – but looking nevertheless very handsome, lighted with countless candles. My goodness, what a lot of jobbing and iniquity must have gone on in those rooms since they were first built.

In April the Morris Firm wrote from Queen Square, Bloomsbury, informing Loo that they had a parcel of stained glass *Annunciation* ready for her; reminding her that on 1 January they had 'sent to mention' a second design – to which evidently no reply had reached them.

Louisa had not forgotten the Carlyles. She wondered whether the little farmhouse at Melchet might be useful to them, for 'that would be *Heaven*. Goodbye, my darling – my own darling.' Towards the end of March she sent Jane a parcel from Mentone: 'Will you use these little candlesticks when you take your bedroom candle, for *my* sake and believe how true and bright my love burns and always will burn.' To Carlyle she sent a piece of olive wood to use as a paperweight. Jane's last letter to her, which Loo subsequently copied out and sent to Carlyle, was written from Cheyne Row a few days after he had delivered his inaugural address at Edinburgh. 'Dearest, sweetest, beautifullest! Oh my darling! How long you stay away, and life so short!' she began, and continued with a description of her hysterical outburst of weeping

RIPE FOR HEAVEN

and relief and recourse to brandy when she heard of Carlyle's triumph. Her death in a London brougham from heart failure a few days later opened the floodgates. Loo wrote two letters to Carlyle from Mentone, one on 25 April the other on the following day. The second of the two, containing some sentiments from the first, was probably the one she sent.

> Oh! my Beloved friend. *Is it true?* is it true that she is gone and *so* gone from us without a word to any of us? that her spirit so glided away to Eternity? What can I say to *you* in this tribulation? I have no words – but tears, tender tears, for her we love so well. I cannot think of Earth without her – bright, tender, brave one – Never again can there come such a friend for me – and for you there is nothing but Desolation – and well do I know the meaning of the word. Would my presence in England be any comfort to you? if so, I gratefully hasten to your side. Surely we are legacies to one another during the remaining days of our pilgrimage. *I* left by 'him', and *you* by *her* – oh! if it is possible, let me be of some use to you – so tenderly will I try. Dearest, and best loved friend, *most* tenderly do I weep with you for the Beloved one – and for yourself.
>
> Thine very gratefully
L. C. ASHBURTON

Touched by her affection for Jane, Carlyle nevertheless begged her not to come, though his brother John Carlyle had reported that she was probably already in England. 'The thought of that was, I confess, as a spark of light for moments; but reflexion even then answered No!' When she came to England for good it would be some consolation, 'but not *before* that, *not* before!' he replied, conscious perhaps of some agitating suspicion of what her irrepressible energy might dictate.

Jane's was the first of two deaths within a month of each other to close a chapter of Loo's life and pierce it with both gain and loss. In Pauline Trevelyan's death, which occurred in May in Neuchâtel, with Sir Walter and Ruskin beside her, Loo lost the one being who could control her eccentricities and speak plainly, though from the heart; while Jane's death secured her a mission. For the remaining fifteen years of Carlyle's life Loo was unremitting in concern for his welfare; ardent in visits to cheer; eager to be a companion to so great a man.

RIPE FOR HEAVEN
121

The Trevelyans and Ruskin had formed with Loo a happy plan to meet at Lake Maggiore, though Pauline, while determined on finding the strength to travel, was so ill that Sir Walter was compelled to write from Paris where they were breaking their journey to warn Loo that she was very weak and no definite date of arrival at the Italian lakes could be relied on. Sir Walter's next letter told of Pauline's death. Louisa was now in Nice and wrote from a full heart:

> It is quite impossible to write what I feel on reading the fatal tidings just received. It quite overwhelmed me. Except my child there is no one in all the world as I loved *her*. She was indeed worthy of *all* our love and I thank God that I knew her. Oh! how tenderly I feel for *you* in the utter desolation that has fallen on your life. Even some Earth looks quite cold simply without *her*; what must it look like to *you*? Our only consolation is that she was long ago ripe for heaven – but the better she was the more our hearts cling to her – dear darling pet – We shall never see her like in any way – and we shall go through life sadder and lonelier the rest of our days without her sweet spirit. Did she know she was so near Eternity? Did she ever mention *me*? Tell me all you can it will be such charity to me. I can only weep for the great cloud that has settled down over our lives.

She asked for something that Pauline had worn or read, or a lock of her hair, and later in the summer went to Neuchâtel to mourn by the grave. Sir Walter sent her some hair and from Wallington wrote that it was now a most desolate house indeed 'without that darling, loving smile which greeted me whenever I came home'. But Loo must have experienced a considerable jolt when towards the end of the year Sir Walter reminded her of a debt owing for eight years (almost to the day). 'Let me have £31.10. in part payment of the sum of £40, which you borrowed of her [Pauline] before you went to Egypt.' A note of ribaldry accompanied a letter from Loo's friend Miss Davenport Bromley who passed on the information told her by a clergyman, that while the Queen was at Balmoral the police were obliged to keep a sharp eye on Buckingham Palace 'as the boys and rabble are always chalking up: "Mrs Brown is out of town."'

RIPE FOR HEAVEN

Louisa was undergoing financial worries and as she dashed to Vichy for the waters and on from there to Switzerland for mountain air, she was undecided whether or not to sell Melchet. Henry Clutton, its architect, had been an associate of William Burges in his early years and worked in northern France where his work on Lille Cathedral had won him a reputation of distinction in the development of the Early French Gothic Revival. He had come under Ruskin's influence in the 1850s and it was most probably this factor which found favour with Louisa – despite his reception into the Church of Rome, for which he suffered grave personal ostracism.[173]

It was intended that Melchet should be completed by Christmas 1866 but there were still decisions to take, oak floors to lay, difficulties with the bath to overcome, and in nearly every letter from Clutton a reminder that Woolner was behind with two commissioned chimneypieces.

> Pray urge on Mr Woolner with the bas reliefs for the two chimney pieces. . . . I fear Mr Woolner has done nothing with regard to the chimney pieces. . . . I fear the chimney pieces are the only things that will keep the completion of the reception rooms back.

Louisa was finding it increasingly difficult to meet the constant demands for further sums, while Clutton was distracted by the idleness of the workmen and Louisa's imprecise instructions from abroad. He was also forced to tell her that Melchet resembled nothing so much as a warehouse filled with furniture and that the beautifully finished interior work was cruelly torn to pieces by the rough treatment of the workmen employed.

> I cannot conceal it from you but the fact is that if your Ladyship continues abroad a first rate responsible person is required to be in residence, to take the entire control of the plan.

The servants were not fitted for the charge unless under superior direction. However, externally things were prospering. The north terrace had been laid out; Loo's order of orchids from India, of which one hundred plants had arrived, were in excellent condition. Cross thought them to have been collected in Brazil though a few of them seemed very like Indian species. The vines in the great vinery were not yet free of mealy-bug but the Aleppo pines were doing

RIPE FOR HEAVEN   123

well and the pomegranates sent from Wiesbaden were flourishing. A discordant note was introduced by Caroline Wilkins, the housekeeper, who wrote to say a bill of five guineas for bedding owing to Standen & Co. of Jermyn Street since 1863 had many times been presented at Bath House without payment having been effected, and Mr Withers, of Romsey, desired fifty or sixty pounds on account for remade mattresses, bolsters and pillows. Meanwhile, Louisa's niece Annie Anstruther acted as a willing slave for her aunt, doing her commissions, tramping London, delivering parcels, ordering two pots of cocoa for Maysie from Manchester since there seemed to be none available in London, countermanding, purchasing. A comb from Floris had proved too stiff and too small, so one was being made – 'they make all their combs so this will cost little more.' Her only failure was not yet to have bought Loo's 'chamois leather sheets'.

Loo considered a precipitate return to England to set matters in order. 'You cannot know', she told Carlyle, 'how I long to see you again and talk of her and of sacred days to us both.' She dreaded a return to Seaton 'without my almost sister Lady Trevelyan', whose grave she was on her way to visit at Neuchâtel (where she hoped also to find a governess for Maysie). From Kaltbad Rigi, Lucerne, she wrote again in July assuring him that if there were a chance of his spending a fair portion of the winter with her at Seaton she might remain there. It was desirable, however, for her to practise economy and this was easier abroad. 'But I *long* to be in harness and blinkers with the small duties of a regular life again', though while meditating on her husband she was moved to reflect that she had really 'only to get ready to follow him'. Carlyle gave her a despondent sketch of how he passed his time.

I am keeping very quiet here, not seeking society or talk, but shunning it, – unravelling with all my faculty, the gloomy imbroglio which my life has suddenly become, and endeavouring to extract from it something which may still be cosmic and feasible. . . . I sit silent, working a little (if it can be called work) over things that belong to the inexorable Past; I walk about a good deal, silent, – especially on long walks towards midnight, along a range of solitary streets, Cremorne and its nauseous uproar heard only faintly in the distance. . . . The sombre gloom of my own thoughts is *less* afflictive to me in

RIPE FOR HEAVEN

general than anything I can hear or speak. . . . What a loss to you too, the death of poor Lady Trevillian! I need *not* say how it rang upon my sad existence even, and awoke memories that are gone into the Eternities, like the years beyond the Flood.

By now Loo had moved on to Zermatt; she heard from Carlyle that once in England she would find him staying with Miss Davenport Bromley at Ripple Court near Walmer, for sea bathing. A year after her departure she returned home for a few hurried days. It would be another year until she was back again. 'She had some sudden call hither,' Carlyle told his brother, 'and is a sudden creature.' She had left again for Calais, 'embarking in a tempest of discordant hurries', but not before she had seen him twice, enthusiastic in her desire for him to join her that winter at Mentone where it was quiet, 'beautiful "society" too, in short it was all beautiful. "Oh it would be so beautiful." '[174] She had barely time while in England to inquire of G. F. Watts if he would undertake what must have been an allegorical memorial picture of Lord Ashburton. In 1864, before death intervened, Frederic Leighton had begun a portrait of her husband and though he had volunteered to finish it 'tant bien que mal' from photographs, it was most probably destroyed. A sketch he made of Maysie was also abandoned though Louisa had wanted to pay the price of it as it stood; this Leighton refused and Loo commissioned a 'fancy picture' for £300, which seems not to have been executed.[175] When Watts was approached in 1866 he replied that though he had 'absolutely given up portraits' he regretted never having painted Lord Ashburton, and since what Louisa proposed could be described as 'subject paintings', he would break through his fixed determination and endeavour to carry out her wishes. Nothing further was heard of this picture.

Once more in Switzerland Louisa fairly battered Carlyle with further inducements. In letters that crossed others from Loo carrying some new and terrible scheme, he gloomily staved off any decision. From Glion she suggested that he should travel out with Leitch who was also expected, but to read Leitch's own letter to Loo on this subject shows how the thought appalled him: 'crushed with a dreadful influenza' he was unable to dream of any foreign travel. Another impetuous offer was that Bailey should go over to England and fetch Carlyle and accompany him back. This

RIPE FOR HEAVEN 125

electrifying proposal was too much for Carlyle. A brief annotation in his handwriting tells of his reaction to such perseverance.

> Goes like the 'High Wind'! I have written in brief absolute *prohibition* for 'Bailey' (the Butler) promising to fix *yes* or *no* at the end of November – if left free – if not, no at once, rather unpleasant to be out in high winds!

She promised him freedom from harassing details of any kind. 'Oh! what a blessing that we have such memories to help and encourage us, who are still wanderers.' Carlyle, yet undecided, felt that 'the kind haven of hospitality and friendly shelter you offer me on that bright shore' might help him but at the moment it was 'flatly impossible: nothing, not one item round me is ready for such an enterprise.' Davos Platz and 'its wild solitudes' had now claimed Louisa and there she heard of Professor Tyndall's determination to bring Carlyle to the south. 'I shall be more than happy to see Professor Tyndall,' Loo wrote in return, 'he is one of my beloved husband's friends I have always *most* wished to know.' This 'cheery thorough going man' as Carlyle called him, this 'strange, lean, ardent kind of soul', was a follower of Darwin and Professor of Natural Philosophy at the Royal Institution where Loo would later attend lectures on his researches into heat radiation from which her interest in its relation to natural gases and vapours would derive. In what concerned this journey Tyndall was 'emphatic and steady on the affirmation side', so that in the middle of December Carlyle wrote finally: 'I do then, at the present moment design to *come.*' She was to fancy them starting out on 21 December, a day in Paris, then to Lyon and on to Marseilles

> and at length, thro' the 150 miles of *tunnel*, emerge at Nice, if all goes well, and find a carriage waiting, which latest circumstance we have never reckoned on.

He dreaded 'those 45 hours of steam machinery and clangorous horror' which filled him with despair, 'but I do mean to venture (under the Ideal of Couriers) for the sake of what lies beyond.' In an earlier letter he had assured her that he could have no doubt left of 'her exceeding friendship and loyal wish to what *is* likely to be best for me'. This it proved to be.

12

Carlyle at Mentone

The last weeks of 1866 found Louisa at the Villa Madonna, Mentone, which she had rented until the spring. A piano was installed, and a coachman, a serving man and a cook engaged; and the daughter of the Neuchâtel clergyman had come as nursery-governess to Maysie. Carlyle's arrival was eagerly awaited; coming from Marseilles, which he thought 'the strangest exotic of sea ports, lanes uglier and darker than anything in old Edinburgh', he found Bailey watching on the road for Tyndall and himself and Loo received him 'with kisses'.[176] The sun was shining and the sky bright as steel. He had his own small cottage joined to the main villa by a little terrace, where he could breakfast by himself – the 'coffee tolerable', if inferior to what he had at home. He worked at his *Reminiscences* until two o'clock, took a breakfast-cup of thick soup, then a drive or walk. 'Return wearied at 5 p.m, sip of brandy, whiff of 'bacco', an hour's sleep, and a fifteen-minute walk between dinner and tea. Loo would probably read aloud till eleven; then, after further reading in his cottage, with a glass of hot milk Carlyle would go to bed.[177] Most days were passed in that way though on Christmas day a picnic was organized by Loo with everyone riding asses to a hilltop village. Despite the bright weather Carlyle wrote home for his warm grey waistcoat and 'old neck flannels', and the parcel was to include Wornum's *Life of Holbein* for Loo, and a Dante, as she now had an Italian Master and was 'sunk in *Dante*'.[178]

Tyndall had left almost immediately and Carlyle did not greatly care for the two Bunsen guests, 'old Madam, and a lame daughter called Emilia', whom later he spoke of as 'much to be avoided if you dislike sententious commonplace, and harmonious cascades of twaddle'.[179]

But Loo had made a friend of a woman whose qualities she could understand and admire and who frequented the Villa Madonna. Lady Marian Alford, sister of the third Marquess of

CARLYLE AT MENTONE

Northampton, was the widowed mother of two sons, of whom the eldest, Earl Brownlow, who had succeeded his grandfather in 1853, was a consumptive invalid with an income of about £100,000. Both he and his younger brother, the Hon. Adelbert Cust, were with their mother at Mentone. Lady Marian, who had spent her childhood in Italy, was an accomplished artist, worldly, extravagant and highly cultivated, lacking only powers of discrimination. She helped to found the Royal School of Needlework and extended her patronage to the arts. The Brownings had known her in Rome; Mrs Browning described her as 'very eager about literature and art and Robert' and seemed to detect 'the least touch of affectation and fussiness'.[180] At Belton House and Ashridge Park, the two country houses that went with the title but were always open to her, she entertained on a large scale, while in London she had built a town house, 'a piece of magnificence',[181] at 11 Princes Gate.

In January 1867 Woolner passed through Mentone and on his return home reported that 'the dear old fellow was in good spirits, and Lady Ashburton was rejoiced in having the mighty man to pet and honour and make cozily comfortable'.[182] It is unlikely that Carlyle was cheerful; nearly ten years later he would look back and still remember the 'winter that I went to Mentone was the saddest of my life'.[183] But everyone was kind,

> nothing can exceed the industry, patience, and continual contrivance of my hospitable Lady Ashburton; and she really has a great deal of sense and substantial veracity of mind – tho' so full of impulses, sudden resolutions, and living so in an element of 'float'.[184]

Caroline Fox, diarist and intellectual, of Quaker descent, was in Mentone in March. Through a cousin she was connected with the de Bunsens and had known the Carlyles close on thirty years; when she paid him a visit she thought he looked 'thin, and aged, and as sad as Jeremiah'.[185] He was reading Shakespeare, clad in a dressing gown, 'a drab comforter wrapped round and round his neck', perhaps one of the neck flannels he had sent for to Cheyne Row. Gladstone on his way from Rome had rested at the Iles Britanniques at Mentone, had a long conversation with Louisa and saw Lord Brownlow 'with deep interest and painful apprehension'[186] – fulfilled when Lord Brownlow died four weeks

128   CARLYLE AT MENTONE

later. Carlyle noted that 'Gladstone made his transit the other day; several hours of him in this house: talk ponderous and copious.'[187] Acquaintance was scraped up with Princess Hélène of Waldeck-Pyrmont, a Lutheran by upbringing and keenly interested in philosophy and literature. (In 1882 her daughter married Queen Victoria's son Prince Leopold, Duke of Albany – after Maysie had declined the honour – and was the mother of Princess Alice, Countess of Athlone.) Loo hurried off a letter to Landseer asking him as a favour 'either to send me a scribble of the picture of me and Mary – or else to send me a photograph of it. A little German Princess is sorely anxious to have a picture of me.'[188]

Quite suddenly Loo could tolerate this regulated life no longer. 'Things are extremely unpredictable here,' Carlyle wrote to his brother on 18 February 1867, 'resolutions changing almost like the wind.'[189] This was followed nine days later with a description which brings vividly to life all the confusion of Loo's impulsive nature.

> Lady Ashburton eager to be off to Italy, or for *something* or *other* – could she but get the many *lines* of her complex affairs to *intersect* handsomely; which she cannot! Her situation here is really intricate; and she makes it by her impetuous handling, often enough not *less* so but more so. . . . And then her own plans, alas, they are manifold, and hardly anything stands *firm*. . . . In short she is the most generous-hearted, but the most tumble-headed (not that she wants sense either, far from that) of existing Hostesses.

On 12 March he wrote again:

> Lady Ashburton is off to Genoa, Florence etc etc suddenly as a whirlwind after all! We were almost glad to see her *go*, strange as our circumstances were; such had *her* dubitations and botherings been for weeks past.[190]

When Loo posted off in her vettura for Florence with what Tyndall called 'her splendid health and life of action', she left behind two guests to look after themselves, as well as Carlyle; he had been to Nice to look at the hotel which ten years before Harriet had left, only to die in Paris, and now it was time for him to be on his way home. Before leaving Louisa had asked Caroline Fox to see him again,

CARLYLE AT MENTONE

for I am very fond of the old man, and I did what I thought was for the best, and I really hope he is the better for it in spite of himself, though sometimes it seems as if it was altogether a failure.

Caroline Fox called on him and 'thought his "Good-bye" so impressive that it felt like parting. . . . It makes one sad to think of him – his look and most of his talk were so dreary.'[191]

Loo's expedition had taken her south to Naples and back to Mentone in three weeks. She missed Carlyle dreadfully. 'I do wish I had had you in a box, and could have unpacked you in the streets of Pompei', for her journey had inspired her to 'read a real course of History!' Her plans were to renew the lease of the villa though to leave it immediately for Nice and Switzerland; she would be at Addiscombe in early June at the latest. In next to no time she was writing from Vichy begging Carlyle to join her at the house she had taken for three weeks, to give the waters a trial. Dr Quain had said these were excellent where there was gout and kidney trouble and Maysie, who had a tendency to acidity, would profit by the baths. She had thought of him and 'the wound that is always bleeding', and 'most thankfully shall I devote my life to being of any use to you that I can'. A short stay at Versailles and at Fontainebleau was mooted (so as not to expose Maysie to the great excitements of Paris), and then forward to Addiscombe. Carlyle grumbled that the 'sooner we *cut* the painter and let Mentone drift, the better we shall get to port'. Another alteration of plan, and Loo was not in England until October.

At Glion the previous year Louisa had formed a friendship with a Hungarian couple, Count and Countess Nakos, and now, when she should have been in Surrey, the English Ambassador in Vienna, Lord Bloomfield, wrote of having seen her in Budapest in June at the coronation of the Emperor of Austria as King of Hungary, in the company of Countess Nakos; Bloomfield made her acquaintance and found her clever and amiable.[192] Maysie had been left in the care of Miss Margaret Trotter (a friend from old days) at St Germain-en-Laye, another of those older single women whose infatuation for Loo was partly reciprocated – though Loo knew how to turn such utter devotion to her own uses. Miss Trotter's was a severe case, adoring, jealous, and hysterical; for the next five years she was, as she herself admitted, 'possessed', and her

130 CARLYLE AT MENTONE

emotional life was dependent, and nourished, on Loo's fluctuating affections. A year later Carlyle noted that Louisa was 'greatly *engouée* with Miss M. Trotter I hear – *à la bonne heure*'.

On her return from Naples in the spring Louisa had spent a short time in Rome and on Lady Marian's recommendation, and probably with Story's blessing, had gone to the apartment and studio of an American sculptress, Harriet Hosmer from Massachussets, three years younger than herself. She had come to Italy in 1852 under the wing of Charlotte Cushman whose passion was said to be 'epicene', who wore a man's collar, cravat, and Wellington boots and whose best known role was that of Romeo.[193] Story described her singing ballads in a 'hoarse and manny voice', requesting people 'recitatively' to forget her not. 'I am sure I shall not,' he commented wryly.[194] Harriet studied under John Gibson, the distinguished English sculptor, and in 1853 successfully modelled the *Clasped Hands* of Elizabeth and Robert Browning. With her mythological subjects, her ideal marble busts, statues, fountains depicting sirens and water-babies, she captured the sentiment of the age and won the accolade for being the leader of the Roman 'white, marmorean flock'.[195] Short of stature, her movements were vigorous and she was a daring rider to hounds in the Campagna. Unaffected, managing and forthright, in appearance she resembled an aging boy in a little forage cap and a man's cravat which in the studio she partly covered with a loose workman's blouse.[196] This middle-aged, emancipated, masculine woman of talent was a friend of the Brownings who looked on her as the 'dearest little creature' with her 'old darling funny face'.[197] Lady Marian Alford who prized and acquired her work knelt down before her in admiration 'and gave her – placed on her finger – the most splendid ring',[198] a heart-shaped ruby surmounted and circled with diamonds.

Hatty, apparently overwhelmed by the presence of her new visitor, remained

> gazing, with no thought of advancing to greet her, for, as I gazed, it seemed to my bewildered senses that the Ludovisi Goddess in person . . . had assumed the stature and the state of mortals and stood before me. There were the same square-cut and grandiose features, whose classic beauty was humanized by a pair of keen, dark eyes. . . . Her chief charm lay . . . in the ever

CARLYLE AT MENTONE

131

varying radiance of expression . . . an exquisitely modulated voice, rich and musical.'[199]

Louisa immediately fell under her spell and recklessly commissioned a *Puck*, a *Will-o'-the-Wisp*, and two *Putti upon Dolphins* with four yellow alabaster pedestals to hold them (for all of which she paid £700), a marble chimneypiece, and two fair-sized pieces of sculpture, the *Sleeping Faun* and the *Waking Faun*. Very many more acquisitions were to follow as Hatty, with a calculating eye swiftly gained an amatory ascendancy over Loo, who volunteered no show of resistance. This new order for a chimneypiece may well have been induced by her vexation with Woolner whose bas-reliefs for the fronts of his had not been begun though the chimneypieces themselves were in place at Melchet. Clutton had written to Mentone of this state of affairs observing that Woolner had long ago obtained very accurate dimensions and he could not imagine for what he was waiting. After her commission to Harriet Woolner's was countermanded; his wife replied for him that if Louisa was unable to wait there was nothing more to be said but that it had been understood that the fronts could be fitted in later. Still on the defensive (and one wonders whether a money advance was expected), Alice Woolner explained the difficulties concerning the *Virgilia*, which now that Clutton had informed them that there was no necessity for the composition to be square in form meant a complete rearrangement of the modelling, a square being one of the worst possible forms for works of art. With the help of the Nakoses Loo had also acquired a set of four Gobelin panels for the covering of the walls in her private dining room at Melchet, but the momentous question on her return was where she should buy a large London house. Her American financial affairs had been settled and money was flowing in. Clutton who acted as agent and adviser had surveyed 10 Connaught Place and had found it large but without attractions, dingy and dirty, and Dr Quain who had also been enlisted agreed, although he found the situation particularly healthy. He dissuaded her from buying Hamilton House in Arlington Street: too great an establishment and not worth the money. Finally 22 Berkeley Square was settled upon and straightway Louisa wished to enlarge it by two storeys over the study. Clutton urged her to hesitate before committing herself to a further outlay, particularly as there was a large sum to pay for the

CARLYLE AT MENTONE

mews stables. Arnold's of Jermyn Street however assured her that the alterations could be effected and 'the glass of the Fern house can be made level with the drawingroom without injury'. It would be a great improvement and look very well.

Loo went at once to Addiscombe on her return in October 1867. 'She falls at last like a blazing aerolith!',[200] Carlyle informed his brother. He was immediately invited to come and see her and he heralded her arrival with unusual cordiality:

> Welcome, welcome, you brightest and strangest of shooting-stars. There have you been, for the last four months darting and dashing thro' all parts of the firmament; most part of the time, uncertain to me where, or whether not gone out of the solar system altogether; and now this morning, sudden as a bolt out of the blue, you are at Addiscombe.

A visit to Lady Marian at Belton was her next digression; Carlyle was there too. 'Lady Ashburton is too absurd, a perfect "*dingle* dousie",' he recorded.[201] Among the guests was Harriet Hosmer who he found uninteresting and of a mediocre intellect though she seems to have done her best to improve it if, as was said of her, she used to go to the Forum ruins in Rome to study the Bible, 'not as a holy book, but, as she took care to tell you, as the *finest prose in the world*'.[202]

Melchet claimed Loo most of the time as there was still much to be done with regard to its decoration, but while at her 'dear hotel', 32 Grosvenor Street (Miss Davenport Bromley's town house), Carlyle sent her a shawl that had once been Jane's – a true mark of trust. 'I cannot tell you *how* much I love that shawl, that precious shawl,' wrote Loo. She was now packing up before her 'southern flight' and repeated her affection for him: 'I value your dear friendship more than most things that are left me.' But she was not without resources for on Boxing Day Edward Lear who was at Cannes entered in his diary: 'Lo! a letter from Lady Ashburton who buys the Cedars for 200 guineas!', and to a friend he wrote on the same day:

> The Cedars are at last sold – not by any means for the sum I wished nor even a third, but still they will be placed, and thoroughly appreciated and I shall get £6 a year out of the critters for the rest of my life, if I can contrive to put my money

CARLYLE AT MENTONE

into three per cents. Louisa, Lady Ashburton, is the purchaser, and they will go to Melchet Court, Romsey, for their fewcherome.[203]

The next summer when Loo was in England the picture was dispatched though Lear was reluctant to part with it. On 18 June he 'worked at stems of Cedars' from 5 a.m. to 8.30 . . . June 25th. Resolved to send Cedars away tomorrow . . . June 26th. Sent away Cedars "so many years a companion" at 11 a.m.'[204]

It was nearly three years since Louisa had first raised Lear's hopes, and Woolner, who had seen him in London this autumn, may have helped her to a decision. Lear's diary account of dining with the Woolners is not without interest and shows clearly that the sculptor and Loo would not long pull well together.

Thomas Woolner is more loud and violent than ever: fool – scoundrel – idiot – blackguard – rascal – all in his mouth each moment and one cannot pass much time with him without some feeling of bitterness added to life.[205]

Louisa was in no haste to give Woolner an answer to a request that he might exhibit the Carlyle bust that summer at the Royal Academy. 'You forgot to say . . . ,' he wrote to her in France in the new year, 'I should be much obliged if you would let me know.' Loo staying in Paris at the Hotel Westminster, rue de la Paix, agreed to take from Hatty a *rosso antico* pedestal with its base, amounting to £70, hoping one day to have a handsome vase to place upon it. The chimneypiece was about to be dispatched to Melchet and work on the *Waking Faun* was progressing. 'The first copy is sacred to you,' Hatty wrote, and shrewdly taking advantage of Loo's enthusiasm hinted that she had set her heart on exhibiting it and its companion in London.

Owning four houses in England, it was time to give up the Mentone villa and after one more visit when Lord Houghton and his family came to stay in early spring ('This place lost all its charm the day you left'),[206] Loo hastened to Rome for holy week, returning to England by Perugia, Venice (at the Danieli), and then to Miss Trotter at St Germain-en-Laye. The Nakoses had invited her on their twenty-six-cabined yacht but this held little appeal as a warning note had accompanied the invitation:

CARLYLE AT MENTONE

Allow me dear Lady to remark that you must have the kindness to be punctual at the rendez-vous, and must repeat that when accepted it is of the highest importance to meet on that day which will be fixed.

Part of the summer was spent at Seaton but hoping for relief from rheumatism Loo established herself with Maysie and Miss Trotter at Malvern for a month, undergoing Dr Gully's celebrated water-cure which she found 'hard work' but was able to tell Carlyle that 'Dr Gully has a deep and affectionate recollection of you'. Hatty joined her at Loch Luichart and was eager for her to buy some magnificent chairs put up for sale in Rome and once the property of a Cardinal. Crimson velvet and gold, three and a half feet high, Hatty felt they were worthy companions to Loo's possessions. Mrs Story had bought four, Hatty four, eight remaining. Prompted partly by Hatty – she being an old friend of his – Loo invited Browning whom she would have seen very occasionally in society over the last years, but, as he wrote to a friend, he simply could not 'get up the steam' to go there.[207]

The house in Berkeley Square was ready for occupation, and besides her portrait which was still with Landseer, Loo needed some of her works of art with which to adorn it and asked Alice Woolner to have crated three marble busts, bronzes and plinths which Miss Davenport Bromley was temporarily housing in Grosvenor Street. In reply Woolner wrote a trifle curtly saying his carpenter had seen to it; later it emerged that some error had been made over the bronzes. Relations with Woolner were worsening. His *Virgilia*, a complex design in high-relief, was still not completed and before long the space intended for it in the Melchet library would be overrun with books and the marble would be stored – to Woolner's vexation – until exhibited at the Royal Academy in 1871. Within a very short time Loo would ask him if he could not dispose of it for her; his reply was the reverse of all she had hoped.

As to the ultimate destination of the 'Virgilia' I should of course be extremely sorry on my own account, if it did not go to Melchet. For me to attempt to arrange differently for it, would I am afraid, be quite impracticable. I have as you know, been already put to a very considerable expense both in time and money about the relief and in case of sculpture, especially of a

CARLYLE AT MENTONE

work of this quasi architectural character, there are unfortunately no facilities in England for disposal. It differs in this respect altogether from the case of a picture.

When W. M. Rossetti, Gabriel's brother, called at Woolner's studio he thought the work very fine but he was told by the sculptor that 'with her wonted caprice' Loo had lost all interest in the work.[208]

Marochetti had died and his son, writing from Onslow Square, suggested that Loo might care to pay the estate the sum still owing for a *Venus*, and a bust of Rinaldo Rinaldi which had been cast and sent to her. A firm of agricultural engineers at Banbury threatened the necessity of litigating if her bill with them were not paid within a week. With Melchet nearing completion it was altogether a harassing time for Loo. Clutton's work, the building of the large country house for entertaining on a grand scale, was finished. He could point with justifiable pride to the lofty saloon, the noble enfilade of library – twenty feet high – two drawing rooms, and dining room measuring sixty feet in length; a billiard room, an outer hall and an inner hall from which sprang the massive staircase rising to the upper floor of bedrooms, boudoir, chapel, tapestry room and a long gallery for the display of marble busts; these stood flanked by vermilion pilasters beneath an ornate plasterwork ceiling. Carved oak doorcases, coffered ceilings and Hatty's marble fireplace of dying wood nymphs and putti framed within fluted columns were in place, and in 1868 Alfred Stevens added his notable contribution to the house. It was the last commission this versatile artist undertook before his death and was a reflection on a small scale of his great gifts, as well as an inspired choice on the part of Louisa, who would have seen his recent work in the dining room of Dorchester House, Park Lane. Painter, architectural sculptor, decorative designer and craftsman, he had studied in Italy in his youth and been employed by Thorvaldsen in Rome. Louisa gave him the grand staircase and ceiling to design and the walls of the inner hall leading to it, and a vaulted corridor. The result was a triumph of colour and conception. The wall of the dark Renaissance staircase was painted Pompeian red with a dado delicately picked out in gold, the polished balusters stained black with gilt sparingly introduced. Above, the ceiling panels were a marvel of classical design, dark

CARLYLE AT MENTONE

and light, and touches of gold predominating, while the walls of the inner hall were repeated in red, the spandrels incorporating medallion portraits of the poets. More exuberantly decorated and with equal success the vaulted corridor was a masterpiece of artistry. Lavishly furnished from The Grange and embellished by paintings, sculpture, tapestries, bronzes, rare china and other inherited or collected works of art, the house contained three organs, four pianofortes (one a grand concert) and a harmonium. Louisa loved her new home with its prospect due south to the Isle of Wight, and the New Forest in the distance, while the splendour of the surrounding park was nicely set off by the formal gardens laid out immediately beneath her windows. The campanile, orangery and lawns were adjacent, the two lakes and the aboretum well situated, while the stable block with the pump house and deep well – for their own water supply came from a chalk stream – stood behind the house. Supplies from outside reached the domestic quarters in carts and were loaded onto trolleys on small railways which took the goods into the house. The household accommodation consisted of the usual succession of laundry, ironing room, drying-ground, still rooms, larders and kitchen premises. There were domestic trials to contend with: 'Do bells ring *any* where?' Loo cried, and a butler was needed for Berkeley Square. But her difficulties with servants were proverbial; once at Loch Luichart with a houseful of guests a retired gamekeeper acted as butler wearing some strange form of dress and served the wine in 'black bottles'.[209] In the fashion of the time not to decant wine was looked on as a near-unpardonable solecism. During her tenure of a house in Stanhope Street in 1871 Lord Houghton came to stay, bringing his valet; besides Loo's own maid and a butler there was no other domestic assistance, not even a cook, and from this time may have stemmed one of Loo's stranger eccentricities, that of having her carriage draw up in front of a restaurant and requiring the meal to be served to her there.

Maysie's education was also in default. Friends were pressed into finding her a governess. Landseer wondered why Loo should trust her child in any hands but her own – perhaps it led him to assume that Maysie's character resembled her mother's – unless, he slyly added, 'she has already formed both character, disposition, temper and mind'.

13

The Widower and the Widow

Loch Luichart, August 1869, and Louisa chose to make a journey across Ross-shire to the west coast to revisit the places she had known in her youth. From Balmacara she wrote nostalgically to Carlyle on the 23rd, the day before she expected to be back at Loch Luichart:

> The dear poor people have been too touchingly affectionate – and my thoughts have been full of sadness – the man who bought all this great principality for many and many a year ardently desired that I should become the mistress of it – and as I leant over the seawall in the drivelling mist, with my *one* little creature gone to bed, and my love gone away from Earth – I could not help shuddering at the contrast of my lonely present, with the full, busy life of earnest usefulness that might have been mine – and then I thought of the old race all gone – almost forgotten – and my mother and husband away!

The letter of a lonely woman, whose 'winning and powerful face, with much intellectual energy and womanly sweetness'[210] were irresistible to many, but who, besides her cherished child, had no beloved companion to determine the course of her life.

On returning to Loch Luichart she found, as she told Carlyle, a letter from W. W. Story who with his sons, daughter Edith and his wife, and Robert Browning, Sarianna his sister and Pen

> were waiting for my arrival at the Inn close by – very reproachful – and there was nothing for me to do but have them all here – so here they came the lendemain . . . I find them very pleasant guests – and Browning a *delightful man*.

When in 1861 Pauline Trevelyan had expressed a hope that Pen might now, at the death of his mother, receive a more reasonable education she was echoing no more than Browning's own intention. The spoilt son of an idolizing mother, the boy was

138 THE WIDOWER AND THE WIDOW

twelve when she died, and although he had settled readily enough in England, his disinclination to study and lack of purpose were causing his devoted father incalculable anxiety. Good-natured but weak, idle and pleasure-loving, his short career at Christ Church, Oxford had begun unfavourably and Browning, tormented by such easygoing ways, was himself physically and mentally exhausted by his prodigious labours of the last years. Since leaving Italy he had seen his wife's *Last Poems* and a collection of essays in book form through the press; his *Poetical Works* in three volumes had been given to the public, while in 1864 he had begun *The Ring and the Book*, his great poem and crowning achievement, which bore on the final page of Book I the royal tribute to his wife. The work had been published in four monthly instalments beginning in the previous November, and Louisa reading of his triumph determined to recover a neglected friendship. In April she sent Browning an invitation which he was obliged to decline.

12 April '69.

Dear Lady Ashburton,
    Indeed I do 'remember you' – I shall be changed miraculously when I cease to do *that*! It is very pleasant to find that you remember *me* – not that I ever doubted it. Thank you exceedingly for your kind invitation – although I cannot accept it, being just about going to Paris for a week or two. . . .

A further overture was made and this time met with success:

1 July '69

I shall indeed be happy to dine with you on the 10th but 'do you the honor'? that is tantalizing to one who would fain do all that infinitely little in his power – but never yet was crazy enough to dream of doing *that*!

To a third invitation there were grounds for refusal and a reply was sent on 29 July:

You may see how reluctantly I forgo your invitation, – *not* the kindness of it, which I shall enjoy in gratitude now and always. I leave town next Saturday with the Storys for – Scotland . . . what a delight it has been to me to find that the best thing in the world does not change and that your friendship remains as of

THE WIDOWER AND THE WIDOW 139

old for Yours ever most truly and, – may I say in right of those
old days, –

affectionately
ROBERT BROWNING

He could have afforded her no happier intelligence than that he
was to be in Scotland. An invitation to Loch Luichart was issued to
them all, probably a day or two after Browning's letter of 30 July to
his friend John Forster.

> I go simply to Scotland – to North Berwick, and there an end. It
> comes of the persuasiveness with Pen of the Storys, who go so far
> and probably farther; all I agree to, is company for a month or
> so, at the roughest place discoverable –afterward, they will
> make visits, I dare say but I mean to return.

Browning was reluctantly coerced into accepting Louisa's
proposition ('through circumstances unforseen and quite out of
my control')[211] for Pen took a delight in shooting and deer-
stalking and to see him occupied and happy would in itself be an
easing of many months of strain. The party promised to be
harmonious and enjoyable, but whether Loo had forgotten her
guests which was unlikely (or pretended, as she seemed to imply to
Carlyle, she had never invited them – though according to
Sarianna 'by main force' she compelled them all to stay)[212] or
whether with her customary unpredictable tendency to follow her
own inclinations she was indifferent to their welfare, on reaching
Loch Luichart they found their hostess absent and no arrangements made to receive them. A nearby inn offered little in the way
of comfort but picnics amongst the heather were enjoyed and
Browning meanwhile read aloud from Scott's *Rob Roy*. He had
not found much refreshment in the 'hideous confusion' of the last
weeks' travelling through Scotland with sporadic sightseeing, and
camping in a 'squalid' hostelry,[213] and the relief of being
established at Loch Luichart was considerable. 'The worst is over
and here, at an old friend's I am comfortable altogether . . . all goes
well now in this beautiful place.'[214]

For close on one hundred years elements comprising the
situation which arose at Loch Luichart during his fortnight's
sojourn have been repeatedly debated. Who made the proposal of
marriage: the widower or the widow? Until quite recently

140   THE WIDOWER AND THE WIDOW

conjecture – or opinion – has been that Robert Browning made the
offer either in 1869 or 1871, qualifying it with the objectionable
remark that his heart was buried in Florence with his wife but that
marriage would be advantageous to Pen; and that his proposal was
rejected with scorn. Fresh letters lend a different interpretation to
this episode.

Louisa had been widowed five years and during that time her
only discipline had been a pecuniary one. Now however she was
free to travel, to build, to spend – and to pursue. Henry James deftly
drew a picture of 'this so striking and interesting a personage, a rich
generous presence that, wherever encountered seemed always to
fill the foreground with colour, with picture, with fine mellow
sound.'[215] There was no question but that she enjoyed having
Browning in her house – 'the accomplished, saturated, sane, sound
man of the London world and of the world of "culture"'[216] She
would have heard of his friendship with Julia Wedgwood, of his
affectionate, 'hearty genial goodwill towards most women';[217]
and to several in particular. Sentiment, sympathy and exaggeration, with which Loo was liberally endowed, were ingredients
suited to the occasion and with these she was well armed to make a
killing. There would have been much discussion of Pen's future (he
was now twenty) and of Maysie's upbringing – each an only child;
of the desolation of death, the loneliness of an empty home, the
need of Maysie for a father. 'Browning has read all day and nearly
all night – Shakespeare, Keats etc etc' she told Carlyle, and what
more conducive to tender susceptibilities in this romantic Highland setting of hill and lake than a celebrated poet (however harsh
his voice was said to be) reading aloud Shakespeare's love sonnets
('we who have him in our very bones and blood, and our very
selves',[218] as Browning once remarked) and the immortal lyrics of
Keats.

An overture to marriage – perhaps not a distinct proposal – most
likely came from Louisa who had many worldly benefits to offer
and needed somebody to shoulder the heavy responsibilities which
she was incurring. Besides, how great the triumph to secure the
laurel-crowned poet. In keeping with Loo's highly charged modes
of expression, and no doubt attuned to the spirit of the place and its
impetuous hostess, perhaps exhilarated by the invigorating air and
momentarily carried away, Browning gave some sympathetic
response as will be seen in a later letter of 1871 in which he writes of

THE WIDOWER AND THE WIDOW 141

'a great exercise of self-denial', and of 'the right course' being 'never very attractive as you know!' The 'great exercise of self-denial' was the substance of his uncommitted, evasive reply to the offer of marriage, one which Louisa may hardly have understood, Browning's obscure style of speech leading her to read into it more than was intended. For Browning had little intention of remarrying; at home his mornings had settled into regular hours of work, his evenings were given to his friends, and the core of his immediate concern was to settle Pen in some honourable path and after that to go back to Italy and live and die there – so he had always told the Storys. Living now among those who were so intimate with Elizabeth and himself, and conversation harking back daily to all their years in Italy, it is inconceivable that Browning would, on no deep acquaintance, have offered marriage to Louisa, with the echo of the dedication to his wife from *The Ring and the Book* – which he must surely have read to them – still ringing in their ears.

> O lyric love, half angel and half bird
> And all a wonder and a wild desire, –
> Boldest of hearts that ever braved the sun . . .
> Never may I commence my song, my due
> To God who best taught song by gift of thee,
> Except with bent head and beseeching hand –
> That still, despite the distance and the dark,
> What was, again may be, . . . some interchange
> Of grace, some splendour once thy very thought,
> Some benediction anciently they smile: . . .
> – Never conclude, but raising hand and head
> Thither where eyes, that cannot reach, yet yearn
> For all hope, all sustainment, all reward,
> Their utmost up and on, – so blessing back
> In those thy realms of help, that heaven thy home. . . .

That there was no rift in the house-party is evident in that it remained cheerful; a rhyming doggerel written in jocular mood on 5 September was sent to Hatty from them all;[219] Lady Marian and Sir Roderick Murchison arrived to swell the gathering and this would have been an occasion to welcome Rossetti as a fellow guest. 'As for that kind, good, overwhelming Lady A,' Rossetti wrote to Allingham in February 1870, 'she has written to me from at least six different parts of the British Islands during the past year, asking

142 THE WIDOWER AND THE WIDOW

me to come down instantly and meet a sympathizing circle';[220] but he was a 'very grubby hole-&-corner old fellow and dont go anywhere,' he told her. By 10 September the Brownings and Storys had left and the Nakoses arrived. Only in London was some alarm felt. Miss Davenport Bromley, knowing Louisa's temperament, observed to Carlyle that she had no news from Loch Luichart 'but with Browning in the house how could she write! The very thoughts of him as an inmate ['of hers' crossed out] make me shudder. That rough voice!'

Loo however found time to write to Lord Houghton of the visit. 'I cannot say what delightful guests I found them. Mr Browning I think a charming man. Is he a friend of yours?'[221] Nevertheless she professed to Carlyle that with the house full of people she longed 'for quiet and solitude – to be done with this Hotel-keeping life – but there is alas! neither quiet nor solitude for me.' She loved the familiar countryside and recognized its beauty and 'my heart glows with highland love', but the railways had destroyed the last remains of solitude, and

> dearly as I love this place, I dont know what I shall do with it . . . farewell – how many memories cluster round us both, to each other – to you, in my name – to me, in you yourself – again farewell.

On leaving Loch Luichart Browning and the Storys went to Naworth Castle, Carlisle, to stay with the George Howards, where Story made drawings of the poet reading from his latest work, and where, as 'the old old Story' told Loo, Browning was 'as full of life as ever, an army in himself'. Moving on to Ashridge they went to

> Mentmore (the Meyer de Rothschilds) yesterday and had an indigestion of bric–a–brac. There were lots of handsome things all tumbled promiscuously together in a sort of head over heels way that made ones head ache.

From Loch Luichart Loo sent Carlyle a haunch of venison and a promise of grouse 'but as my shooting lodge is filled with a succession of artists, musicians, literary men, and scientific savants, the game laughs at us and the forester is in despair.' Ten days later nothing had reached Cheyne Row. 'Some hunting thief in some railway station must have seized and eaten it, as I am told their frequent custom is,' wrote Carlyle. 'Never mind them,

THE WIDOWER AND THE WIDOW 143

miserable spongers', and though the venison did not arrive 'the bright kindness of it did'. Loo tried again: 'I send 5 grouse – will they fly straight and take all the messages I give them? or will they subside into the inside of some Railway knave?' A batch of six partridges and a hare followed soon after carrying a message: 'Eat these for my sake.' Loo would have been touched by his gratitude for she worked hard to please him. 'Surely in loving kindness you have no rival living,' he told her on 1 October. 'No man of my acquaintance was, at any time, valued so far beyond his worth.'

At the close of 1870 plans for Pen to stay at Melchet were afloat.

If your arrangements allow [Browning wrote to her there on 29 December] (and you will never stand on anything like ceremony with me, I hope) he shall go to you on January 2nd. . . . And so ends another year! The best of wishes for you and Maysie – together with the poor suffering world – for the next one.

Ever yours affectionately,
ROBERT BROWNING

Ten days later Browning received two notes, one from Pen and the other from Louisa. He replied to hers at once:

Besides your note, comes a word from Pen to tell me . . . 'While I write Lady Ashburton – who is kindness itself – is drawing from a cast, Maysie is playing the piano, and Miss Ronan [governess] is reading aloud from a French book': so I see you, – and am prepared for 'kindness itself' speaking so kindly of Pen to me. . . . Thank you for that and all else: most of all for what I dare not doubt is true, – since you again assure me of it – that you have 'wished for me much'. I cannot take in such assurances as if they were mere breath and vanity – nor do I suppose that you believe I do so. If I secure no good to you, and therefore to myself, by a great exercise of self-denial, there has been one more great mistake made by me who have made many – but few that, by reason of this difficulty, looked so like the right course – never very attractive you know! If it is clear to me, at any time, that I can give you a moment's pleasure with no pain – as a consequence, neither the miles between here and Melchet, nor the leagues further to South Africa if there you should happen to be in the flesh, – shall separate us. Perhaps some instinct will tell me when I am really wanted, – I partly or altogether believe in

144 THE WIDOWER AND THE WIDOW

such warnings, but you are copying your cast, and Maysie is playing and both are listening to the French book, and I confess I feel I am best here, now – however I may feel one day, what cast I wonder! Pen might have mentioned it. . . . And it only remains that I wish you goodbye: remember me whenever you come to town, and, if it can be without inconvenience, apprise me and let me see you for a few minutes.

God bless you ever.

R.B.

Browning must have composed this letter with some care, dealing as best he could with her provocative expressions of missing him and her evident desire to have him at Melchet ('I am better here'); if seeing him would give her a modicum of pleasure 'with no pain as a consequence' – no regrets at his refusal to subscribe to marriage – he would come and see her. Some instinct would tell him when he was 'really' wanted; no sudden whim or capricious desire would bring him – but only when 'really' wanted. The hope of seeing her for a few minutes if she came to London probably expressed precisely what he felt. It was both a friendly and a conciliatory letter; Loo had shown immeasurable kindness to him and Pen and had placed herself in an equivocal position at Loch Luichart, which owing to his usual gallantry with women Browning may well have considered his fault. By temporizing and not seeing her, Louisa's enthusiasm – always unpredictable – 'her liberal oddity', her 'genial incoherence'[222] might favour some other victim or object.

On the contrary however, for now began her 'nine or ten months' teazing with her invitations',[223] which were to end only in October by which time he had resisted her 'cajoleries and pathetic appeals for two years together'[224] – ever since he had left Loch Luichart in September 1869. In March he sent the eleven-year-old Maysie a book, ending an affectionate letter with: 'The gift is small, the love is all',[225] and on the publication of his *Balaustion's Adventure* a copy was sent to Loo at Loch Luichart by his publisher. The poem was written in May, just ten years after Elizabeth's death, which occurrence it may have been designed to commemorate, and since it was a narration of the espousal of death rather than remarriage, the author may have hoped that in sending it he would convey to Louisa his lasting fidelity to his wife.

THE WIDOWER AND THE WIDOW 145

Browning was staying with friends in Perthshire in August and September 1871, a visit he enjoyed and which he would have liked to prolong – 'far from as wild and grandiose, however, as Loch Luichart where we hope to be tomorrow night',[226] he had written on 1 October. Pen had proved a failure academically and enjoyed an indolent and extravagant life; once again he had been invited to Loch Luichart for the deer-stalking and Louisa had insisted on Browning coming over from Glen Fincastle. Unwillingly he did so on 2 October and there he found Louisa, who, according to his letter to Edith Story six months later,

> knowing she had only succeeded after nine or ten months' teazing with her invitations to get me to promise to visit her for one day, and so get handsomely done with it all, – wanted to have the air of shutting the door in my face with a final bang, – fancying that she could coax me round the back-way the very next day[227] [as she had done by asking him to the house she had rented in Park Lane for the winter]. I have told her my mind so thoroughly about *that* and so effectually relieved myself from any further bother of the kind that I need not bring up the nauseating remembrance.

On his arrival she would have again raised the question of marriage, wanting a decision, at which Browning, tried beyond bearing and in self-defence, probably then spoke outright what he had often cloaked more tactfully:

> My heart is buried in Florence, and the attractiveness of marriage with her lay in its advantage to Pen: two simple facts, – as I told her, – which I have never left her in ignorance about, for a moment.

This was the root of her quarrel with him, 'concerning which she foamed out into the couple of letters she bespattered me with'[228] and 'exploded in all the madness of wounded vanity'.[229] Browning kept these letters on Story's advice (while sending him copies, since he had been an onlooker from the start) as they were a simple answer to Loo's charge 'that I had been making endeavours to renew a relationship of even ordinary acquaintance', when he had done his utmost to elude her. The letters were evidence enough of Loo's dissemblings. At the time he was unaware 'of what I have had abundant knowledge of since – how

146   THE WIDOWER AND THE WIDOW

thoroughly her character as a calumniator was understood by those most intimately connected with her'.[230]

When Pen and his father reached Loch Luichart sometime on 2 October they found the house overflowing with visitors; in addition there were Lord and Lady Houghton and a daughter, and Loo's recently married niece Mary (later Lady St Helier, 'a sort of amiable lion-huntress',[231] daughter of Keith Stewart-Mackenzie) with her husband 'little Johnny Stanley'[232] who had served in the Crimea and on Lord Canning's staff in India. Perhaps it was not altogether fortuitous that Lord Fortescue, a widower of four years was also a guest.[233] Loo had the inconvenient habit of inviting more people than she could accommodate and in this over-abundance of hospitality the surplus were lodged at Brahan Castle accepting the infliction 'with a kind of traditional charmed, amused patience'.[234] This then was surely the circumstance in which Lord Houghton and Browning (and probably the Stanleys) were sent down to Brahan to find rooms there. Writing almost forty years after the event, Lady St Helier (never too precise a chronicler) referred to the occasion as having taken place during her girlhood,[235] but so far as is known it was the only time during Browning's two visits to Loch Luichart (1869, 1871) that Houghton was a fellow guest. The distance was too great to allow Browning to return to Perthshire on the very evening of his arrival and in this crisis Brahan would seem a natural shelter for the night of 2 October. Lord Houghton, an inveterate talker, only surpassed by Browning himself, would have relished the situation.

At the end of March 1872 Browning was at Belton as a guest of Lady Marian who though an intimate of Loo evidently felt no repugnance towards him. Brookfield was there, as was Mary, Gladstone's daughter, who left a record of their being the sole daily worshippers at morning chapel; but she did not care greatly for him until later for he 'talked so loud and breathed into one's face and grasped one's arm', and when Louisa arrived with Carlyle on 5 April and Browning departed the next day leaving the field to Loo, she wrote: 'We all supposed he [Browning] was proposing to Lady Ashburton . . . at least she let it be thought so.'[236] But as they were so few hours together Loo must have made her innuendoes after his departure, presumably to counteract any rumours disparaging to herself. On the day before her arrival Browning had written to Edith Story that he had met Loo once only since October 'and I felt

John Ruskin and Louisa at Wallington Hall, 1857

Brahan Castle

Louisa, c. 1859

The Grange

Louisa wearing mourning (perhaps for her mother), c. 1862

Louisa from a marble bust by Marochetti, 1861

Louisa and Maysie, by Landseer, 1862

Lord Ashburton, c. 1860

Harriet Hosmer, c. late 1860s

Thomas Carlyle, mid 1860s

Loch Luichart

Robert Browning, probably reading from *The Ring and the Book*, Naworth Castle, 1869

Melchet Court

Louisa in old age

THE WIDOWER AND THE WIDOW   147

excused from even looking at – much less speaking to her'.[237] But when in July 1872 part of Melchet was destroyed by fire, Browning, knowing the scale of the tragedy to Loo and willing to heal the breach, wrote her a condoling letter:

> There never was a more unnecessary word, dear Friend, than this I am going to write; but I shall formally write, nevertheless, that all circumstances considered, I believe there can be nobody in the whole world so profoundly moved for you as myself. I take comfort only in your magnanimity, of which I am happily certain. It would have been too great a privilege to try and be the least good to you directly – but let the good only go to you through the offices of others, and I shall be happy and satisfied. . . . I leave London next week and shall hear no more of you for a long while: but hope is easy now that I have experience how you can become all the stronger for a calamity like this. Forgive the poor expressions, the first that come, which do not attempt to represent the feeling beneath them. And pray return no answer: I know you will accept the sympathy I should be too pained in attempting to stifle altogether. God bless you ever, dear friend, above the chances and changes of this life!
>
> ROBERT BROWNING

Far from relations being renewed Browning told Story in 1874 that he saw 'every now and then that contemptible Lady Ashburton, and mind her no more than any other black beetle – so long as it dont crawl up my sleeve.'[238] He avoided her wherever possible and the following year it was probably of her that he was thinking when he observed that he had kept away from Carlyle on account of 'someone who visits him.'[239] Hatty too had been active, and on Loo's behalf, trying to stir up trouble between Browning and the Storys, but apparently with no effect.

In the late spring of 1873, as she journeyed to Marienbad, Loo had been pursued by letters from Hatty with whom she had spent a Roman winter and to whom she had given before leaving 'some interesting' letters to read. In particular, one from Browning which 'shows what a double dealer he is', wrote the outraged Hatty to Perugia, and instantly wished for permission to show it to the Storys since it concerned his disloyalty to them. She had put it under lock and key until she received a reply, and 'Now goodnight darling and hold me in your arms – you can do that figuratively

148 THE WIDOWER AND THE WIDOW

speaking and I wish you could physically.' From Bologna Loo wrote in June to forbid its exposure; this did not satisfy Hatty.

> It ought to be shown since he [Browning] has denied ever being disloyal to the Ss. . . . Oh that miserable nature – I mean B. *She* was the one who made him spread his wings and soar above himself; when she left him he began to sink and sink and now is *very* near the earth.

With a little further coaxing Hatty obtained what she wanted and prepared also to read to the Storys that portion of Loo's accompanying letter ('which is entirely worthy of you') in which she said it seemed so like revenge to allow it to be scrutinized.

> Having [as Hatty said] shifted the act upon my own shoulders I put it (B's letter) into Mr S's hands and asked him to read it aloud. 'Well I never,' said Mrs Story with much expression and much indignation. 'A most improper letter to have written' said Mr Story. 'That is not the best of letters I should expect a man who calls himself my friend to write to me.' I told them that after the experience of last year their eyes were but very impartially opened. They are leaving tonight for Dieppe – stop short of England, I believe the reason is they do not care to see Mr B.

The Storys were in Scotland as usual that autumn and there appears to have been no rift in either friendship or correspondence with Browning. Neither the date or the occasion of Browning's letter of disloyalty is revealed, nor indeed if it was addressed to Loo or whether it had been sent to her by some correspondent with the 'other interesting letters'. 'The experience of last year' (1872) might have been a report reaching the Storys in which Hatty had concerned herself in making mischief between Browning and others, though Browning had always supposed her to be Loo's 'cat's paw'.[240]

Thirteen years after this incident of the letter, when referring to Louisa's actions in 1871, Browning was moved to say: 'So, enough of an odious experience – which had, however, the effect of enabling you and Mrs Story to prove yourselves effectually and admirably my friends.'[241] They continued to preserve a coolness towards Loo until 1875 when she thought it politic to be on friendly terms again and she resolved upon a 'fathom-deep burial of the hatchet', Story told his wife. 'She is affectionately mine.

THE WIDOWER AND THE WIDOW   149

Well! no matter – let by-gone be byegones.'[242] In about 1878 Loo '"tried on" conciliation' with Browning in Story's London rooms but he was too wearied by the 'hateful subject'[243] to wish for any kind of resumption of friendship.

He was angered by Hatty attempting in 1887 to win favour with him again. 'You may as well know,' he told the Storys, 'how the chief agent in that business of the eighteen seventies professes to feel for me whom she so slandered.'[244] In his *Parleying with Daniel Bartoli* of the same year, Browning exposed a female apparition, surely in the guise of Louisa:

> . . . brisk-marching bold she-shape,
> A terror with those black-balled worlds of eyes,
> The black hair bristling solid-built from nape
> To crown its coils above.

and thus with one avenging stroke repaid Louisa for the fabrications with which she had bedevilled him. Small wonder, perhaps, that when the next year an acquaintance witnessed 'a furious outburst from Lady Ashburton against Browning' it seemed to him that 'the fury of her language was a storm unappeased'.[245]

14
Schemes and Crises

Venison and game had been Louisa's contribution to the newly augmented household at Cheyne Row, for Carlyle on leaving Scotland at the end of the summer of 1869 had brought back his niece, Mary Carlyle Aitken, to be a companion in that lonely house. He in his turn 'in obedience to your royal command', as he wrote to Loo,

> had a hand, indeed both hands plaster-cast the other day, under Woolner's inspection. [Most certainly inspired by Hatty Hosmer's *Clasped Hands* of the Brownings.] Accept it as a little gift from me, a bit of humble obedience . . . I said there were two hands; Woolner would not have it otherwise than that they should be *disjoined*, and quite independent of each other: coming home I felt this would be absurd; that the right hand which is back uppermost with a pen in it should be yours.

From his letters to his brother it is possible to chart something of Louisa's movements that winter.

> 26 October [1869]
> Lady A. I saw for a moment (by accident) – hurrying home to Melchet, with her Hungarians sent on ahead: 'back here in a week', will then be plentifully visible 'for 4 or 5 days'. . . .
>
> 12 November
> Lady A. is here, came down last Friday after dinner, and cut off my sleep, but has done no other *mischief* with her kindness. . . .
>
> 10 December
> Lady A's letter after three weeks of utter silence came to me, – like a shot from a covy.[246]

But Loo was not the only friend to interfere with his sleep. Ruskin too had arrived forty minutes before he was expected, 'just while I was lying down to siesta, cost me two nights'.[247] It

SCHEMES AND CRISES

151

was Carlyle's habit to sleep before his evening walk and on returning at about nine o'clock to have tea, bread and butter and plum cake, after which he would sit on the floor beside the fire with his long clay pipe and carry on a monologue with whoever was his visitor, sometimes for two hours at a time.[248] With Louisa the talk was less likely to be so one-sided and from Loch Luichart several years later she exclaimed: 'I must sit up by night light to have a chat with you – alas! not on the floor, and with a pipe, as it has been, in dear days gone by.'

Carlyle and Mary Aitken had been at Melchet early in 1870, one of the 'best-appointed, beautifullest and solidly resourceful houses in England' and his hostess's generosity 'unsurpassable, or indeed unequallable.' On his return to London he found to his delight a Valentine present awaiting him from Brookfield in the form of a large grey owl made into a fire-screen with a verse pinned to it:

> To wisdom lit with fires divine
> Minerva comes as Valentine.
> Tu whit tu whoo she says to you
> Your part the wit, and hers to woo.

Loo had now reached the conclusion that her London house did not suit her, and in February Lord Houghton, who was deciding whether or not to keep his own house in Upper Brook Street, passed it one day 'with a bill in the window and was thinking of going in and buying it'. She told him she had sold it for 'about exactly' what she had given for it, and while casting about for land on which to build herself a house, she moved to 6 Stanhope Street for a year. When her choice fell upon Kent House facing the late-eighteenth-century barracks and riding school of the Household Brigade on the edge of Hyde Park, Dr Quain hastened to caution her against building, for there would be no limit to the cost. The house had been lived in at the beginning of the century by the Duke of Kent with Madame de Saint-Laurent and had subsequently passed to the Villierses. Since Louisa preferred to build, rather than to purchase the old house, it was pulled down in 1870 and she acquired the site; the following year tenders were put out for building. The lowest was for £15,000 and Henry Clutton was again chosen as architect.

SCHEMES AND CRISES

Besides building schemes Louisa was concocting a capital plan for the summer. She had talked to Carlyle 'about sailing to Norway, to America even; about having a yacht of her own etc, but since the Easter days she has vanished – and may have gone to the Ecumenic Council for all I know'. By June Loo's 'fine yacht speculation' seemed extinct 'if it ever deserved to be called alive'. In its place she proposed that Carlyle should go to Loch Luichart with her and to 'lone sea hamlets on the coast of Skye; but I *dont* bite at that kind of bait, knowing how aerial *it* is.'[249] But Loo was not well and decided to let Loch Luichart and take the waters at Strathpeffer nearby, remarkable for the treatment of rheumatism and indigestion, and if the better for her cure would cross to the Lews with Maysie for a few weeks. Before leaving Melchet for Scotland she begged an autograph from Carlyle for the Duke of Rutland's gardener who told her that his guide and text book had been *Sartor*, 'and who nearly went down before your bust. The desire of his soul is a bit of your writing. I have walked with him till I am nearly dead.' Carlyle had gone as usual to Dumfries and Loo writing from Strathpeffer was 'dreadfully sorry to pass near Dumfries and not stop', but she was so unwell that she wanted to get to the waters. The country had never seemed to her more beautiful 'but it feels sad and forlorn enough to me – with all its sacred memories of those beloved ones who gladdened it to my heart'. Unhappily for Loo those sacred memories were not proof against what she referred to as 'the cruel unkindness of the Barings' calumnies' from which she had been 'made afresh to bleed'; she needed some words of 'comforting and strengthening' from Carlyle – 'any random words of yours are sure to be helpful to me.' The Barings had probably heard of her desire to build a town house and were appalled at her extravagance, still owning as she did Addiscombe villa and farm, Seaforth Lodge, Loch Luichart with its deer forest and grouse moor, and Melchet Court. She had heard it said that she had behaved like the most 'avaricious of women' on leaving The Grange and had torn down all the bell wires out of spite. She lamented that her husband had left no memorandum concerning her conduct during their married years as the kind of report that was being put about ran like 'a black thread through my life'.

She took Maysie with her that autumn to St Moritz and was joined there by Hatty Hosmer but she was at Melchet at the end of

SCHEMES AND CRISES

the year, grappling with her child's education. Having turned to Carlyle for advice (for which she thanked her 'dearly beloved friend') she was able to tell him that for the first time in her life Maysie was getting a fair chance of instruction. Miss Trotter had come from France to teach her music; she had a governess, Mademoiselle Ronan, for French, and the schoolmaster from the village school – 'a nice earnest man' – to come every morning for two hours 'for the harder drier things', arithmetic, writing, geography and Latin. Maysie would soon be eleven and daughter and devoted mother were seldom apart. She was still 'the same truthful *child* with so much of the noble simplicity of her father'.

Dickie Doyle and others had been to stay; Pen Browning, if not his father, was expected in the new year and Loo herself had so benefited from 'the dear Highland waters' that she felt too young for her increasing age. Her energy was devoted to bringing beauty and order to her garden which had once been chaos. Very many years earlier she must have read William Morris's *Story of an Unknown Church* in the first number of the *Oxford and Cambridge Magazine* (1856) and had remembered his description of a cloister and garden. She wrote to him now asking him to come to Melchet and lay out her garden. In his romance she had read of a marble fountain in the midst of a lawn, of a cloister around whose pillars

> crept passion-flowers and roses . . . in the garden were trellises covered over with roses and convolvulus and the great-leaved fiery nasturtium . . . the hollyhocks . . . great spires of pink, and orange, and red, and white . . . lush green briony . . . red berry with purple.[250]

Her hopes were dashed when in reply Morris told her that he could not get away (he was correcting proofs of *The Earthly Paradise*, iv) and that his wife was not well (sciatica and lumbago) and, besides, the laying out of a garden on any large scale was beyond him, nor did he know of any landscape gardener who would enter into his views.

Carlyle was seventy-five in December and as a small celebration Annie Thackeray arranged the presentation of a clock at Lady Stanley of Alderley's house in Dover Street in late February 1871. Louisa and Emily Tennyson were among the fourteen women who contributed. Alexander Munro had died the previous month;

SCHEMES AND CRISES

there had earlier been some financial discussion in which the sculptor forbade his sister to send Loo a bust 'and all the other things' until she saw Louisa's cheque, which should be in guineas, not pounds, and now at his death Loo was housing at Stanhope Street, either as her property or in his widow's name, a small nymph, a *Phryne*, and a bust of the actress Adelaide Ristori.[251] But this house was about to be given up in favour of a lease of 16 Park Lane while a contract for building the new Kent House was being prepared, and with constant visitors at Melchet and a variety of demands on her time in London, Loo's days were passed in whirlwind activity. With the Houghtons and Mrs Cowper-Temple (her Broadlands neighbour in Hampshire) she made up a party at George Eliot's house one March afternoon;[252] Rossetti was pressing her to purchase a watercolour of *Romeo and Juliet* by Madox Brown whom he considered

> one of the greatest painters now living anywhere, though the intensity of expression in his works places them beyond the appreciation of common-place people. I am truly delighted to find you so responsive to their appeal.

Loo's interest in natural science had revived and she ordered a new microscope. Professor Tyndall was rebuked for failing to come and see her, but he could see or visit nobody. He wrote:

> No doubt you are offended with me: but behold my life! Up at seven, working till half past seven and going down giddy and exhausted to my club to take my chop and claret at eight. Offended or not, I do not forget and cannot forget all your kindness to me. I am giddy *now*.

In May Carlyle and Mary were her guests in the country and Turgenev, who had arrived in England and wished to see Carlyle, was also welcome as a visitor for two days. When Loo took flight for London after his departure Carlyle remarked to his brother:

> It only increases ones freedom, with hour of dinner *certain* . . . but certainly this noble hostess excels in genial effusive kindness of heart . . . all that one could object to is laxity of purpose as to time and space, whereby much gets *jumbled* daily.[253]

Mary Aitken had proved a great favourite and Loo had demonstrated her affection by giving her a gold watch as a 'shining

SCHEMES AND CRISES 155

testimony'.[254] Regretting losing 'two days of your beloved society' Loo sped back to Carlyle at Melchet, prodigal of summer plans, but owing to her 'disrespect for the rigorous nature of Time' Carlyle and Mary missed their homeward train, but not before a summer excursion was mapped out –

> a fine little programme about going to the Island of Lewis . . . I to go with her to lodge in some aristocratic summer cottage close by solitary shore and there bathe and swim – till 10 August when above said cottage would be required again by aristocratic owner . . . I had only to assent. She overjoyed will at once go into preliminary enquiries and at an early date ('June 4' she said; but let us call it June 10 or 20th) begin executing.

Again on 28 May Carlyle wrote: 'Not seen Lady A., she is of flighty fitful habit in her appointments – this we already knew!' and the next month: 'Lady A's plans all gone to windy uncertainty';[255] but she was unrelenting in her determination and she succeeded in having him at Loch Luichart for most of the summer of 1871 though he had left before Browning's arrival on 2 October. It was probably this autumn that despite rain and snow Millais enjoyed the deer-stalking and killed four stags.[256] His wife had not accompanied him; perhaps she had not forgiven Louisa's continuing friendship with Ruskin after the annulment, though with eighteen years behind them the meeting might have prospered. Both were large women, Loo 'though stout, a commanding presence', and Effie according to Henry James, 'a very big, handsome, coarse, vulgar, jolly, easy, friendly Scotchwoman',[257] not inconsistent with Carlyle's view of Louisa: 'Just a bonnie Highland lassie, a free-spoken and open-hearted creature as ever was.'[258]

Loo was not well that winter and early spring of 1872 for besides suffering from rheumatism she had also some form of heart condition. The ubiquitous Miss Trotter was of great assistance in overseeing some few improvements at Seaforth Lodge, helping with Maysie generally, and in discharging various duties in connection with Loo's philanthropic concerns. The two women were sentimentally infatuated, but Loo, capricious in her affections as in the ordering of her life, had scampered off to Buxton with Hatty Hosmer; this evoked a spate of recriminations from Miss Trotter who charged her with cruelty and infidelity, of 'going

156 SCHEMES AND CRISES

after other loves and other caprices'. 'Oh, that I should have to pray you to remember me who have lived for you for three years,' she wrote. Loo was 'crucifying my heart', had 'put me away and said I was no use'. She had thought of Loo while singing hymns in Gloucester Cathedral,

> but why trouble about her said I, when she is where and how and with whom she most desires. I could cry; I wish I were near you but you are with your delight. Dont throw me off, it would I think almost break my heart.

Loo's response, immediate and at vast length, was an instance of her eagerness to make amends where she had wounded.

> Forgive me all the pain and misery I unwittingly have brought you, forgive me for loving you too much – and too madly –*my love* is *unalterable. Nothing* can alter my sweet memories of the Past – you who are to me a sort of Revelation; again and again forgive *me* all the pain I have brought you – my most Beloved, and adored one. I shall pour out my heart every day to you and throw it into the flames, FORGIVE me all the misery I have brought one I love better than myself. Forgive me whatever was sinful, remember whatever was sweet in those five beloved months, *to me so full of sweetness, so free from sin.* Trust my *truth* – my *loyalty* and my *constancy.* If you knew (4 in the morning) the *hours* of weeping your letter has caused me – you would pity me.

Miss Trotter dropped from Louisa's life soon after for Hatty Hosmer's star was in the ascendant and would blaze forth in their shared Roman winter. Lady Bloomfield was also a devoted slave, causing Hatty to write:

> The note from Lady Bloomfield to my sposa is quite pathetic. How many hearts has my sposa disturbed in the course of her flighty life?

Despite ill health and fractured susceptibilities, Loo was still procuring pictures for Melchet. From G. F. Watts in the new year of 1872 she asked for his *Love and Death.*

> I need not say [he wrote from Little Holland House] how much it would gratify me to think it might hang amongst the noble

SCHEMES AND CRISES

works you possess. This is one of the few pictures upon which I intend to found my claim among real artists (I am thinking of the great names of old).

He priced it at 1,500 guineas. Loo settled for a smaller version which, he was able to tell her, was 'universally preferred to the large one'. *Time and Death* had also been asked for as a pendant and both pictures were ready by the end of July, Watts inquiring at the same time whether, if Loo built Kent House, she would consider

> affording me the opportunity of painting the Titans on a grand scale. . . . Please don't think I am asking for a commission. I am only thinking about finding an opportunity of writing my name legibly in Time's book.

As a young man, having seen the Sistine Chapel, he had been fired with enthusiasm to produce, on a gigantic scale, a mural, *Chaos*, depicting figures of titanic dimensions, studies of which Louisa had seen. She was rapturous at the suggestion of Watts working in her house – though the house must needs be built first.

At Melchet on 2 August Loo suffered one of the severest blows she had yet had to face. Soon after breakfast fire was discovered on the first floor. It was impossible to bring it swiftly under control because the water-pump, on which all depended, was undergoing repairs. Three fire engines from Romsey were able to gain a supply of water from the large ornamental pond in the formal gardens and work went on to save the house until midnight. Of the large reception rooms and the principal bedrooms above them, all that remained were bare and blackened walls. The roof was cut away above the hall in the hopes of arresting the flames but the great staircase was ruined and Stevens's noble work irremediably lost. Every possible effort was made to rescue the furniture, pictures, and objets de vertu and these were soon covering space around the house, presenting a scene of wreck and confusion. Many of the paintings were cut from their frames; the conservatory was hastily stripped of its palms and ferns, which were strewed about on the ground outside. Louisa had returned from Seaton a few days previously having left Carlyle and Maysie at the seaside; suffering from shock she was carried on a sofa to the walled flower-garden some

158 SCHEMES AND CRISES

short distance from the back of the house and remained there in a state of semi-consciousness with a doctor in attendance until evening, when William Cowper-Temple, who had been directing the salvaging of the effects from the house, carried her back to Broadlands for the night. Ably supported by his pious and high-minded wife, the Hon. William Cowper-Temple, Member of Parliament and putative son of Lord Palmerston, was a man of outstanding rectitude and of great religious fervour. Before long Broadlands would be the scene of religious conferences where Mrs Cowper-Temple was venerated as High Priestess of the Quakers, Evangelists, preaching negresses, Shakers, ritualistic curates, even clairvoyantes. All were welcome, and Louisa would find common ground with such godly zealots. But now her first care was to spare Maysie any anxiety. Carlyle was immediately reassuring; her daughter's first reaction was concern for Loo's health, exclaiming that she was 'so weak, oh you don't know how weak!', but learning that her mother was safe Maysie was now 'brilliantly well'. 'A bonny little woman,' concluded Carlyle.

The destruction of a large part of the house was a major disaster but with characteristic fortitude Louisa decided to rebuild in spite of John Forster's warning of the very great outlay it would involve. This burly, cultivated, domineering man, historian, critic, and art collector, began to assume a position of influence over Louisa. Outwardly brusque of manner and dogmatic, he had a gift for friendship and counted many literary giants among his intimates, Charles Lamb, Landor, Dickens, Trollope, Landseer and Maclise, and from the first Carlyle valued his sincerity and his generous heart.

Loo's health had suffered a setback and an attack of mumps at the end of the year strengthened her resolve to go abroad. The Park Lane house had long since been given up, Melchet was uninhabitable and Kent House would not be ready till next year. Besides, there had been a grave misunderstanding àt Cheyne Row which to Louisa in her debilitated state assumed woeful proportions and made her the more eager to join Hatty in Rome. She had been to see Carlyle before leaving for Buxton when he had apparently told her that Mary Aitken, misinterpreting Loo's exaggerated manner and unremitting kindnesses and ever predisposed to perceive in her uncle's friends an irregular interest in him (prescribing this to anticipatory hopes of money or marriage), had, it seemed, let it be

SCHEMES AND CRISES

known that in Louisa she recognized a dangerous contender for matrimony.

That evening, bidding him burn it, Louisa wrote what she called 'only a little word from me to you':

> My dearly loved friend – I cannot tell you with what feelings of sorrow, and perplexity I left you today. How can it be otherwise? As far as my poor judgment on my own conduct serves me, I feel I have nothing to reproach myself with. How can I fail to revere and love you? – you who were my young enthusiasm, the prophet of my soul – (for I still recall the enchantment with which in the days of my girlhood I used to read Sartor and the french Rev under the old fir trees in the wild wood at Brahan) – you who were the chosen friend of my husband – the only person as he often told me, whose approval or disapproval were of real importance to him – and who have been my unchanging friend all these years. It grieves me to the very soul to feel that I have been so misunderstood. My only comfort is that the one who sees all ones motives as well as ones conduct and judges us through and through is the one I turn to as my judge in this bit of my life, without fear.

From Buxton she wrote again, enclosing a letter to be forwarded to Mrs Aitken, Carlyle's sister, to whom Mary had evidently reported her conclusions. Carlyle was undecided whether or not to send it deeming it wiser 'not to speak again at all on that inane and mad affair. . . . All yesterday my notion was to destroy the generous little document, and let my own mind be the only record of its creation.' Either he would send it to his brother first, or else burn it. Very disturbed by Carlyle's procrastination Loo wrote again begging that some of his family might see what she had written.

> When you are gone away and your niece still continues to hold the opinions she does of me, and will not be restrained from expressing them by fear of your displeasure, or your pain, there is no saying what harm my good name may endure.

In justice to herself she wished him to send the letter to Mrs Aitken 'as it is quite clear the poisoned tongue of calumny added to the natural inclination to believe her own child, has made your sister take a jaundiced view of the matter.' The letter was at last sent

SCHEMES AND CRISES

to Dr Carlyle urging him to deliver it at once to their sister for 'the poor Lady, much in a pucker about the non-delivery' was very anxious. 'These *incipiences* which have now grown to such a blessed *maturity*,' Carlyle groaned, while to Loo he wrote:

Dismiss wholly the anxiety I entreat you! No shadow of mendacity, or mean dishonourable malice, is in poor luckless Mary herself; only self-deception.

A year previously Mary had assured Louisa that she would always value the gold watch for Loo's sake and would often think of her uncle's friend who had given it to her. But back came the watch on 29 October with a curt note from Mary:

Madam,
I return with this the watch that I received from you. Your Ladyship lately took the trouble to send a letter to my mother, but you, knowing that it contained an untruth, that in fact the sense of it was untrue, will not be surprised that it made small impression on my mother's mind.

She knew it to be of little importance to Louisa what the opinion of the family was in regard to her

and I beg to inform you that it is a matter of the utmost indifference to them as it is to myself what you are pleased to think in regard to me and my motives.

In December, taking Maysie with her and staying for a brief time at Villa Hanbury, La Mortola, Louisa exchanged the London gloom and the hampering situation at Cheyne Row for the palliative of Roman skies and the welcoming arms of Hatty Hosmer.

15
Clutton and Nesfield Censured

Harriet Hosmer's studio in the via Quattro Fontane was said to be the most delightful in Rome. A small courtyard formed the threshold to three rooms where busts and ideal figures were aligned against the walls. Beyond was her workroom; above, the private apartments which Loo and Maysie shared with her from January 1873 until May. 'What fun we had in our little box' of a dining room, Hatty exclaimed, though had it been possible to obtain the house by the Trinità de' Monti, so eagerly desired for the following winter, they would have shared it with Lady Marian Alford, each contributing £2,000. 'It would be lovely if we could have a house conjointly. It would seem then quite hubby and wife,' Hatty thought.

'We have had a *most delightful* winter with dear Miss Hosmer,' Loo told Lord Houghton. 'We three were made to live together. She is the kindest sister to me and is a charming friend.[259] A sister relationship was not one associated with the two women. Hatty constituted herself the man – the husband –in this strangely assorted ménage that included a thirteen year-old girl who from birth had been seasoned to a delicate vagabondage, with no settled home, her mother's constant companion and martyr to her eccentricities. An association was formed between Hatty and Louisa stronger and more lasting than any of Loo's earlier female infatuations, so that Hatty could justly remark: 'I know my little sposa would do anything for her little unworthy hubby.' When apart, Hatty's letters were a combination of skilful professional manoeuvring for commissions, and expressions of fervid love.

My darling I embrace you – and whisper in your ear – you know what – and love me as I love you. . . . I am off to bed [she wrote], I wish I could take you with me. . . . What would I not do to have you in my arms to kiss you and tell you how dearly I love you.

There were the exchanges of flower petals:

CLUTTON AND NESFIELD CENSURED

You see I forestalled your wish and *did* send you one of the rose leaves full of kisses. Send it back to me. . . . Here is a verbena leaf covered with kisses both sides.

Lady Paget, wife of the British Ambassador in Rome, summed up the situation: 'Louisa Lady Ashburton . . . always lived in Miss Hosmer's house and bought her statues';[260] earlier she had commented tersely that Miss Hosmer did not 'frequent the haunts of men'.[261]

Walburga Paget, a Prussian by birth – and very highly-born by her own account – found Louisa 'most attractive and very remarkable', and though by her capriciousness she seemed immature and impossible to take seriously, Lady Paget neverthe-less was attracted by the warmth of Loo's friendliness. She thought her 'very Scotch', for 'with all her *engouement* for people and her enthusiasm for artists, a certain vein of grim matter-of-factness ran through her, and told its own story'. Swayed by the impression of the moment, Loo was necessarily dominated by someone; artists, tradespeople and adventurers thought her to be enormously rich since she spent extravagantly and generously on any newly formed whim.[262]

Louisa settled happily into the mixed society of Romans and Anglo-Americans. The Storys avoided her, but Henry James, living in the Corso that spring, made her acquaintance at a dinner given by the mother of Marion Crawford the novelist. The party was

> small and select at the request of its heroine, Lady Ashburton, who is a great swell and, I believe, makes the terms on which she is entertained. In this case . . . that she should keep us waiting exactly an hour.

But sitting beside her he found her 'very amiable and humble-minded in her talk'.[263] Emerson, the American poet and essayist and friend of Carlyle for over forty years, was also in Rome and immediately upon arrival was subjected to invitations from Louisa. 'I do most highly value the privilege of making the acquaintance of one whom I have so long revered and worshipped, with my intelligence,' she told him and engineered a meeting between him and the Duke of Sermoneta, with herself making the introduction, though in the event Hatty was obliged to 'pilot him' as Loo was unable to attend.

CLUTTON AND NESFIELD CENSURED   163

Don Michelangelo Caetani, Duke of Sermoneta, was a widower for a second time and an intrigue was set afoot (though surely without Hatty's connivance) to establish Louisa as his present Duchess.[264] Perhaps she favoured and encouraged the report as in the case of Browning – and as with Carlyle, for Lady Paget referred to Carlyle's desire to marry Loo,[265] and only Loo could have circulated such a statement given one's knowledge of the situation at Cheyne Row the previous autumn. The Duke, now completely blind at sixty- nine, was a man of high intellectual ability, a great Dante scholar, brilliant and witty in conversation, the owner of vast properties in the Pontine Marshes, and with a vacillating propensity towards marriage with the fifty-nine-year-old Miss Baby Seymour. ('It didnt take you and me so long to make up our minds' to marrying, Hatty exclaimed to Loo.)

Other acquaintances of this time included Augustus Hare, the diarist, notorious – though always welcome – as a near-professional country-house guest, a 'dapper little man with a narrow aquiline nose and rather beady penetrating eyes',[266] eyes which so impressed Carlyle that summer by their softness that he would not forget them, though the 'singular cutting tone of voice' did not go unnoticed. Hare had been very ill and Loo with her customary benevolence showered benefits upon him, but in the middle of February, when restored in health, he was to give a lecture on the Palace of the Caesars (the first of a series) to Queen Victoria's third son, Prince Arthur, then in Rome. Through the good offices of Hare and with the consent of His Royal Highness, Louisa and Maysie were to make up the party, Loo insisting upon fetching Hare to transport him to the Palatine, he strenuously opposing it, knowing her incapable of being punctual. Prince Arthur and his suite were pacing the ground when Loo and the lecturer arrived ten minutes late. 'It was a terrible beginning'[267] for Hare but his next two expeditions with Louisa were more favourable – a drive with five carriages to the Etruscan city of Veii with 'quite a banquet near the waterfall',[268] followed a week later by a picnic at Castel Fusano where the wild cyclamen carpeted the ground and daphne and rosemary grew in profusion.[269] When writing of Rome to Lord Houghton Loo could not express 'how rich I feel my memory with lovely things, and tokens, never to be forgotten'; and as to her main delight:

164 CLUTTON AND NESFIELD CENSURED

Oh! what a revelation the Campagna is! the thing of all others at Rome, the most beautiful and the most mysterious – altogether it is certainly a new life, going to that city of the great dead.[270]

She had regained her strength and by the end of May was at Perugia on her way to Marienbad in Bohemia, Hatty's letters regarding Browning's infamy and disloyalty to the Storys following her on her way. At Verona she walked in the moonlight with Sir Coutts Lindsay, that great arbiter of taste, who undertook to take charge of the decoration of Kent House. Louisa had left behind her in England a multitude of complications centring on the rebuilding of Melchet, and on her London house where Henry Clutton was suffering from the ill-advised interference of Forster whom Loo had set up to overlook and control his work. She had wanted to dismiss Clutton, probably on grounds of extravagance and, to her mind, general ineptitude, but Forster was aware of the difficulty of 'coming to open and bitter rupture with this Mr Clutton' while he was entrusted with the contracts and general arrangements at Kent House. Carlyle had written to Louisa in Rome that he noticed her new house

in Kensington Gower when I pass that way; it looks very stately and fashionable . . . but I am sorry to understand there is again internally some haggle with that arch-quack and son of Beelzebub, Architect Clutton!

At Melchet, and probably on Cowper-Temple's advice, Loo had called in W. Eden Nesfield, an architect of distinction, to rebuild what had been destroyed. She knew his work at Broadlands where he had built the Gate Lodge, and the school in Station Road at Romsey; when Chief Commissioner of Works, Cowper-Temple had given him his first commission at Kew and the Regent's Park and so felt that Louisa was in safe hands. Immediately after the Melchet fire Nesfield had made a careful report on the state of the house and was anxious to start work at once. Letters poured from his office in Argyll Street, but whereas he was of consummate amiability and genuinely good-natured (according to the artist Simeon Solomon),[271] and not without charm, he was his own master, while Clutton's task must have been a thankless one, for at Kent House John Forster was in authority, diligently writing damaging letters to Loo about him.

CLUTTON AND NESFIELD CENSURED

I should have been glad to get rid of Clutton altogether . . . [though] despite the degree of blame attributable in regard to the obstructions and hindrances, without clearer confirmation I could hardly advise you to sanction the extreme step of dismissal, even with the end so near.

Hatty too was needling Louisa with letters drawing attention to Clutton's incompetence and suggesting alternatives. Loo had commissioned pieces of statuary and sculpture from her while in Rome, two marble dogs (to be modelled from Loo's mastiffs), a *Psyche*, two large bas-reliefs, a *Hermes*, a pair of marble gates and a further chimneypiece for which Hatty sent a sketch of the frieze round the Barberini Palace, adapting it to suit a variation on the *Hours of the Night* from a fountain she had made for Lady Marian, to the *Hours Sleep*, the *Hours Wake, Aurora Veils the Stars*. Most winningly she urged Loo to let her copy in *rosso di Levante* a yellow alabaster vase in the Vatican, adding a pedestal. Louisa hesitated and Hatty suggested as a cheaper method modelling it in clay and casting it in bronze in London. Clutton weighed in believing that the whole concern was proportionately on too large a scale for the hallway at Kent House. Forster must have slapped him down for Hatty wrote derisively: 'He keeps the old Jesuit in his right place', but reckoning on Loo's impetuosity she called for prudence: 'When you havent your Hatty at your elbow you are so erratic and immeasurable that nobody can manage you; it is only conjugal authority that you acknowledge', and made a blot on the paper: 'Where I have kissed it.' The stables too enabled Hatty to proffer advice from Rome, particularly with regard to the harness room – which Forster ignored, calling attention rather to the lack of room for standing eight horses and six carriages, which had been Loo's wish. His suggestion was adopted of putting two loose boxes for hacks and six carriages on the ground floor and constructing an inclined ramp for the remaining six horses upstairs. Besides the coachman's house Loo favoured grooms' rooms but this Forster firmly rejected on the grounds of expense. Perhaps he was in an irritable mood as he was suffering from what Quain called 'undeveloped gout' which had attacked him after putting 'Lord Lytton in his last bed in Westminster Abbey – a rather superfluous operation', Carlyle thought.

The new house was an imposing building of red brick with stone

166 CLUTTON AND NESFIELD CENSURED

dressings. As originally designed the rooms for entertaining were on the first floor, allowing space if required for a study or billiard room below. By early 1873 however, with no likelihood of Browning or an alternative male joining the household permanently, the dining room was redisposed downstairs, while above three large communicating drawing rooms each over forty feet long, their double doors folding back into the thickness of the walls, led to a library and to a roof garden or conservatory – with an open view westward.[272] The dining room, once built, was then modified at the cost of £1,300, the ceiling being raised eighteen inches. A magnificent room, and Loo must have felt her trust in Sir Coutts Lindsay rewarded. Its walls – and the room repeated the length of that above – were covered with gold *repoussé* leather, surely anticipating by a year or more Jeckyll's gilt-leather dining-room walls for Leyland the shipbuilder in Prince's Gate, afterwards to suffer transformation into Whistler's celebrated Peacock Room. A high elaborate black and gold chimneypiece supported by twisted columns flaunted an apposite text: 'Eat to live and live to serve',[273] and the black polished doors of superb workmanship offered a further foil to the golden walls which by mellow candlelight proved an effective background to two of Lear's large oil paintings which came to hang there. At the windows, on the outside and covering the lower halves, were fine wooden, dark brown grilles, curved towards their base, emulating their Mediterranean counterpart.[274] The black and white marble paving of the hall led to the broad stone staircase which rose two floors beneath a glassed dome. It was on the wall of Pompeian red beside the first flight of stairs that Woolner's *Virgilia* would come to rest, though not for long.

In April 1873, shortly before Louisa had left Rome, Forster advised her that 'the Woolner piece of sculpture is not yet placed', and by August he expected Sir Coutts 'to order and if possible superintend' the placing of the work. He was not aware that Loo had been busily scheming to rid herself of what she had long considered a costly encumbrance. She had paid £2,000 for it, besides a large sum annually for its keep in a warehouse, and now fearing from what she heard that because of its immense size it would hang so low and close to the eye it could not be seen to advantage, she had determined to dispose of it. From

CLUTTON AND NESFIELD CENSURED 167

Marienbad at the end of June she asked Carlyle to find out from Woolner from her what he would wish done with it.

> For although Mr Woolner for some reasons *quite unknown* to me has lately taken to ignoring me when I have had the honour of seeing him I do not wish to behave to him in any but an honourable and ladylike manner. Would he like to take the work off my hands himself?

She added that she did not wish Mary Aitken to know of her inquiry. Carlyle found this an unwelcome proposition but devised a solution.

> From the first moment it was evident to me that there was not the faintest chance of Woolner doing anything but roughly refuse to help you in *selling* this thrice unfortunate bit of sculpture and that I never could, or must for your own honour's sake whisper of such a proposal: nay, furthermore it was distinctly evident that neither Woolner nor any other person *could* possibly sell this piece of sculpture within any comfortable length of time, but that it must keep painfully lumbering after us year after year.

He could now flatter himself 'to have shoved that miserable business into its final posture' by hitting on the idea – which he had long ago suggested to Woolner – of the sculptor making some clear indication by some ingenious inscription in Latin or the like,

> of what the real subject of it was, or what it meant to tell one – which was otherwise a total blot of darkness . . . more to be avoided altogether than *sought after* at such an expense.

He would ask Woolner to assist in choosing the best position for this 'thrice wearisome bit of sculpture' (though Carlyle believed it to be a meritorious work and the position meant for it appropriate), and

> this I have no doubt he will gladly do and take perhaps as a compliment to himself to be asked to do so. The sculpture will then be off *your* hands, out of your thoughts altogether.

This was not at all to Louisa's way of thinking. The fact was that she needed the money, perhaps to pay for Hatty's work. Perhaps, too, Hatty's feelings were to be considered – Woolner's large

168 CLUTTON AND NESFIELD CENSURED

high-relief might overshadow the *Puck*, the *Hermes*, the *Psyche*. She retorted that two or three years earlier Woolner had asked her what

> 'I would take for my bargain', to use his own expression – but I did not imagine till it was explained to me, that he meant to ask *what* I would sell him the piece of art for – so never answered the question.

She would be glad 'to be quit of a large thing that never hit my fancy'; however, she must accept the inevitable. This was a transient mood for in September 1874 the builder at Kent House submitted an account for 418 hours' additional work. This included unloading cases of marble from Salisbury (presumably sculpture was on the move from Melchet), loading and unloading marble statuary and chimneypieces, removing statuary and, finally, 'moving marble entablature on principal stairs' – the last discordant intimation of Woolner's hapless *Virgilia*. But before this occurred Louisa had already settled her account – with Woolner – in her own fashion. In the last days of 1873 she accompanied Augustus Hare on a visit to Cheyne Row and perhaps then, with his help, and under Mary Aitken's jealous eye, she cajoled Carlyle into agreeing to sit to Boehm, the prominent sculptor much favoured by the Queen, for a statuette to be cast in bronze later in the spring. (This was so successful an image that in 1882 after Carlyle's death a larger statue by Boehm, but taken from this earlier work, was unveiled on Chelsea Embankment.) At the close of this end-of-year visit to Carlyle the three left the house together and Hare thought that in his long gown and tall, broad-brimmed felt hat from Bavaria, Carlyle had the air of an old magician. His gait was slow and shuffling and as the trio walked along Cheyne Row, past the old brick houses, Louisa on one side, Hare on the other, the cab-drivers pointed and laughed at the astonishing figure, 'and indeed it was no wonder.'[275]

A new house afforded space for a greater accumulation of objects, just as large rooms meant large wall surfaces to cover and Louisa's mania for collecting needed no keener stimulus. She had not forgotten the dazzling ambition of a fresco-painted wall at Kent House and discussed it with Watts. Still eager to undertake the great work which would be in the nature of the Sistine Chapel or the Raphael Stanze, he wished to be paid only his daily

CLUTTON AND NESFIELD CENSURED   169

expenses like an Old Master, but first he must free himself of all engagements. Supposing himself to be capable of achieving 'the object of my aim in style of form and sentiment of colour, I won't fail altogether.' But the painting was never achieved though Louisa generously offered to store his pictures at a critical moment in 1875 when Little Holland House was about to be pulled down and Watts had not yet a home for his canvases. Artists and their work were never far from Loo's objective and later this year Rossetti executed a sensitive drawing of Maysie, who at fifteen required serious teaching in art. Rossetti, always anxious to do his friends a good turn, wished to promote Madox Brown's fortunes, 'for she has a real turn for art, and is generally a charming genuine creature, of the sweetest looks and temper', but unreasonable where pupils were concerned, Brown would have replied forcefully. 'I suppose I must not encourage Miss Baring if she should prove to have bent her heart on becoming your pupil', Rossetti rejoined, 'though if you only saw her you would find her irresistible.' The suggestion of Arthur Hughes was discarded as it seemed likely that failing Brown – of whose work Loo spoke enthusiastically to Rossetti – Legros, already an acquaintance, would be selected.[276]

Meanwhile difficulties at Melchet were emerging. Nesfield, who had gained Loo's entire approval at the outset, had been charged with some building at Loch Luichart as well as the development of the Addiscombe estate, staking out plots of land there, making roads, seeing to drainage, and advertising for contracts. Since Loo had now rather abandoned the place it was time to put the whole concern on a more profitable basis. Nesfield hoped the first roads to be opened would be the Bingham and Baring Roads (which still exist today). At Loch Luichart he ran into trouble concerning the transport of the much-needed bricks from a field at Culloden, and the masons and quarrymen he employed went on strike. Then Louisa disliked the new porch he had built her. At Melchet the heating apparatus was ineffective and the pumping system broke down and the desired decorative tiles were unobtainable – only such as were 'half Japanese half cockney'. Work extended to 1875 by which time Loo was charging him with dilatoriness and extravagance. Nesfield, who was building his notable Kinmel Park, Denbighshire, during these years and was often absent from London, remained buoyant though repeatedly applying for remittances to be paid him. He was 'dreadfully vexed' in having

CLUTTON AND NESFIELD CENSURED

incurred Loo's displeasure for neglect and remissness, though could she but know the labour and red tape involved she would not accuse him. Louisa dismissed him and asked him to return her letters which he agreed to 'most cheerfully'. But association seems not to have entirely ceased for in 1876 Nesfield was again in communication regarding a bargain he was making for her with the manager of the Croydon racecourse who wanted the mould excavated from the drains on the estate, for levelling the course. Nesfield thought '£50 a very fair and capital price'. Two years later financial matters were brought to a head when Nesfield was involved in a law suit owing to Loo's negligence in paying him arrears; these were defrayed but not before he felt that the publicity had had an adverse effect on his reputation.

During so many preoccupations Loo had been lax in her letters to Hatty who wrote deprecatingly from Rome: 'Now my beloved, will you not deign to send me a word of love; is this the tone I am obliged to assume after a year of marriage?' She thought it would be a consolation to Miss Trotter to know to what straits she was reduced. 'You are ever in my thoughts,' Hatty declared, 'as deep down as even a jealous lover like yourself could desire.'

A matter of perplexity to Louisa was how to convey to Carlyle that she did not wish him to show her letters to his niece. She hoped to enrol John Forster as her representative, but 'for the present at least' he replied 'I cannot reconcile myself to saying it', and Loo could only resume her unwearying kindness under a critical eye. She was enchanted with Boehm's statuette and wrote to Carlyle accordingly:

> I must thank you for allowing me to possess that beautiful work of art – and delightful likeness. The *only* thing of you that gives any just representation – it is indeed precious – and will become more and more so. Goodnight – God keep all evil from you.

She reaffirmed that to see him was her greatest happiness. There had been a moment's pause at Seaton that Easter ('You will rest your little legs at Seaton as at nowhere else,' Hatty had told her) from where Loo breathlessly informed Carlyle: 'We are revelling in the French Revolution. Here comes a bevy of visitors so goodbye ever dearly loved and revered.'

CLUTTON AND NESFIELD CENSURED 171

Early in February 1875 with Melchet nearing completion despite Nesfield's supposed idleness, Loo asked Forster to come and give his opinion on the work. 'The mountain must go to the goddess,' he wrote, 'if the goddess cannot come to the mountain', and in August, on a second visit, he was able to write in admiration to Loch Luichart:

The appetite grows by what it feeds on when it has these Rubens, Del Sarto and Poussin drawings for the Banquet, Edwin too – the Watts colour landscape. I never saw finer Reynoldses, Turners, Rembrandts and Albert Dürers.

But Louisa had not yet done; more and still more was needed for Kent House. From Rome Hatty wrote of her attempt to induce Don Marcello, a priest at the Vatican with a very valuable collection of pictures for sale, to part with a Raphael, a Murillo, and a portrait of Vittoria Colonna. Hatty herself was shipping over to Loo a *Mars*, a bust, an *Amazon*. In June, before Louisa went north, Augustus Hare returned with her to Kent House after a 'very pleasant party in the Duke of Argyll's garden' and noticed her 'semi-ruined cartoons of Paolo Veronese upon the staircase'.[277] Five days previously she had commissioned a large painting, ten feet in length, of *Mount Kinchinjunga, from Darjeeling* from Lear, whom she had found dining among the eight other guests with Lord and Lady Lyttelton on 24 June. In London from San Remo to exhibit his drawings he noted in his diary that it had been a pleasant evening, and on 25 June that Louisa had given him a commission 'for a large *Kinchinjunga*'. Within ten days he replied, pricing the picture at 700 guineas, to which Loo agreed.

Lord Northbrook, one of the executors of Lord Ashburton's will, had been appointed Viceroy of India in 1872 and had invited Lear – a friend of thirty years – to join him and make drawings which he could work up and sell at home. Lear had reached India in late 1873 and at Barrackpore at the end of that year had walked in the terraced garden and seen Lady Canning's tomb; in mid January he was looking at the Himalayas for the first time. Kinchinjunga was not, to him, 'a sympathetic mountain; it is so far off, so very God-like and stupendous' that he felt the impossibility of rendering such a mighty scene, and that it would 'make up a rather distracting and repelling whole'.[278] Two days later he responded enthusiastically: at sunrise Kinchinjunga was 'a glory not to be

172 CLUTTON AND NESFIELD CENSURED

forgotten', and in the afternoon 'a wonderful hash of Turneresque colour and mist and space'.[279] It became for him 'a sort of mountain epic, controls and absorbs every interest.'[280] With Loo's heartening commission on hand he wrote from the 'Vickeridge' at '7 Oax' in September that 'I go into HARD WORK – Louisa, Lady A's' painting . . . if Lady A's picture thrives. . . . '[281]

Meanwhile Louisa was travelling all over the country on country-house visits with Maysie as usual accompanying her. From Inveraray she told Carlyle that Princess Louise (the Queen's daughter, and wife of the Duke of Argyll's son and heir) was also there. 'I am quite bewitched by her – so much intelligence, fun, high feeling and distinction in all ways.' Loo was imbibing 'this pure, good atmosphere of cultivation and refinement'. Her whole life was spent, she said, in trying to make up to Maysie for the loss of her father, but she was sad at going south, 'away from the dear North countrie', and she must not venture to think of Skye or Lewis, 'both of which are holding out their hands temptingly'. They were on their way to Ford Castle in Northumberland to stay with Louisa Lady Waterford, also a widow, but childless and very devout, beautiful, distinguished, and a gifted artist, though, according to a friend who was staying there 'quite devoid of courage and treads the path of conventionality and respectability and is rather excited for Royalty in the shape of those insipid Christians [Prince and Princess] are coming over from Floors'. Lady Waterford found Loo and Maysie 'both very pleasant', so she told Hare. Maysie, 'a charming girl – magnificent, gentle, unspoiled, clever, and delightful', and with perhaps a shade more reticence: 'Lady A also interests me very much.'[282] Possibly Louisa had arrived with her Highland gillie in place of a lady's maid – a favourite foible in which she indulged. (She was reported to have once bade him enter her room backwards as she was not fully dressed and placing a hipbath directly in his way watched him splash into the water.)[283] Pausing on their way south at Castle Ashby, the home of the Northamptons where no doubt they found Lady Marian, Louisa and Maysie spent a few weeks at Seaton, preparing themselves for what was becoming the most fashionable trip abroad that a wealthy person could take.

16

The Last Adventure

Heading her letter 'On the Nile. Decr. 25th 1875', Loo told Carlyle that at Cairo she had been swindled out of £600 by the iniquity of a 'sort of gentleman courier' but that they had a delightful boat, their doctor was a 'pleasant gentlemanly addition' and their dragoman, known as 'Hippopotamus Johnnie', was the man who had brought the first hippopotamus to London which had created such a stir in 1850. Whereas seventeen years ago Loo had recognized the fascination of this 'cradle of humanity', 'how *much more* I delight in it now.' While closing her letter by committing Carlyle – 'as always' – to God, she added her gratitude to him for gaining her Forster's friendship. But this was to be sadly ruptured and mourned for in her next letter. 'Beloved friend,' she wrote from Denderah on 27 February 1876, 'we are brothers in sorrow having both lost what we never more can find again.' She grieved with Carlyle in the death of 'dear beloved Mr Forster', 'this blessed sign that God sent me is taken away – and I must resume my journey again *alone*.' Hatty might have been sceptical of this last fanciful sentiment but Loo wrote with the warmth of her heart; her friendships were true and deep, while they lasted. But Hatty and the happiness of their 'married life' were awaiting her in Rome, with plans for further handiwork for Kent House. Hatty was sending over one of her men with a plaster cast to be set up for a competition, and after Loo had left for England she wrote careful instructions of how to souse the principal figure in tea to give it the colour of wax. It had been damaged in her studio but Loo was to say 'injured in transmission'.

News of John Tyndall's marriage to Louisa, daughter of Lord Claud Hamilton, an old friend, had caught up with Loo abroad. Carlyle had attended the wedding in Westminster Abbey and contrary to expectation had found it 'very grand

174 THE LAST ADVENTURE

and solemn. . . . Lord Claud himself who gave her away was almost at the crying.' Loo thought that in his marriage Tyndall was

> uniting all that dear vain creature could desire, youth, connection and continual worship. Oh! how nice and how sweet it must make Earth appear to him – radiant with prismatic light.

Hearing that Loo was in Rome Edward Lear wrote trusting she might come along the 'Cornice' from Genoa and stop at San Remo 'for a twinkling' on her way home that he might show what he had so far accomplished on the *Kinchinjunga* canvas. If he held out hopes of some payment in advance he had to be content with a letter from Florence telling him that until the Himalayan picture was completed she would hang the *Cedars* in its place at Kent House. He thought she would not object to having the text 'The Lord Breaketh the Cedars of Lebanon' removed from the frame for it was 'so injudiciously divided as to be a mistake', and were there any difference in the light at the two ends of the room he desired she might give the *Cedars* the darker wall. Louisa had been on a friendly footing with Story since the previous year; now in Rome she requested a *Sibyl* and an *Alcestes* but when in 1877 Story wrote that the former was far advanced and the *Alcestes* completely ready and that the pedestals of grey-veined Ravaccione marble cost £200 each, and might he now have payment in full, he met with some captiousness, but pressed home his advantage. When finished, he told her, the statues were absolutely her own property and the risk became hers as clearly stated in the contract, and should he now forward them to London? The cost of the pedestals at which Loo demurred was only what the workmen charged – dearer in England and he was only trying to help her. Finally in August one figure was already on its way, the other ready to depart. 'I was sorry to gather from an expression in your last letter a shadow of feeling that was not quite pleasant,' he said. He was sorry, too, to be obliged to mention payment but he required the money for his journey to America.

Another appeal for money came to her from Noel Paton, George Square, Edinburgh, who felt he was 'projecting a rocket wildly into space', not knowing where she might be. Dr John

THE LAST ADVENTURE

Brown was a victim for a second time to the sad malady in which his mind was 'overclouded'. A sum of not less than £5,000 was being raised to ensure that he would be relieved from anxiety in the future.

Hatty was at Melchet this summer; in September Lady Paget, 'succumbing to Lady Ashburton's blandishments', was a guest at Loch Luichart and left a record[284] of physical discomfort and of conduct so egregiously fanciful on the part of the hostess that, though criticized by her friends, it yet shows Loo in her fiftieth year as spirited as in her youth and still as arrogantly inconsiderate. This was a trait more apparent in the Highlands where there still existed a feudal respect for the Clan Mackenzie of which she was an honoured representative, still owning great tracts of land, caring in a rather random though devoted manner for her people, and looked on in her own country as having 'an hereditry vein of heroic blood in her'.[285]

On this occasion Walburga Paget, with her children, had travelled all night but was unable to take possession of her room at Loch Luichart till midday, its occupancy being disputed, and once established there was no certainty that Loo would not 'make hay' of the bedrooms, allocating them to new arrivals. The unreliability of the dinner hour was also a considerable vexation, as it had been to Carlyle. Lady Paget, with the good manners that characterized her behaviour (and which she never failed to emphasize), readily overlooked these shortcomings but she was sorely tried on the day before departure when the house-party was to go over to Arthur Balfour's (the twenty-eight-year-old Member for Hertford), seven miles distant, to watch Highland games preceded by an early lunch. It was not until the afternoon that Louisa marshalled her famished guests and set out under a menacingly storm-laden sky through treeless bog-land, arriving in a drizzle to find the games over and nothing but a few cold scraps remaining from luncheon. Hearing that there was a gillie ball that evening Louisa suddenly elected to stay the night and, to the dismay of Balfour's sister who had no beds for so large a party, declared herself too weary to move. This was as distasteful to Lady Paget as it had been unforeseen: 'What! without even a toothbrush?' With an early train to catch on the morrow she hoisted herself and children on to ponies and accompanied by a gillie braved the bogs and the

176 THE LAST ADVENTURE

silence, the oncoming dark and the loneliness of the hills. Louisa returned in the middle of the night with her party.

A recollection of distant anguish may have stirred Loo when she learned in March 1877 of the remarriage (following the two-year interval since his wife's death) of the man she had loved and sighed for in her youth. Caroline Norton was free at last to crown their long romance with matrimony, but its fulfilment was short-lived; within four months she was dead and William Stirling-Maxwell followed her soon after. There was no one left with whom Loo could recall her youth or speak to of that far-off love, and despair. But there were new friends, and new causes to foster. Her charitable designs were expanding and would before very long take first place in her expenditure. But not yet. There were three Turner watercolours to purchase at Christie's and besides Lear's *Kinchinjunga* – now completed – she had bought his *Philae, Crag that Fronts the Even* – an illustration to Tennyson's poem 'Eleanore', the landscape depicting Kasr Es Saad, on the Nile – and *Mount Tomohrit*, 'begun and toiled at in 1849 and I went to Harting near Petersfield to study the Beach trees in Upark'.[286] The picture was laid by for years in the Pantechnicon and worked upon from 1870 onwards at San Remo. *Kinchinjunga* was shown in Lear's rooms in Duchess Street in June and was much commended. At midday on 11 June he walked across Hyde Park to Kent House and saw Louisa.[287]

> She was profuse in apologies and said she had written (N.B. No letter *came*) but had forgotten my Bankers: Later she owned all had escaped her memory. She made a difficulty about paying now – having no money – but at length, seeing I was seriously bent on tin – she wrote a note to her Agent (Morgan's) begging him to pay £500 into Drummonds – afterwards she added £30 for the Philae.

She composed a memorandum of what she still owed for the four paintings, and '(I think) arranged to pay remaining 1000£ in next August. Truly wonderful female!' On the 13th, a sketch in his diary of the seating at table recorded dining with Louisa where he sat on her left while Hare acted host opposite Loo, Maysie on his left. 'Very very pleasant evening and nice dinner' with 'no end of pleasant converse' and 'cab home by 12'. Two days later on applying to his bank Lear found 'Lady A had really paid the £500

THE LAST ADVENTURE 177

for the Tomohrit'. At Christmas that year he wrote to Maysie from San Remo begging her to accept two small Nile drawings and hang them in some space of unfilled wall and keep them 'as a remembrance of the Artist's recognition of her Mother's help'. He knew Loo had liked them 'but she would not let me give them to her as she was so vexed about not being able to pay for her pictures at the time she intended to do so.' He only regretted that his pictures 'were the cause of any annoyance'. When he saw his paintings again, shown off to perfection in the dining room of Kent House he was delighted.

> I saw my 'Crag that fronts the even' let into the wall in a vast black frame all the room being gilt leather. Never saw anything so fine of my own doing before and walked ever afterwards with a nelevated and superb deportment and a sweet smile on everyone I met.[288]

Carlyle was not forgotten though he was feeble now and rarely came to Kent House. Loo still sought to distract him. In June she offered to take him to Grosvenor House, lent by the Duke of Westminster for the occasion, to witness a representation of passages from the second part of *Pilgrim's Progress* in aid of funds for an orphanage at Ham Common, acted by George MacDonald (poet and novelist, whose work often mystical in character was much admired), his wife, their twelve children and two adopted. The audience was moved and 'cried most sympathetically'.[289] Later in the summer Hatty was at Melchet and was still there in November when Louisa Waterford made a day's expedition from her own house on the Hampshire coast. It was a day full of incident. Her drive through the New Forest was a delight with 'droves of lovely *black* pigs – fat yet slender, giving a sort of wild boar' medieval character to the forest. Besides Hatty and her hostess she found Louisa Baring and a spinster of exceeding piety whom she hoped to capture to come and address some navvies. They drove over to friends to admire their pictures and from there to the rector of Romsey whose invention of collapsing boats fired their interest, and then to Broadlands. Stimulated by this dissimilarity to her usual well-regulated life it seemed to Lady Waterford on her return home as if she had been away a month.[290]

178   THE LAST ADVENTURE

Broadlands was near enough to Melchet for Loo to descend
unheralded and often unsought. Mrs Cowper-Temple, whose
gentle patience was highly tested, spoke of Louisa as 'dashing
down upon us – dear woman at all sorts of unexpected times',
alone or with a host of people; 'her brain is so excitable.'[291]
Augustus Hare was often Loo's companion; in tendencies they
were perhaps well suited. Together they drove to Woburn after
Christmas, lunching in the Canaletto Room and looking at the
church close by in a field (now the village) where Clutton had been
turned loose and told 'to produce what he could. He *did* produce a
very poor mongrel building, neither gothic nor romanesque,[292]
Hare observed testily. In January he dined at Kent House and
found Hatty there; her two designs for fountains, *The Dolphin* and
The Mermaid's Cradle were in place in the formal gardens at
Melchet; Loo was suggesting renting a London studio for her.
Hatty would postpone for a few weeks a spring crossing to the
United States: 'This will enable us to do a Laocooning even more,'
she wrote. 'I will fancy when you get this that we have already
begun laocooning and my arms around you.'

In Devonshire the month of May (1878) was of particular
beauty and Hare who had been invited to Seaforth Lodge found it
'an enchanting little paradise'[293] with walks through miniature
groves of tamarisk and ilex, and roses blooming in the blue haze
of an early summer's day. True to custom, his 'erratic hostess'
was not there to welcome him, having taken herself to Torquay
for two days, but the day after her return an early morning train
brought them to Yeovil where orchards were full of blossom and
Montacute in prospect.

Maysie was eighteen now and out in society – 'the only child of
an *exigeante* mother,' it was said.[294] With Loo she concerned
herself with charitable work and read to patients at St George's
Hospital in the Ratcliffe Ward. She was still receiving instruction
in drawing; the previous year John Varley had offered her the use
of his studio in Thistle Grove, now that it was tidy, where she could
copy his drawings. Legros, director of the Slade School of Art, had
been asked whether he would take her as a pupil but with a full
complement of students he could only give her limited help in his
own studio once a week. He took the opportunity of forwarding
his copy of a Giorgione made for Loo many years ago – and
presumably never paid for. Louisa was in a severe financial

THE LAST ADVENTURE 179

position, still spending extravagantly, as much on others as on herself, sending frantic messages to Mr Waterhouse her man of business. A solicitor, he was in frequent attendance at Kent House and dealt with accounts, paid the servants and wrote her business letters. 'Not a penny at Drummonds' and I daily expect that they will refuse to honour my cheques – tell me what I am to do?' she cried. But this in no way crippled her entertaining for Maysie on a large scale. Balls and dinners included a very grand one in the summer of 1879 for the Hereditary Grand Duke of Baden and the Prince Royal of Sweden and Norway at which Hare committed a solecism which must have tried him sorely though he passed it off in his memoirs with urbane complacency.[295] For an evening concert the well-known contralto Antoinette Sterling (not unlike Louisa in feature) would charge twenty-five guineas. Her repertoire consisted chiefly of religious and moralizing ballads (Sullivan's 'Lost Chord' being a great favourite) which were probably sung at Kent House, or at Melchet where Loo, in an abundance of prodigality, would gather a houseful of pious zealots and refresh them with singers and evangelists.

Maysie was not short of admirers, of whom one was said to be Arthur Balfour. More than an 'understanding' existed between her and Prince Leopold, the Queen's invalid son, a match that had probably been forwarded by Princess Louise to whom he was much attached. Judging from the Queen's letter to Louisa the Prince's affection was not fully reciprocated.

Windsor Castle

May 8th 1880. . . . How *entirely* I agree as a *Mother* and can enter into your feelings about your beloved Child. I know too well what it is to part with a daughter and what a wrench it must ever be. I also have felt that my dear Child's health would be an anxiety and a great difficulty. I still believe he *is* much better in *most* ways. . . . I however entirely agree in the advisability of delay . . . he is much devoted to your dear daughter. Leopold is willing to accede to your request. There is one point which I think however *due* to him and which I hope *you* and your daughter will agree to. It is, that while she (as well as he) are to be considered free – that I do not think she *ought* to allow any one to make advances to her *till* Leopold has returned from Canada. If after she sees him again, and *after* having seen others

THE LAST ADVENTURE

(irrespective of his health and supposing he returns well) she does *not* care for him sufficiently to accept him, then of course she is entirely free to accept anyone else.

In begging for delay to a decisive reply to the proposal of marriage, Louisa was probably activated by fears for the Prince's health, and though he had considerable intellect Court life was not one into which Maysie had ever ventured.

Carlyle's life was nearing its end. On one of Louisa's last visits she had borrowed a book and wrote to thank him:

I have the book – and thank you with all my heart. It was a treat to me seeing you again – but I wish I never lost you.

Yours with a sweet Goodnight

He died on 4 February 1881; in a codicil to his will he had left her the large oil painting *The Little Drummer* (a copy from the original) depicting Frederick II as a child, with his sister. This had been a present to Jane from Lord Ashburton many years earlier and Carlyle was here returning it in recognition of her affection and unvarying kindness to him for so many years. He had, however, by his friendship bestowed a greater gift, for without it her name might scarcely have survived oblivion. In April Loo's letters to Carlyle had probably been returned to her by Froude; she had hoped to see him, but writing from 5 Onslow Gardens on 21 April he spoke of being

entirely drowned in Carlyle papers; weeks ago I was up to the neck in them, and now they are flowing over my head, and only by desperately sticking to the work can I hope to escape suffocation.

In June he had come across two further letters which he enclosed observing that 'there must not be so much as a chance' of their falling into the niece's hands.

Loo travelled abroad less, but her energy sustained her for some years still. In London Mary Gladstone observed her at the Burne-Joneses' house 'panting enthusiastically', with Ruskin ('quite mad') for company, and Burne-Jones 'flitting like a ghost in and out'; and the next year again she was 'thrilling a good deal' at a dinner party.[296]

A new adventure brightened the summer of 1882. Although

THE LAST ADVENTURE
181

she had not seen him lately Loo grieved for Rossetti's death in the spring and begged his assistant, Treffry Dunn, to buy a Chinese vase for her at the Cheyne Walk sale as a memento of the painter. There had also been a worrying affair in which Loo had bought three pictures at the Conduit Street exhibition in April for 700 guineas, with a promise to pay at midsummer. Money was not forthcoming and she claimed that the 'sham' Turner and Old Crome must be returned. This led to a threat of litigation, so that active plans for a yachting cruise were a welcome diversion. *Titania*, of 306 tons, was chosen, commended by Lord Ducie as 'a likely vessel – good steam power, good coal carrying capacity. Price £420 per month (lunar)'. An agent in Glasgow supplied an estimate of victualling ('to be of a superior class') for ten persons for two months at ten shillings and sixpence a head per day, admitting of tea, coffee and cocoa with cream, toast and biscuit from six to seven in the morning; at breakfast, fish, ham and eggs, Irish stew, lamb or mutton cutlets, tea, coffee, jams and toast; for luncheon, cold meats would be supplied, sardines, Stilton, Gorgonzola and Roquefort cheese, and Irish butter; for dinner, soup, fish, two entrées, three joints, vegetables, entremets, dessert and coffee; for supper '(if necessary)', cold meats. The hire of a first-class chef nine pounds per month and an experienced steward at seven. Wine was not included but whisky, in a blend of 'Long John' and 'Ardbeg', could be had at twenty-three shillings per Imperial gallon. With Captain Bond at the helm (already inquiring for cash and board wages for officers and steward) *Titania* sailed from Southampton on 24 June with Greenock as her destination where she would pick up the sailing party and a piano and head for the Lews. Louisa had always felt an irresistible attraction for the sea, connecting it with her birth on the Western Isles. Sometimes she claimed that her birthplace was the source of her having been named Louisa, and after Lewis was sold by her parents she maintained a deeply rooted attachment for what she felt should have been her own inheritance. On a later visit to Stornoway she was greeted with fireworks and demonstrations of loyalty as befitted the last representative of an old and revered family.

In 1884 Maysie's marriage to Lord William Compton, later fifth Marquess of Northampton, and nephew of Lady Marian Alford, was a blending of happiness and pain for Louisa. 'My Beloved's wedding. May all best blessings rest on her sweet life,' Loo wrote

THE LAST ADVENTURE

on her own order of service. The loosening of ties with a loved daughter and constant companion was compensated by the forging of so strong a link with a family Loo had long known; and with Castle Ashby she was well acquainted. Louisa herself gave the bride away at St Margaret's, Westminster on 30 April when Archdeacon Eric Farrar gave the blessing and Gladstone and Lord Northbrook were among those who signed the register. Following the wedding breakfast at Kent House the married couple went for their honeymoon to Compton Wynyates, a second Northampton property.

After her daughter's marriage Loo's philanthropic activities redoubled and engaged most of her time and money. Her friendship with Florence Nightingale sustained a second flowering and in the spring of 1880 she put Seaforth Lodge at Florence's disposal ('which your kindness has made so doubly dear,' Florence wrote), giving strict instructions that she was not to be disturbed. She then went there herself from Melchet and enjoyed 'the deep joy of communion with my beloved'.[297] But in London it was a friendship by proxy of letters only as Florence refused even her closest friends to her tower room in South Street where she laboured unceasingly.

I wish [wrote Loo] that you would let me sit like a poor rat in the corner, while you are at dinner; it is much wholesomer not to eat in solitude.

And when she had received Florence's blessing on the charitable work in hand she replied with gratitude:

I am humbled in the dust when I think of what you say to me – poor wretched, profitableless me, and yourself the guiding-star to so many of our lives.[298]

All the enthusiasm that had gone to the building of houses and buying of art treasures was now lavished on the afflicted; the love and urge to help her fellow men found an outlet in charitable causes of which the Mission to Seamen in Victoria Dock Road, Canning Town played the greatest part. There, from a row of cottages and shops she constructed the Ashburton Home of Rest with a coffee tavern and mission hall, herself conducting services, carrying on the work of evangelization, the fervour with which she spoke in her clear musical voice winning many to her side. She would drive

THE LAST ADVENTURE 183

down to the docks every day and if, as often happened, she returned late for her own dinner-party at Kent House, 'she was always held excused because of her good works. For the Cause she was prepared to make any sacrifice.' The money she gave for fishermen's buildings at Yarmouth indicated perhaps again her love for the sea; she subscribed to the Metropolitan Tabernacle at Newington, to the Tower Hamlets Mission where Edward Clifford, artist and friend, was in charge, to Joseph Fry's Metropolitan Drinking Fountain and Cattle Trough Association, Holy Trinity Mission Fund, Bethnal Green, and numerous others besides, and she laid the foundation stone of the Shaftesbury Memorial Hall at Poplar. She also undertook to purchase the Utambanyama coffee plantation in Nyassa, British Central Africa, to be developed as an industrial mission station and agreed to provide funds for a year until the first annual coffee crop was realized.

Closer home and of great interest was the trust formed to administer three homes at Addiscombe, the 'Rest' and the 'Dovecote' for adults, and one, the 'Nest', to be devoted to children. The Temperance cause at Romsey was given a strong impetus when Loo presided 'with much dignity and sweetness'. Previously a Canon Barker had delighted his audience with his address, though it was thought 'he condescended a little too much and unnecessarily to the level of their language for our taste'. Canon Wilberforce had also given a powerful and eloquent speech, but Louisa was the 'moving spring'. She paid for the care of two orphan children Cecile and Flossie at a home, first at Hornsey where 'the keen air on the hill was not favourable for Flossie' who had a wonderful gift for singing, and then at a cottage with a view 'sweetly picturesque' behind the Alexandra Palace. When money for two quarters did not materialize, 'Kindly send a cheque' followed, and thereafter nothing further is heard of these two waifs.

In spite of this all-engrossing work – and in 1881 Florence wrote of Loo at Marienbad distributing 'Bibles and Tracts in Czech-ish'[299] – Loo welcomed old and new friends as enthusiastically as ever she had done. Tennyson hoped to propose himself for the day; Marie Corelli wished not to lose sight of her; Lord Tankerville thought of her 'and all your heartiness which is so refreshing in our commonplace plodding thro' the world'.

THE LAST ADVENTURE

Augustus Hare was still dining – 'a quiet party, with all the beautiful Kent House pictures lighted up. Mr Henschel whistled like a bull finch after dinner.'[300] She was always prepared to lend her pictures for exhibitions at the Royal Academy, Grosvenor Gallery, New Gallery, and she was still adding to her collections, if on a more moderate scale, though it is startling to find Boehm quoting her 300 guineas for a marble bust in 1889. Earlier she had inquired of him a plaster cast of General Gordon, 'without that stupid Fez which he hated,' Boehm told her, 'and *never wore* but once'; while from Alfred Gilbert she asked for a small copy of his bust of G. F. Watts. Kate Greenaway had sent her drawings to look over as desired; Paton had suggested his *Dream of Latmos*, and C. E. Hallé, the artist, wrote twice for the balance of £50 on a portrait of Maysie.

Domestic and financial cares figure largely in the 1890s. Loo's niece Annie, who had run errands for her in the past, was active again, crossing and recrossing London in all weathers to serve her aunt, sending 'books and tracts for sailors but it came on to rain', looking out her red flannel petticoats, attending to Loo's hopelessly involved tax returns from which the Surveyor at Westminster, a newly appointed 'civil man', failed to discover why no return had been made for two years nor why it had risen from £16 to £2,000. 'I find you have nothing to pay, *really*,' Annie concluded ingenuously. A groom was required and a John Pygroves applied with a reference confirming him as 'genuine case of conversion to God and a pledged abstainer'. He was anxious to get among Christians. Another could recommend a cook, who though 'inclined to be rough and coarse in her entrées' was honest and obliging and 'about as economical as most professed cooks are'. When a footman was needed for hall duty Loo applied to the Barracks of the Corps of the Commissionaires and a guardsman with twelve years' service in the 2nd Life Guards was sent to be interviewed. A Mr Marshall of Bell Street, Romsey, was 'again oblidged to ask your Ladyship' for a cheque for £43 and she could not be aware of the inconvenience he was put to – 'being quite a young beginner in business trusting I shall receive it per-return.'

Mr Waterhouse spent many hours at Kent House – seven on one occasion – in an attempt to unravel Loo's labyrinthine transactions. She had paid twice a cheque of over £100 to the YMCA; Belgravia Dairies were pressing for a £50 account outstanding; she

THE LAST ADVENTURE 185

had insured several pictures twice over with two different companies. Finally, his despairing cry: 'The case at the docks you wrote me about contains an Indian cabinet – not orchids – Is it intended for you?'

Poor health in 1894 brought a message of affection from Florence Nightingale who 'trusted in God that He will raise you up again soon – dearest child of God. Ever in His name your loving F.N.' Activity was still the essence of Loo's life and in 1898 another journey to Egypt was in prospect. Thirty-nine years ago her marriage had led her there with an ailing husband and now it was she who was being cautioned by Florence not to 'run any risks till you go off to Cairo – dear Cairo'.

The new century brought its death-blow in a double sense. Maysie the adored, the loving, the only child, now wife and mother, had been an invalid for some time before death claimed her in the summer of 1902, an annihilation so crushing that Louisa could not recover. Her own health too was failing; she knew she was suffering from cancer of the breast which she gallantly referred to as 'a very fashionable trouble'. Once she had written to Carlyle: 'Oh! how nice to know one is *so* insignificant, nobody will want to write my life and cut me up for inspection when I am gone', yet she had kept the mass of letters written to her since young womanhood. Froude had returned to her the dual correspondence with Carlyle, some from Browning she had destroyed; other letters she might have allowed to perish. Had she had some thought that perhaps among her friends someone might write an account of her as Lord Houghton had done of Harriet Ashburton, or did she follow simply the common practice of the day in keeping her letters, the garner of a not unadventurous life?

Her finances were in chaos. Once a vast fortune, it had now been dissipated. Insolvent at death, the main portion of her valuables and Melchet and Kent House would be sold to pay legacies and creditors. Lear's great Indian picture would go for seven pounds, the *Crag* for five, his *Cedars* for twelve guineas, and Woolner's *Virgilia* which had cost her £2,000 and much irritation was bought for £8.18s.6d. Where by her wealth and possessions she had thought to demonstrate her affection for her three grandchildren – most particularly dear since their mother's death – her wild extravagance vitiated her intention; and from

THE LAST ADVENTURE

the younger boy, most loved of the three, on whom Loo wished to lavish the greatest part, the holocaust of battle would exact its savage due.

With her daughter's death the flame burned low and sank. Louisa died at Kent House in the early morning of 2 February 1903 within four weeks of her seventy-sixth birthday. At St Paul's, Onslow Square, a church strongly Evangelical in character where she had worshipped for many years, a memorial service was held simultaneously with her funeral in Scotland. She had not chosen to sleep in Fortrose Cathedral with her kin whose monuments crowd the wall, but in Highland soil on her own land in the embrace of her church and its small burial enclosure.

If in Louisa was reflected her mother's 'almost lawless spirit of adventure',[301] then surely, at the close of the glen at the foot of rising hills, where the wind sweeps and storm clouds mass, and as so often in her life of contradictions the dark gives place in turn to light, so ardent a spirit would not linger in her massive tomb, free now for some new adventure or some timeless quest, or to make a haven of her lost inheritance, the sea-girt Western Isles.

Bibliography and Notes

Bibliography

All books are published in London unless otherwise stated

Airlie, Mabell, Countess of, *Lady Palmerston and Her Times*, i, 1922.
Allingham, Helen, and Williams, B. E., edd., *Letters to William Allingham*, 1911.
Barrington, Mrs Russell, *Life, Letters and Work of Frederic Leighton*, ii, 1906.
Bloomfield, Baroness, *Reminiscences of Diplomatic Life*, ii, 1883.
Bornand, Odette, ed., *The Diary of W. M. Rossetti, 1870–73*, Oxford, 1977.
Boucourechliev, André, *Chopin, A Pictorial Biography*, 1963.
Brookfield, A. M., *Annals of a Chequered Life*, 1930.
Brookfield, Charles and Frances, *Mrs Brookfield and Her Circle*, ii, 1906.
Browning, Oscar, *Memories of Sixty Years*, 1910.
Carlyle, Alexander, ed., *New Letters of Thomas Carlyle*, ii, 1894.
Carr, Cornelia, *Harriet Hosmer, Letters and Memories*, 1913.
Chanler, Mrs W., *Roman Spring*, Boston, 1934.
Chapple, J. A. V., and Pollard, A., edd., *The Letters of Mrs Gaskell*, Manchester, 1966.
Colebrook, Sir T. E., Bt., *The Life of the Hon. Mountstuart Elphinstone*, i, 1884.
Collier, Hon. E. C. F., ed., *Victorian Diarist, Lady Monkswell*, i, 1944.
Cook, Sir Edward, *Florence Nightingale*, i, ii, 1913.
Corkran, Henriette, *Celebrities and I*, 1902.
Donnachie, Ian, and Macleod, Innes, *Old Galloway*, Newton Abbot, 1974.
Doughty, Oswald, and Wahl, J. R., edd., *Letters of Dante Gabriel Rossetti*, ii, iii, Oxford, 1965, 1967.
Edel, Leon, ed., *Henry James Letters*, i, ii, 1974, 1975.
Elliot, F., *Roman Gossip*, 1896.
Foss, Arthur, *The Ionian Islands*, 1969.
Froude, J. A., *Thomas Carlyle: A History of His Life in London*, ii, 1890.
Grierson, H. J. C., ed., *Letters of Sir Walter Scott*, ii, iii, iv, 1932, 1934.
Gunn, Peter, *Vernon Lee*, Oxford, 1964.
Haight, Gordon S., *George Eliot*, Oxford, 1968.
Hanson, Laurence and Elizabeth, *Necessary Evil*, 1952.

190 BIBLIOGRAPHY

Hardman, W., and Ellis, S. M., *Mid-Victorian Pepys*, 1923.

Hare, Augustus, *The Story of My Life*, iv, v, vi, 1900.

Hare, Augustus, *The Story of Two Noble Lives*, iii, 1893.

Hawthorne, Nathaniel, *Passages from the French and Italian Note-Books*, i, ii, 1871.

Hill, G. Birkbeck, ed., *Letters of Dante Gabriel Rossetti to William Allingham, 1854-70*, 1897.

Horsman, E. A., ed., *The Diary of Alfred Domett, 1872–1885*, 1953.

Hudson, G. R., ed., *Browning to his American Friends*, 1965.

James, Henry, *William Wetmore Story*, i, ii, 1903.

Kenyon, F. G., ed., *Letters of Elizabeth Barrett Browning*, ii, 1897.

Lang, Cecil Y., *The Swinburne Letters*, ii, Yale, New Haven, 1959.

Leach, J., *Bright Particular Star*, Yale, New Haven, 1970.

Lear, Edward, Diaries.

Lennie, Campbell, *Landseer*, 1976.

Liddell, A. G. C., *Notes from the Life of an Ordinary Mortal*, 1911.

McAleer, Edward C., *Dearest Isa: Robert Browning's Letters to Isabella Blagden*, Austin, Texas, 1951.

Mackenzie, Alexander, *The History of the Mackenzies*, Inverness, 1894.

Mackenzie, Alexander, *The Prophecies of the Brahan Seer*, Inverness, 1875.

Masterman, Lucy, ed., *Mary Gladstone (Mrs Drew): Her Diaries and Letters*, 1930.

Matthew, H. C. G., ed., *The Gladstone Diaries*, v, vi, Oxford, 1978.

Millais, J. G., *The Life and Letters of Sir John Everett Millais*, ii, 1899.

Miller, Betty, *Robert Browning, A Portrait*, 1952.

Milnes, R. Monckton, *Monographs: Personal and Social*, 1873.

Mitford, Hon. Nancy, *The Stanleys of Alderley*, 1939.

Mitford, Hon. Nancy, *The Ladies of Alderley*, 1967.

Morris, May, ed., *The Collected Works of William Morris*, i, 1910.

Murphy, Ray, ed., *Edward Lear's Indian Journal*, 1953.

Noble, Sir Humphrey, Bt., *Life in a Noble House*, 1967.

Noakes, Vivien, *Edward Lear, The Life of a Wanderer*, 1968.

Oman, Carola, *The Wizard of the North*, 1973.

Orr, Mrs Sutherland, *The Life and Letters of Robert Browning*, 2nd ed., 1891.

Paget, Walburga, Lady, *Embassies of Other Days*, i, 1923.

Paget, Walburga, Lady, *The Linings of Life*, i, 1928.

Partington, Wilfred, ed., *Sir Walter's Post-Bag*, 1932.

Pope-Hennessy, James, *The Years of Promise*, 1949.

Pope-Hennessy, James, *The Flight of Youth*, 1951.

Pollock, Sir Frederick, Bt., *Personal Remembrances*, ii, 1887.

BIBLIOGRAPHY   191

Pym, H. N., ed., *Caroline Fox: Memories of Old Friends*, ii, 1882.

Roth, Cecil, *A History of the Jews in England*, 3rd ed., Oxford, 1964.

Russell, Bertrand and Patricia, edd., *The Amberley Papers*, i, 1937.

Russell, G. W. E., *Portraits of the Seventies*, 1916.

St Helier, Lady, *Memories of Fifty Years*, 1909.

Sanders, Charles Richard, and Fielding, Kenneth J., edd., *The Collected Letters of Thomas and Jane Welsh Carlyle*, v, Duke, Durham, N. C., 1977.

Smalley, G. W., *London Letters*, i, 1890.

S.P.C.K., *Dr Lee of Lambeth*, 1851.

Strachey, Lady, ed., *The Later Years of Edward Lear*, 1911.

Stirling-Maxwell, Sir William, Bt., *Diaries*.

Surtees, Virginia, ed., *Reflections of a Friendship*, 1979.

Teignmouth, Lord, *Reminiscences of Many Years*, i, Edinburgh, 1878.

Wagner, Sir Anthony, *English Genealogy*, Oxford, 1960.

Ward, Maisie, *Robert Browning and His World*, ii, 1969.

West, Sir Algernon, *Recollections*, i, 1869.

Wilson, D. A., *Carlyle to Threescore-and-Ten (1853–65)*, 1929.

Wilson, D. A., and MacArthur, D. W., edd., *Carlyle in Old Age (1865–81)*, 1934.

Notes

N.L.S. The National Library of Scotland
P.T.P. Pauline Trevelyan Papers
T.P. Trevelyan Papers

1 J. A. Froude, *Thomas Carlyle: A History of His Life in London*, 126.
2 Sir W. Stirling-Maxwell, Diaries.
3 C. Carr, *Harriet Hosmer, Letters and Memories*, 97.
4 Sometimes given erroneously as May.
5 Elevation and plans at the Soane Museum. Information regarding Glasserton given me by Mr Ian Donnachie.
6 Seaforth Muniments, Scottish Record Office, Edinburgh.
7 Information regarding Pereiras and d'Aguilars is derived from Sir Anthony Wagner, *English Genealogy*, 231–2; C. Roth, *History of the Jews in England*, 288–9; Spanish and Portuguese Jews' Synagogue, London; Islington Local History Library.
8 *Gentleman's Magazine*, 24 July 1795.
9 A. Mackenzie, *The Prophecies of the Brahan Seer*, 92.
10 A. Mackenzie, *History of the Mackenzies*, 340.
11 Ibid., 342.
12 H. J. C. Grierson, *Letters of Sir Walter Scott*, iv, 13, 14.
13 Ibid., iii, 393.
14 Ibid., 471.
15 *North British Review*, 1863.
16 C. Oman, *The Wizard of the North*, 153.
17 N.L.S.
18 Ibid.
19 Grierson, ii, 307–8.
20 Ibid., 344.
21 W. Partington, *Sir Walter's Post Bag*, 56.
22 Grierson, ii, 317.
23 N.L.S.
24 'And locks flung back, and lips apart/Like monument of Grecian art', *The Lady of the Lake*, I, xvii.
25 Grierson, ii, 534.
26 Ibid., 540.
27 Lady St Helier, *Memories of Fifty Years*, 12.
28 Sir T. E. Colebrook, Bt., *The Life of the Hon Mountstuart Elphinstone*, 254.
29 Ibid., 262.
30 Ibid., 270.

NOTES

31 Grierson, iv, 19.
32 Ibid., 13, 14, 22.
33 N.L.S.
34 Grierson, iv, 136.
35 Colebrook, 315.
36 N.L.S.
37 Grierson, iv, 458–9.
38 C. R. Sanders and K. J. Fielding, *The Collected Letters of Thomas and Jane Welsh Carlyle*, v, 385.
39 Oman, 220.
40 N.L.S.
41 Ibid.
42 Seaforth Muniments.
43 Ibid.
44 Ibid.
45 Ibid.
46 Richmond Reference Library.
47 P.T.P. Spencer Library, University of Kansas.
48 Seaforth Muniments.
49 P.T.P.
50 Ibid.
51 P.T.P.
52 T.P. University Library, Newcastle upon Tyne.
53 P.T.P.
54 Grierson, ii, 481.
55 P.T.P.
56 Seaforth Muniments.
57 A. Foss, *The Ionian Islands*, 206–7.
58 J. Pope-Hennessy, *The Years of Promise*, 305.
59 Henry James, *William Wetmore Story and His Friends*, i, 364.
60 N. Hawthorne, *Passages from the French and Italian Note-Books*, i, 240–1.
61 N. Mitford, *The Ladies of Alderley*, 211.
62 T.P.
63 Seaforth Muniments.
64 Ibid.
65 Ibid.
66 Royal Archives, Windsor Castle.
67 P.T.P. Lord Reidhaven succeeded as seventh Earl of Seafield; he married in 1850 and it seems unlikely that he ever proposed to Louisa.
68 Sir Algernon West, *Reflections*, 88.
69 P.T.P.
70 V. Surtees, ed., *Reflections of a Friendship*, 35.

194   NOTES

71 A. Boucourechliev, *Chopin, A Pictorial Biography*, 119.
72 Stirling-Maxwell Diaries.
73 P.T.P. and T.P.
74 Stirling-Maxwell Diaries.
75 Private information.
76 P.T.P.
77 Ibid.
78 Cheshire County Record Office.
79 P.T.P.
80 Ibid.
81 British Library.
82 C. Lennie, *Landseer*, 149.
83 B. and P. Russell, *The Amberley Papers*, 421.
84 P.T.P.
85 Ibid.
86 J. A. V. Chapple and A. Pollard, *The Letters of Mrs Gaskell*, 359.
87 Mitford, *The Stanleys of Alderley*, 83.
88 Mabell, Countess of Airlie, *Lady Palmerston and Her Times*, 168.
89 C. and F. Brookfield, *Mrs Brookfield and Her Circle*, 382.
90 N.L.S.
91 Ibid.
92 Chapple and Pollard, 556.
93 N.L.S.
94 Brookfield, 468, 471.
95 P. A. Motteux, Translation from Rabelais *Gargantua and Pantagruel*, Bk. iv, ch. 24, slightly misquoted.
96 Mitford, *Stanleys*, 269.
97 N.L.S.
98 Bodleian Library, Oxford.
99 Pope-Hennessy, *The Flight of Youth*, 103.
100 T.P.
101 R. Monckton Milnes, *Monographs: Personal and Social*, 228.
102 N.L.S.
103 Houghton Library, Harvard University.
104 Ibid.
105 British Library.
106 Cheshire County Record Office.
107 Sir Edward Cook, *Florence Nightingale*, i, 37.
108 Mitford, *Stanleys*, 261.
109 N.L.S.
110 Mitford, *Stanleys*, 261.
111 Brookfield, 485.

NOTES

112 Ibid.
113 Houghton Library, Harvard University.
114 Mitford, *Stanleys*, 261.
115 N.L.S.
116 *Dr Lee of Lambeth* (S.P.C.K.), 16.
117 Sir F. Pollock, Bt., *Personal Remembrances*, 147.
118 A. M. Brookfield, *Annals of a Chequered Life*, 17.
119 Brookfield, 487.
120 D. A. Wilson, *Carlyle to Threescore-and-Ten*, 237.
121 N.L.S.
122 A. M. Brookfield, 16.
123 N.L.S.
124 Ibid.
125 Drawings exist at the R.I.B.A.
126 L. and E. Hanson, *Necessary Evil*, 499.
127 Wilson, v, 401–2.
128 T.P.
129 N.L.S.
130 Ibid.
131 James, ii, 199.
132 N.L.S.
133 Ibid.
134 Ibid.
135 Mitford, *Stanleys*, 338.
136 Trinity College Library, Cambridge.
137 W. Hardman and S. M. Ellis, *Mid Victorian Pepys*, 192.
138 H. C. G. Matthew, *The Gladstone Diaries*, v, lxiv.
139 G. R. Hudson, *Browning to his American Friends*, 133.
140 James, ii, 88, 89.
141 G. W. E. Russell, *Portraits of the Seventies*, 288.
142 H. Corkran, *Celebrities and I*, 264–5.
143 O. Browning, *Memories of Sixty Years*, 118.
144 Hawthorne, ii, 68.
145 Hudson, 95.
146 Chapple and Pollard, 422.
147 P.T.P.
148 Trinity College Library, Cambridge.
149 N.L.S.
150 Walburga, Lady Paget, *Embassies of Other Days*, 280.
151 Bodleian Library, Oxford.
152 Munro Papers.
153 Unpublished letter to Ellen Heaton, of Leeds.
154 Munro Papers.
155 O. Doughty and J. R. Wahl, *Letters of D. G. Rossetti*, 522, 523.

156 Fitzwilliam Museum Library, Cambridge.
157 Wilson, 556.
158 Cheshire County Record Office.
159 Trinity College Library, Cambridge.
160 Ibid.
161 P.T.P.
162 Ibid. A fragment of the account of the Jewish nation from Tacitus *Histories*, Bk. V.
163 Trinity College Library, Cambridge.
164 N.L.S.
165 P.T.P.
166 Cheshire County Record Office.
167 Edward Lear Diaries.
168 Bodleian Library, Oxford.
169 V. Noakes, *Edward Lear*, 180, 185, 186, 191.
170 Lear Diaries.
171 N.L.S.
172 P.T.P.
173 Information derived from Penelope Hunting's thesis 'The Life and Work of Henry Clutton', 1979.
174 N.L.S.
175 Mrs Russell Barrington, *Life, Letters and Work of Frederic Leighton*, 123. A *Mother and Child* by Lord Leighton was sold among other of Louisa's pictures at Christie's, 8 July 1905. A portrait exists of Maysie, by Watts, executed at about this time.
176 N.L.S.
177 Ibid.
178 Ibid.
179 Ibid.
180 F. G. Kenyon, *Letters of E. B. Browning*, 392.
181 E. McAleer, *Dearest Isa*, 378.
182 H. Allingham and E. Baumer Williams, *Letters to W. Allingham*, 292.
183 D. A. Wilson and D. W. MacArthur, *Carlyle in Old Age*, 379.
184 A. Carlyle, *New Letters of Thomas Carlyle*, 244.
185 H. N. Pym, *Caroline Fox, Memories of Old Friends*, 300.
186 Matthew, vi, 494.
187 Spencer Library, University of Kansas.
188 Victoria and Albert Museum Library.
189 N.L.S.
190 Ibid.
191 Pym, 304, 305.
192 Baroness Bloomfield, *Reminiscences of Court and Diplomatic Life*, 281.

NOTES

193 J. Leach, *Bright Particular Star*, 114.
194 James, i, 255.
195 Ibid., 257.
196 Hawthorne, i, 190.
197 McAleer, 24.
198 F. G. Kenyon, 392.
199 Carr, 355–6.
200 N.L.S.
201 Ibid. 'Dingle-dowsie', probably used here as meaning an over-busy person whirling about. This was the sense attached to it by Jane Carlyle in 1856. I am grateful to Professor K. J. Fielding for this information.
202 F. Elliot, *Roman Gossip*, 276.
203 Lady Strachey, *Later Letters of Edward Lear*, 88–9.
204 Lear Diaries.
205 Ibid.
206 Pope-Hennessy, *Flight of Youth*, 210.
207 McAleer, 331.
208 O. Bornand, *Diary of W. M. Rossetti*, 52.
209 A. G. C. Liddell, *Notes from the Life of an Ordinary Mortal*, 206.
210 Pym, 304.
211 McAleer, 322.
212 Armstrong Browning Library, Baylor University, Waco, Texas.
213 James, ii, 197.
214 McAleer, 322.
215 James, ii, 196.
216 Ibid., 88.
217 Corkran, 166.
218 Mrs Sutherland Orr, *Life and Letters of Robert Browning*, 268.
219 Carr, 275–6.
220 G. B. Hill, *Letters of D. G. Rossetti to W. Allingham*, 288.
221 Trinity College Library, Cambridge.
222 James, ii, 197.
223 Hudson, 170.
224 Ibid., 186.
225 B. Miller, *Robert Browning, A Portrait*, 253.
226 McAleer, 367.
227 Hudson, 170.
228 Ibid., 170–1.
229 Ibid., 186.
230 Ibid., 186–7.
231 Peter Gunn, *Vernon Lee*, 108.
232 A. Hare, *The Story of Two Noble Lives*, 144.

NOTES

233 Visitor's Book, Loch Luichart.
234 James, ii, 196.
235 St Helier, 158.
236 L. Masterman, *Mary Gladstone*, 454.
237 Hudson, 170.
238 Ibid., 175.
239 E. A. Horsman, *The Diary of Alfred Domett*, 165.
240 Hudson, 170.
241 Ibid., 187.
242 Ibid., 172.
243 Ibid., 190.
244 Ibid.
245 M. Ward, *Robert Browning and His World*, 79.
246 N.L.S.
247 Ibid.
248 G. W. Smalley, *London Letters*, 293.
249 N.L.S.
250 M. Morris, *The Collected Works of William Morris*, 150–1.
251 Munro Papers.
252 G. S. Haight, *George Eliot*, 453.
253 N.L.S.
254 Ibid.
255 Ibid.
256 J. G. Millais, *Life and Letters of Sir John Everett Millais*, 24–5.
257 L. Edel, *Henry James Letters*, ii, 236–7.
258 Hare, *The Story of My Life*, iv, 123.
259 Trinity College Library, Cambridge.
260 Paget, *Embassies*, 280.
261 Paget, *The Linings of Life*, 222.
262 Paget, *Embassies*, 281.
263 Edel, *Letters*, i, 371.
264 Private information.
265 Paget, *Embassies*, 280.
266 Mrs W. Chanler, *Roman Spring*, 18.
267 Hare, iv, 90–2.
268 Ibid., 95.
269 Ibid., 99.
270 Trinity College Library, Cambridge.
271 C. Y. Lang, *The Swinburne Letters*, ii, 32.
272 Sir Humphrey Noble, Bt., *Life in a Noble House*.
273 Information from Lady Gladwyn.
274 Ibid.
275 Hare, iv, 154–5.
276 Doughty and Wahl, iii, 1321, 1322.

NOTES

277 Hare, iv, 329.
278 R. Murphy, *Edward Lear's Indian Journal*, 63.
279 Ibid., 64.
280 Ibid., 110.
281 Strachey, *Later Letters of Edward Lear*, 187.
282 Hare, *Noble Lives*, 361.
283 Private information.
284 Paget, *Linings*, 265–6.
285 W. Grote to Carlyle.
286 Lear Diaries.
287 Ibid.
288 Strachey, 231.
289 Hare, v, 30.
290 Hare, *Noble Lives*, 382–3.
291 Munro Papers.
292 Hare, v, 60.
293 Ibid., 73.
294 E. C. F. Collier, *Victorian Diarist, Lady Monkswell*, 149.
295 Hare, v, 211.
296 Masterman, 191, 217.
297 Cook, ii, 324.
298 Ibid., 314.
299 Ibid., 391.
300 Hare, vi, 454.
301 Lord Teignmouth, *Reminiscences of Many Years*, 351.

Index

Index

Aberdeen, 4th Earl of, 51

Addiscombe Villa, 35, 59, 105, 107, 112, 129, 152, 169

Aitken, Mary Carlyle, 150, 151, 179; attitude to L, 158–60, 167, 168, 170

Albert, Prince Consort, 1, 87, 94

Alexander I, Tzar, 82

Alexandra, Princess of Denmark, 94

Alford, Lady Marian, 126–7, 130, 146, 161, 165, 172, 181

Alfred, Prince, 68

Alice, Princess, Countess of Athlone, 128

Anstruther, Annie, 65, 123, 184

Anstruther, Hon. Mrs Philip (Mary), 28, 112

Argyll, 8th Duke of, and Duchess, 87, 171, 172

Arnold, Dr Thomas, 28, 29

Arthur, Prince, 163

Ashburton, William Bingham Baring, 2nd Baron, 1, 2, 46, 48, 83; ancestry 54, 59; career, 59; ill health, 59, 65, 66, 71, 72, 87, 88, in Paris, 91–6; character, 56, 77, 89, 102; reports of remarriage, 58, 60; plans wedding, 62, 63, 64; honeymoon, 56, 66, 68–73; message from Carlyle, 94; death, 68, 98, 99, 101, 102, 104, 107, 112, 113; his will, 106, 107, 108, 109, 110, 117, 171; portraits of, 81, 85, 86, 102, 110, 111, 118, 124

Ashburton, Lady (Harriet, 1st wife), Carlyle's friendship for, 2, 46, 55, 56, 128; death, 54, 56, 128; appearance, 55; her opinion of Barings, 67

Ashburton, Louisa Lady, ancestry, 2, 7, 8, 57; birth, 4; religion, 2, 35; upbringing, 25, 28, 101; appearance, 2, 30, 33, 41, 46, 47, 49, 65, 68, 69, 72, 74, 80, 82, 101, 116, 130, 155; her interests, 2, 28, 154; characteristics, 2, 3, 11, 33, 40, 50, 57, 59, 64, 65, 69, 74, 76–7, 84, 89, 96, 98, 101, 127, 128, 137, 163, 173; motives for marriage, 2, 58, 69, 108; allusions to marriage, 35, 37–8, 48, 58, 59, 60, 65, 145, 146, 163; love for Stirling, 2, 38, 42, 43–4, 45, 46, 47, 48, 176; ill health, 40, 68, 96, 104, 152, 155, 156, 158, 185; and Ruskin, 40, 47, 49, 58, 98, 101, 120; and Landseer, 2, 52, 53, 60–1, 69, 76, 85–6; attempts at swimming, 53, 73; her finances, 114, 122, 131, 167, 178–9, 184; manoeuvres for marriage, 57, 58–59, 61; marriage, 65, 66; relationship with husband, 69, 70, 72–3, 74, 78, 88, 91, 92, 99, 108; infecundity, 71, 72; in society, 74, 76–7; pregnancy, 76, 78, 88, 91; fondness for Carlyle, 2, 78, 105, 112, 113, 120, 123, 126, 127, 129, 132, 170, 180, 129; portraits of, 46, 82, 85–6, 117, 134; as collector, 82, 89, 96, 97–8, 101, 102, 103, 104, 114, 116, 118–9, 131, 132, 156, 157, 165, 168, 171, 174, 176, 184; and philanthropy, 83, 99, 105, 155, 178, 182–3; miscarriage, 88, 91; relationship with Barings, 68, 91–2, 95, 107, 108, 109, 110, 152;

204 INDEX

deficiency in discharging debts, 103, 121, 122, 123, 135, 170, 174, 178, 183, 188; borrows money, 58, 121; leaves The Grange, 106, 109, 152; her inheritance, 106, 107, 108; offers to return works of art, 109, 110; inserts notice in *The Times*, 110; lends bust of Carlyle, 118, 133; urges Mentone to Carlyle, 124–5; rents villa at Mentone, 126; seeks London house, 131, 151; and servants, 68–9, 71, 122, 136, 184; relationship with Browning, 138, 139, 140–1, 143–7, 149; at Belton, 146; summer plans, 152, 155; discord with Aitkens, 158–60; in Rome, 130, 133, 158, 160, 161, 162, 163, 174; is threatened with litigation, 135, 181; hires yacht, 181; insolvent, 185; death and burial, 186. Lavishes affection on: Jane Carlyle, 78, 81, Harriet Hosmer, 95, 131, 156, 161–2, 170, Florence Nightingale, 35, 84, Jane Stirling, 38, 41, 42, 45, Pauline Trevelyan, 32, 120, 121, Miss Trotter, 95, 129–30, 155–6. At home and abroad: Bad Homburg, 40, Baden, 80, Balmacara, 36, 38, 137, Bath, 104, 105, Beulah Spa, 50, Bologna, 148, Budapest, 129, Buxton, 155, 159, Carlsruhe, 35, 117, 119, Ceylon, 27, 28, 112, Corfu, 30, 33, 34, 112, Davos, 125, Egypt, 69–70, 71–2, 121, 173, Embley, 50, Exeter, 112, Florence, 128, Folkestone, 88–9, Frankfort, 40, Glion, 124, 129, Lucerne, 123, Malta, 68, 96, Malvern, 134, Marienbad, 147, 164, 167, 183, Mentone, 35, 119, Naples, 129, Neuchâtel, 121, 123, Paris, 36, 41, 68, 90–6, 133, Perugia, 133, 164, Roker, 43, 47, 48, St Moritz, 152, San Sebastian, 73, Sidmouth, 112, Spittal, 53, Strathpeffer, 152, Torquay, 178,

Venice, 133, Verona, 164, Vichy, 122, 129, Whitby, 43, Wiesbaden, 114, 116, 117, Zermatt, 124
Athenaeum, 54

Bailey (manservant), 91, 93, 113, 124, 125, 126
Balfour, Arthur, 175, 179
Ballantyne, James, 19
Baring, Hon. Emily, 64, 67, 68, 92, 107, 109–10
Baring, Hon. Francis (later 3rd Baron Ashburton), 64, 87, 91, 92, 108, 109; and wife, 64, 92, 95
Baring, Hon. and Revd Frederick, 64, 87, 107, 108, 109; and wife, 64, 95
Baring, Hon. Louisa, 64, 67, 68, 87, 105, 108, 111, 112, 177
Baring, Hon. Mary Florence (Maysie), 84, 107, 108, 109, 117, 134; birth, 79, 80; ill health, 87, 93, 129, 185; at Nice, 91, 93, 129, 185; character, 93, 153, 172; education, 123, 126, 136, 153; portraits of, 85–6, 124, 169; receives drawings from Lear, 177; in society, 178, 179; marriage, 181–2; death, 185, 186
Barnard, Lady Anne, 13
Bath, Dowager Marchioness of, 64, 72, 104
Bath House, 1, 35, 46, 47, 59, 77; marriage at, 65; improvements at, 82, 83; entertaining at, 83, 94; paintings from, copied, 82, 103, 111, 178; and terms of will, 106–7, 109; stripped, 113
Belton House, 127, 132, 146
Berry, Mary, 13
Bloomfield, 2nd Baron, 129; and wife, 156
Boehm, Joseph E., 95, 168, 170, 184
Bracebridge, Mr and Mrs, 36, 50
Brahan Castle, 11, 12, 22, 23, 35, 36, 49, 50, 75, 146; construction of, 8; description of, 25–6, 27
Brewster, Sir David, 42, 48

INDEX

205

Brighton, 54, 66, 68

Bromley, Charlotte Davenport, 95, 112, 121, 124, 132, 134, 142

Brookfield, Revd W. H., 55, 85, 94, 101, 106, 119, 146; characteristics, 60, 76; sends Valentine, 151

Brookfield, Mrs W. H. (Jane), 55, 56, 76, 94, 119

Brown, Ford Madox, 104, 154, 169

Brown, Dr John, 44, 72, 98; admires L, 46, 48, 74, 99, 111; illness, 174–5

Browning, Elizabeth Barrett, 36, 41, 42, 43, 130; and Lady Marian, 127; death, 84, 97, 138, 145; dedication inscribed to, 138, 141; *Last Poems*, 138

Browning, Robert, 84, 88, 90, 127, 130, 134; in Paris, 36, 41, 42; relationship with L, 101, 140–2, 143–6, 148–9; delivers photographs, 98; characteristics, 141, 142, 144, 146; at Loch Luichart, 137–42, 146, 155; correspondence with L, 138–9, 140, 143–4, 147, 185; at Naworth, 142, Mentmore, 142, Belton, 146; *Balaustion's Adventure*, 144; *Parleying with Daniel Bartoli*, 149; *Poetical Works*, 138; *The Ring and the Book*, 97, 138, 141, 142

Browning, Robert Wiedeman (Pen), education, 84, 138, 145; at Loch Luichart, 137, 139–42, 145, 146; at Melchet, 143, 144, 153

Browning, Sarianna, 137, 139

Brownlow, 2nd Earl, and brother, 128

Bunsen, Baron, and family, 64, 70, 117, 126, 127

Burges, Williams, 122

Burne-Jones, Edward, 104, 180

Butterfield, William, 79

Canning, 1st Earl, 146; and wife, 171

Carlyle, Thomas, 1, 24, 44–5, 75, 97; character, 46, 77; obsession

for Harriet, 2, 46–7, 55, 56, 81; relations with wife, 56; at The Grange, 55, 77, 81, 87, 90, 98; his opinion of L, 57, 81, 120, 132, 143, 152, 154, 155; relations with L, 100, 180; receives horse, 95, dressing gown, 95, bequest, 99, olive wood, 119, game, 143, 150; encourages L, 100, 105; at Seaton, 112–13, 157, 158; sits to Woolner, 113; mourns his wife, 123–4; staves off visit to Mentone, 124–5; at Mentone, 126, 127, 128, 129, at Belton, 146; cast of hands, 150; at Addiscombe, 132; at Melchet, 151, 154; appearance, 127, 168; to Grosvenor House, 177; death and bequest, 179; *Frederick the Great*, 77, 89, 113; *French Revolution*, 113, 170; *Reminiscences*, 126; *Sartor Resartus*, 152

Carlyle, Mrs Thomas (Jane), 67, 75, 76, 80, 94, 97, 105; visits The Grange, 55, 77, 78, 81, 87, 90, 98; and L, 62, 78, 79, 82, 91, 99, 102, 105, 111, 114; and Nero, 77, 78; her gift to L, 82–3, 89, 94; at Folkestone, 88–9; ill health, 98, 102; to Woolner, 102; at Seaton, 112–13; receives horse, 105, candlesticks, 119; her shawl, 132; death, 115, 120

Carlyle, Dr John, 120, 124, 128, 132, 150, 154, 159, 160

Castle Ashby, 172, 182

Chapman, George, 103

Chopin, Frédéric, 41

Christian, Prince and Princess, 172

Christison, Dr, 91, 95, 96, 99

Clifford, Edward, 183

Clough, Arthur Hugh, 55, 70

Clutton, Henry, 101, 104, 112, 131, 178; and Melchet, 88, 122, 135; and Kent House, 151, 165

Coltman, William, 59

Compton, Lord William, 181

Conway, Moncure, 105

Corelli, Marie, 183

INDEX

Corfu, 30, 33
Cowper-Temple, Hon. William, 158, 164
Cowper-Temple, Hon. Mrs William, 154, 158, 178
Crawford, Marion, 162
Cross (gardener), 116, 122
Cumberland, Duke of, 13
Cushman, Charlotte, 113, 130

d'Aguilar, Ephraim Lopez Pereira, Baron of Highbury, 6, 7
d'Aguilar, Georgiana Simha, 2, 5, 6, 7
d'Aguilar, Moses Lopez Pereira, 6
Darwin, Charles, 87, 125
Daubigny, C. F., 96, 99
Davy, Lady, 34
Derby Day, 49, 83
de Staël, Madame Auguste, 95
Dickinson, Lowes, 58
Dingwall, 8, 37, 75
Douro, Marquess, 1
Doyle, Richard (Dickie), 83, 153
Drummond, Henry, 66
Dyce, William, 115

Edinburgh Annual Register, 19
Edward, Prince of Wales, 94
Eliot, George, 154
Elphinstone, Hon. Mountstuart, 20–1, 23
Emerson, R. W., 162
Erskine, Thomas, 41
Eugénie, Empress, 68
Euston, Earl and Countess of (later Grafton, 6th Duke of, and Duchess), 64, 95

Fantin-Latour, Henri, 103
Farrar, Ven. Eric, 182
Forster, John, 139, 158, 166, 170; interferes, 164–5; his opinion of Melchet, 171; death, 173
Fortrose, 37, 93, 186
Fox, Caroline, 127, 129
Froude, J. A., 55–6, 115, 179, 185

Galloway, Earls of, 5

Gaskell, Mrs, 54, 59, 115
George IV, King, 15, 18, 19, 23, 30
Gibson, John, 131
Gladstone, Mary (Drew), 146, 180
Gladstone, W. E., 64, 83, 96, 118, 127, 128, 182; and wife, 83
Glenfinlas, 47, 48
Goodall, Frederick, 70
Grange, The, 35, 59; entertaining at, 46, 55, 76, 77, 87, 90; description of, 66–7, 77, 98; improvements at, 78–9; and church, 79, 98; photography at, 90; and terms of will, 106–7, 109–10
Grant, Francis, 85
Great Britain, S.S., 36
Greenaway, Kate, 184
Grote, Mrs, 52
Gully, Dr, 134

Haag, Carl, 70
Hallé, C. E., 184
Hamilton, Lord Claud, 173, 174
Hare, Augustus, 163, 168, 171, 176, 178, 179, 184
Harford, Revd Frederick, 96
Hawthorne, Nathaniel, 90
Haydon, B. R., 88
Henschel, George, 184
Hertford, Marchioness of, 19
Hood, Vice-Admiral Sir Samuel, Bt., 12, 13, 14, 15, 19, 20, 21, 22
Hood, Lady, see Stewart-Mackenzie, Hon. Mrs James Alexander
Hosmer, Harriet, 152, 155, 162, 177; appearance, 130; achievements, 130, 135; characteristics, 130, 131, 161, 162; relationship with L, 2, 95, 130–1, 147, 148, 156, 161–2, 165, 170, 173, 178; Carlyle's opinion of, 132; her studio, 130, 161, 174; urges purchases on L, 133, 134, 161, 165, 171; and Browning, 130, 147, 148, 149; *Amazon*, 171; *Clasped Hands*, 130, 150; *Dolphin*, 178; *Hermes*, 165, 168; *Mars*, 171;

INDEX

207

Mermaid's Cradle, 178; *Psyche*, 165, 168; *Puck*, 131, 168; *Putti*, 131; *Sleeping Faun* and *Waking Faun*, 131, 133; *Will-o'-the Wisp*, 131

Houghton, 1st Baron, 44, 64, 94, 96, 99, 106, 107, 108, 142, 146; considers marriage, 35; at The Grange, 55, 77, 87; with L at British Museum, 116, and Mentone, 133; *Monographs*, 114, 186

Howard, George and Hon. Mrs, 142

Hunt, Mr and Mrs Leigh, 112

Hunt, W. Holman, 116

Ionian Islands, 28, 29, 30, 64

James, Henry, 97, 140, 155, 162

Jameson, Mrs Anna, 2, 36, 46, 47, 53

Jowett, Benjamin, 35

Kent House, 4, 35, 157, 182, 185, 186; previous owners, 151; building of, 151, 152, 154, 158; description of, 164, 166, 184

Kingsley, Revd Charles and Mrs, 70, 87

Landseer, Sir Edwin, 83, 88, 136; as suitor, 2, 60, 61; career, 52, 61, 117; health, 53, 86; at Brahan, 26, 52, 61, 85; correspondence with L, 60, 61, 85–6; expectation of marriage, 61, and dejection, 69; at Loch Luichart, 85; portraits by, 85, 86, 102, 117, 128, 134; *Attachment*, 96; *Flood in the Highlands*, 69; *Rent Day in the Wilderness*, 8

Lansdowne, 3rd Marquess of, 44

Lawrence, Sir Thomas, 9, 30, 109, 110

Lear, Edward, 28; expectation of sale to L, 114, 132–3, 172; opinion of Woolner, 133; in India, 171; financial dealings with L, 171, 176; dines with L,

171, 176; *Cedars of Lebanon*, 114–15, 132–3, 174, 185; *Crag that Fronts the Even*, 176, 177, 185; *Mount Tomohrit*, 176, 177; *Philae*, 176; *Mount Kinchinjunga . . . from Darjeeling*, 171, 174, 176, 185

Lee, James Prince, 28, 29

Legros, Alphonse, 103, 169, 178

Leighton, 1st Baron, 124

Leitch, W. W., 82, 111, 112, 115, 124

Lemon, Mark, 84

Leopold, Prince, 128, 179

Lewis, Isle of, 4, 11, 25, 155, 172, 181, 186; sale of, 35, 38, 181

Lind, Jenny, 84

Lindsay, Sir Coutts, 164, 166

Little Holland House, 49–50, 156, 169

Loch Luichart, 36, 59, 60, 95–6, 107, 169; description of, 49, 75; Carlyle and, 57, 155; Hatty at, 134; Browning at, 137, 139–42, 145, 146, 155

Locock, Sir Charles, 93, 94

Londonderry, 3rd Marquess of, 1

Louise, Princess, 172, 179

Ludovisi Goddess, The, 2, 130

Lushington, Franklin, 28

Lytton, Lord, 165

MacDonald, George, 54, 177

Mackenzie aunts, 22, 27, 28, 29, 40

Mackenzie, Hon. Caroline, 22, 26

Mackenzie, Hon. Maria Frederika (Mary), *see* Stewart-Mackenzie, Mrs James Alexander

Mackenzie curse, 4, 7, 8, 9, 22, 26

Macready, W. C., 113

Malmesbury, 3rd Earl of, 1

Marochetti, Baron, 82, 117, 118, 135

Martin, John, 49

Matheson, Alexander, 38

Maugham, R. O., 93

Maurice, F. D., 45, 114

Melbourne, 2nd Viscount, 38–9, 52

INDEX

Melchet Court, 35, 107, 111, 112, 151, 153, 169, 179, 185; purchase of, 87, 92; building of, 97, 106, 114, 122; decoration of, 101, 131, 135–6; fire at, 147, 157–8, 164
Mendelssohn, F., 2
Millais, (Sir) John Everett, 47, 49, 50, 53–4, 58, 115, 155; and William, 47
Milman, Very Revd Henry, 1, 8
Milnes, Richard Monckton, *see* Houghton, Baron
Mohl, Madame, 35, 41
Morning Chronicle, 65
Morris, William, 104, 153
Morris Firm, 89, 104, 119
Morritt, John, 16, 22, 24
Munro, Alexander, 82, 97, 101, 102, 110, 153, 154
Murchison, Donald, 8
Murchison, Sir Roderick, 8, 141
Museum of Practical Geology, The, 49

Nakos, Count and Countess, 129, 131, 133–4, 142, 150
Nelson, Vice-Admiral Horatio, Viscount, 12
Nesfield, W. Eden, 101, 164, 169–70, 171
Nettlecombe Court, 32, 36, 106
Newton, Charles, 116
Nice, 62, 90, 128; L journeys to, 94, 119, 121, 130
Nightingale, Florence, 50, 54, 80; affection for L, 35, 182, 185; refuses marriage proposal, 35; at Harley Street, 50; and Crimea, 36, 50, 54; ill health, 59; suggests books, 70; retrieves letters, 84; tardy sympathy for L, 99–100; to Seaton, 182; 'the guiding star', 182
Nightingale, Parthenope (Lady Verney), 35, 50, 54, 59, 78; and husband, 78
Northbrook, 1st Earl of, 106, 109, 171, 182

Norton, Caroline (Hon. Mrs George), 38–9, 42, 45, 46, 48, 52; imaginary letter to, 65; death, 176

Paget, Lady (Walburga), 162, 163, 175
Palmerston, Viscountess, 55, 64, 94
Panizzi, (Sir) Anthony, 44–5
Paton, Noel, 82, 174, 184
Petre, Mrs John, *see* Stewart-Mackenzie, Caroline
Price, Miss E., 27, 30, 34, 112
Prince Regent, *see* George IV
Prince of Wales, *see* George IV
Prinsep, Mr and Mrs Thoby, 50
Punch, 84

Quain, Dr Richard, 74, 87, 89, 96, 129, 131, 151, 165

Reidhaven, Lord, 37–8
Reynolds, Sir Joshua, 6, 118, 171
Ronan, Mademoiselle, 143, 153
Rossetti, D. G., 89, 103, 104, 154; refuses L's invitations, 104, 141–2; his sale, 181; *Joan of Arc*, 103, 112; portrait of Maysie, 169; *Salutation of Beatrice*, 97, 98; *Venus Verticordia*, 103
Rossetti, W. M., 135
Rubens, Sir Peter Paul, 82, 83, 103
Ruskin, John, 40, 48, 84, 94, 119; at Wallington, 47, 58; and L, 41, 45, 58, 98, 101, 123, 155, 179; Landseer's opinion of, 60; and Turner, 96; and Pauline's death, 121; and Carlyle, 150
Ruskin, Mrs John (Effie), 40, 45, 49, 54; her praise of L, 41, 46, 47; characteristics, 41, 157; at Wallington, 47
Russell, 1st Earl, 119

St George's, Hanover Square, 64, 80
St Paul's Cathedral, 1, 21
Sandwich, Dowager Countess of, 62, 65, 75, 81
Saturday Review, The, 106

INDEX

209

Scotsman, The, 32

Scott, Sophia, 17, 25

Scott, (Sir) Walter, 34; describes Border country, 14, and wearing of a plaid, 18; relationship with Mary, 11, 13, 14, 15, 16, 20–1, 22, 23–4; death, 26; *Lady of the Lake,* 16, 17; *Lament for the Last of the Seaforths,* 9–10; *Marmion,* 14; *Rob Roy,* 139; *Vision of Don Roderick,* 19

Scott, William Bell, 57, 58

Seaforth, Lord (Francis Humberston Mackenzie), ancestry, 8; characteristics, 9, 13; career, 9; death, 4, 10, 51; funeral, 22; and wife, 11, 24

Seaton, Seaforth Lodge, 35, 107, 119, 152, 155, 170; plans for building, 95, 97, 104; house completed, 104, 111

Sermoneta, Duke of, 162, 163

Serpentine, The, 81

Seymour, Hon. Mary, 37

Smith, Sydney, 55

Stafford, Lady, 13, 21, 22

Stanley of Alderley, 2nd Baron, 48–9, 61, 74, 75, 76, 91, 106; and wife, 153

Stanley, Revd Arthur, 80

Stanley, Catherine, 36, 80, 114

Stanley, Rt Revd Edward, 36, 48; and wife, 36, 74

Stanley, Colonel Hon. John and Mrs (later St Helier), 146

Stanley, Maria Josepha, Dowager Lady, 55

Stanley, Mary, 36, 80, 114

Sterling, Antoinette, 179

Stevens, Alfred, 135

Stewart, James Alexander, *see* Stewart-Mackenzie

Stewart, Admiral Hon. Keith, 5, 7

Stewart-Mackenzie, Caroline (Mrs John Petre), 25, 27, 29, 33, 37, 54

Stewart-Mackenzie, Frank (Francis), 25, 27, 28, 29, 37

Stewart-Mackenzie, George, 25, 27, 37, 42, 43

Stewart-Mackenzie, Mrs George, 42–3, 85, 91, 93

Stewart-Mackenzie, James Alexander, ancestry, 5, 7; marriage, 4, 23, 25; appearance, 24; characteristics, 4, 24, 29, 33, 34; career, 25, 26, 27, 28, 29, 34; religious convictions, 29, 33, 34

Stewart-Mackenzie, Hon. Mrs James Alexander (Mary), ancestry, 4, 7; birth, 11; appearance, 11, 15; marriages, 4, 10, 12, 23; characteristics, 4, 11, 12, 13, 15, 16, 21, 22, 29, 33, 186; friendship with Scott, 11, 14, 15, 20–1; model for Ellen, 17, 18; and India, 20–1; travels with L, 40, 41; ill health, 44, 50, 54, 60, 62, 85; claims peerage, 51; at L's marriage, 66 receives financial help, 70; death, 93–4

Stewart-Mackenzie, Keith, 25, 27, 51, 146; unseemly behaviour, 25, 37, 66, 93

Stewart-Mackenzie, Louisa Caroline, *see* Ashburton, Louisa Lady

Stirling, Jane, 38, 41, 42, 43, 44, 47, 72

Stirling, Mrs, 84

Stirling, William, *see* Stirling-Maxwell

Stirling-Maxwell, Sir William, Bt., 1, 38, 44, 47, 48, 176; attached to another, 2, 38, 42, 43, 45; rejects L, 43, 45

Story, W. W., career, 90; at Loch Luichart, 137, 141–2; relations with L, 101, 103, 148–9, 162, 174; and Hatty, 130, 147, 148; makes sketch of Browning, 145; and L's letters to Browning, 145; *Alcestes,* 174; *Cleopatra,* 90, 102–3; *Roba di Roma,* 97; *Sibyl,* 90, 174

Story, Mrs W. W., 134, 137, 138, 141, 142, 148, 162; and daughter, 137, 145, 146

Stuart, Lady Louisa, 4, 12

Surtees, Robert, 14, 16

INDEX

Swinburne, Algernon, 114
Swinton, James, 46, 53

Taylor, Tom, 84
Tennyson, Alfred, Lord, 97, 106, 176, 183; and wife, 153
Thackeray, W. M., 55, 87, 98, 106
Thistlethwayte, Mrs (Laura Bell), 96
Thorvaldsen, B., 135
Times, The, 110
Trench, Very Revd R. Chenevix, 94
Trevelyan, Sir Walter, 79, 83, 96, 112; characteristics, 32; his tips, 33, 36–7; as landowner, 32, 95, 104; at Corfu, 31, 33; visits and travels with L, 36, 46, 47, 48, 54, 80; reads aloud, 43; Ruskin's letter to, 49; Pauline's death, 120, 121
Trevelyan, Lady (Pauline), 31, 80, 82; characteristics, 32, 35; affection for L, 32, 33, 99, 101; at Brahan, 36; visits and journeys with L, 36, 43, 45, 46, 47, 48, 49, 50, 54, 81, 90; values L's jewellery, 58; intimation of L's engagement, 58; meets Ashburton, 65; and bazaars, 83, 105–6; in Paris, 95; at The Grange, 98; at Seaton, 98, 104, 112, 113, 115, 119; ill health, 119, 121, 132; summer plans, 119; death, 50, 101, 120, 121, 124
Trollope, Anthony, 95
Trotter, Miss, 134, 153, 170; passion for L, 41, 95, 129–30, 155–6
Trumpeters' House, Richmond, 26–7, 29, 35
Turgenev, Ivan, 154
Turner, J. M. W., 47, 96, 171, 176, 181
Tyndall, Professor John, 117, 125, 126, 128, 154, 173–4

Varley, John (Jr), 178
Vaughan, Dr C. J., 36

Venables, S. V., 106, 108, 109, 110, 112, 114
Victoria, Queen, 51, 68, 82, 93, 94, 111, 121, 128, 163, 168, 172, 179–80

Waldeck-Pyrmont, Princess Hélène and daughter, 128
Waldegrave, Lady (Frances), 74
Wales, Princess of (Caroline), 13, 15
Wallington Hall, 31, 32; L at 43, 47, 57, 58, 75, 84; Ruskin at, 47, 58
Waterford, Louisa Lady, 172, 177
Waterhouse, Mr, 108, 179, 184, 185
Watts, G. F., 50, 124, 168–9; Gilbert's bust of, 184; *Chaos*, 157, 168; *Love and Death*, 156; *Time and Death*, 157
Wellington, Duke of, 1, 19, 23, 44; and wife, 13, 19, 23
Whistler, James McNeill, 103, 112, 166
Wilberforce, Rt Revd Samuel, 55, 63, 64, 65, 87, 90
Wilkie, Sir David, 26
Wilton Place, London, 37, 45
Windus, B. D., 47
Wiseman, Cardinal, 114
Within and Without (George MacDonald), 54
Woolner, Thomas, 97, 116; characteristics, 117–18; commissions from L, 101–2, 113, 115, 150, and his tardiness in execution of, 115, 122, 131; portrait busts, 101, 111, 113, 115; at Seaton, 112, 113; at Mentone, 127; discord with L, 101, 118, 134, 167–8; *Puck*, 115, 118; *Virgilia Bewailing . . . Coriolanus*, 115, 118, 131, 134, 167, 185
Woolner, Mrs Thomas, 112, 113, 118, 131
Wooster, D., 53, 79